History of
The Wheelwright Grammar Schools

by
W. Pickles

To

My late Mother and Father.

To

Dorothy

and

To all past, present and

future staffs and pupils

of the Wheelwright Schools

in Dewsbury.

Contents

First Published March, 1973

Published by
W. PICKLES
"Dimple Dale" 24 Glebelands Close,
Garforth, Leeds

Printed in Times New Roman 10 on 11pt.
by
JOSEPH WARD & CO. (PRINTERS) LTD.
Wesley Place, Wellington Road,
Dewsbury, Yorkshire

Preface

You owe this attempted history of the Wheelwright Grammar Schools to several causes. Except the two theses by K. Bamford and E. J. Green, the first touching on John Wheelwright's effect on education and the latter on the general history of education in the County Borough of Dewsbury, no one has bothered to write a full history of the School before. My father had great interest in local matters and even whilst I was a pupil at the Victoria Jubilee School (now the Victoria Modern School), he used to tell me how the street adjacent to this school got its name (Wheelwright Street) and of the struggle and the high feelings which were aroused in the town at the time when Dr. Hinchliffe left his money for the education of the children of Dewsbury, and how the working people of the borough were afraid that the money might be lost in litigation etc. He used to tell me stories of his experiences at Rodger's College (Daw Green Charity School), which he attended before going to Boothroyd Lane Board School, as a result of the passing of the Education Act of 1870.

The "Wheelwright", as the schools have always been known to Dewsburians, was always held up to me as some wonderful institution by my father who deeply regretted that he had not had the privilege of going there.

It is no wonder that I entered its portals on that September day in 1919 with considerable trepidation and met Mr. Sadler for the first time. He appeared to me as a very stately giant and someone not to be trifled with as he told us new-comers to remain in the Hall after the assembly. Mr. Evans took charge of us and we were quickly seated at desks and paper and pens given to us and an examination conducted in Arithmetic and English. Before starting the former, Mr. Evans prowled up and down the aisles, hands behind his back, his aquiline face very stern; then he slowly turned on his heels and said, "I want your own work, boys. Don't copy. To copy is to be dishonest and to be dishonest is the first step on the slippery slope to hell."

I passed through the School without bringing it any honour, I am sorry to say, but owing it a great debt of gratitude. Like so many other of its pupils, I've been too busy making a living and my interests have been in other directions, and so I failed to realise that none of its great sons or daughters (far more qualified than I am to write such a dissertation) had attempted a complete history of the School.

It was in the course of perusing the copies of the *Dewsbury Reporter* from 1870 to 1933 in connection with another piece of research a few years ago that I came across the account of the House of Lords Appeal against the West Riding County Council on behalf of "Wheelwright" that my interest was re-awakened. I decided to contact Mr. Lancaster, the present Headmaster, and discuss the possibility of a history of the school. From that day to the completion of this research both Mr. Lancaster and Miss Levitt (Headmistress of the Girls' School) encouraged me forward. To both I owe a great debt of gratitude.

I beg the readers to overlook any faults and failings (and these must be legion) and any omissions. This latter applies particularly to the account of the Girls' School. If this appears somewhat short and stilted in comparison with that of the Boys' School, there is a very good reason for it. As the Boys' School remained in the 1893 building after 1934 I have taken its history through to 1970 first, so that much information which is included in that account equally applies to the Girls' School and has therefore not been repeated in the account of the Girls' School. The fact that the account of the Boys' School comes first is entirely due to it remaining in the old building in 1934 and no slight of any kind whatever is intended to the Girls' School.

I hope that this book will fill a gap and be interesting to all old scholars, not too dry and not too wordy. I have tried to obey the motto of the School, *Res Non Verba*. Through this little effort I hope to try to repay to some degree the debt of gratitude I shall always owe to my Alma Mater.

W.P.
Garforth, Leeds LS25 1HY.
December, 1971.

Acknowledgements

I wish to acknowledge my very deepest thanks to all who have helped me in any way whatever with this research and in particular the following: Mr. W. B. Lancaster (Headmaster of the Boys' School) and Miss D. Levitt (Headmistress of the Girls' School) for their criticism of the MS. chapter by chapter and for putting at my disposal all the information at the schools, magazines, libraries, etc., and their encouragement throughout; Miss E. Moore (Secretary of the Wheelwright Trustees) and the Wheelwright Trustees themselves for giving me access to the minutes of the Wheelwright Charity; Mr. F. Smith (the Dewsbury Borough Librarian) for great help and encouragement and his staff (in particular Miss M. Roberts and Mrs. B. Chappell) in the Reference Library at Dewsbury Central Library for their patience with me and their ever ready help; The Bishop of Wakefield (Dr. E. Treacy); the Chief Education Officer of Dewsbury (Mr. J. Clitheroe) for great assistance and very ready access to the minutes of the Dewsbury Endowed Schools Foundation and the minutes of the Dewsbury Education Committee; Mrs. Knowles and Miss Sykes (Secretaries respectively to the Headmaster and Headmistress of the Wheelwright Grammar Schools); Mr. W. Bolton (former Headmaster of the Boys' School); Miss N. W. Truelove (former Headmistress of the Girls' School); the late Miss A. D. Baker (former Headmistress of the Girls' School); the staffs of both schools and in particular R. B. Crowther, P. Biggin, S. G. Hamilton, J. Crompton, H. Benton, J. Lister (for copies of photographs), G. Robinson, Miss E. Secker, Miss B. Smith and other members of the Girls' School staff for plying me with welcome sustenance in the staff room; The Rector of Thornhill (Rev. N. D. J. Webb), Revs. J. M. Furness, Richton, M. Lister, Humphreys, R. D. S. Trapps, the late Canon B. A. Smith; Canon H. J. Hammerton, Revs. K. Law, A. Crow, and J. T. Abell; Mrs. A. D. Glover, Mrs. M. Withers, Mrs. B. Nuttall, Mrs. E. C. Sadler, Mrs. F. Dennison; Mrs. F. Driver, Miss M. Turner, Mrs. N. Senior, Miss P. Wilkinson; Miss E. Saynor; Miss F. Cropper; Messrs. H. Newbould; C. L. Spurr; R. Townend; C. M. Jones; H. M. Docton; H. Kaye, H. Perkins; J. D. Ingram; T. Aveyard; J. E. Scatcherd; C. V. Chester; A. B. Clegg; A. E. Coghill; T. Turner; the late Dr. L. Wakefield; Dr. P. B. Walker; Mr. M. Wheelwright, The Department of Education and Science; The Trustees of Harrison's Charity; The Charity Commissioners (Northern Office); The Wakefield Diocesan Registrar (C. E. Coles); The Headmaster of Ilkley Grammar School (R. Hughes); The Librarian of H.M. Customs and Excise; The Estate Surveyor of British Rail (Eastern Region); Mrs. S. Mallorie for typing certain appendices, etc., The Old Girls' Association and the Old Boys' Association.

The photographs are acknowledged beneath each one.

Besides all these I wish to thank especially Miss D. Ramsden for reading and criticising the early drafts of each chapter of the MS. and for her encouragement throughout the work; Miss M. Driver for typing the final

MS. and for bearing with me whilst this was being accomplished and finally my wife for her patience, encouragement and for enduring so gladly many hours of "Wheelwright widowhood" so that this work would see the light of day.

SECTION 1

CHAPTER I

"Res Non Verba"
John Wheelwright and the Early History of the School

Thousands of boys and girls in Dewsbury and the surrounding district have worn caps, hats or blazers on which have been enbroidered a coat of arms with three wheels and underneath the motto *Res Non Verba*. Some boys and girls in the earlier days of the Wheelwright Grammar School's existence wore a silver shield which was sewn either on to the navy blue cap or on the navy blue hatband, with red zig-zag stripe, which surrounded the hats which were ordained to be worn by the girls of that period.

This coat of arms and the motto is that of the Wheelwright family[1] who originally held quite large areas of land in the Halifax and Dewsbury districts; one descendant of the family still lives in Nidderdale to this day.

That thousands of children have had the privilege of wearing this coat of arms and attending the Wheelwright Grammar Schools in Dewsbury is due in the first place to one John Wheelwright, who died at North Shields on 26th October, 1724 and was buried in the Parish Church of Sandal Magna, near Wakefield. He was a "collecter" of Salt Duties as it is spelt on his grave slab in that church. In his will, dated 14th October, 1724, he left his estate to provide for the education of the children of his tenants, both boys and girls, and this should also include the inculcation of the doctrines of the Church of England as by Law Established, by the foundation of a school at Rishworth, near Halifax, and the continuation of a school which he had already established at Dewsbury. This clause regarding the teaching of the doctrine of the Church of England was later to be the subject of bitter trouble between the Wheelwright Trustees and the Governors of the Schools on one side and the Local Education Authority of that period on the other.

John Wheelwright was born at Gawthorpe, which is now in the Borough of Ossett but which in those days was in the ancient parish of Dewsbury, and he is described as a bachelor of frugal habits. He was the son of Michael Wheelwright and Dorothy Norton, widow of the late Michael Norton.

1

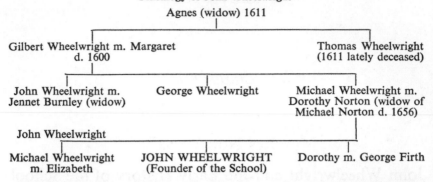

Genealogy of John Wheelwright[2]

Agnes (widow) 1611

Gilbert Wheelwright m. Margaret
d. 1600

Thomas Wheelwright
(1611 lately deceased)

John Wheelwright m.
Jennet Burnley (widow)

George Wheelwright

Michael Wheelwright m.
Dorothy Norton (widow of
Michael Norton d. 1656)

John Wheelwright

Michael Wheelwright
m. Elizabeth

JOHN WHEELWRIGHT
(Founder of the School)

Dorothy m. George Firth

In adult life John Wheelwright became a collector of Salt Duties by profession. Salt was among the first goods liable to Excise Duty in 1643 and this appears to have ceased at the time of the Restoration (1660). In 1694 another Excise Duty of 2/– per bushel was imposed for a period of three years with a countervailing duty on imported salt. The term of duty was extended and in 1702 the management of it was taken from the Board of Excise and placed under a new Board of Commissioners. The Salt duty was repealed in 1730, some six years after John Wheelwright's death and then it was revived in 1732, passing back to the management of the Board of Excise in 1798. It was a very unpopular tax and regarded as far more of a nuisance than its revenue warranted. In the early days, the offices of Collectors of Salt Duties were "farmed" out; but this appears to have ceased around 1680 so that John Wheelwright would be employed by some department of the Crown.[3] These offices appear to have been very lucrative at times and this possibly helps to account for the large areas of land which John Wheelwright was able to own both in Halifax and in Rishworth etc. besides the lands inherited by him from his forebears.[2] There is plenty of evidence to show how the family and ultimately, John Wheelwright acquired property in Ossett, Dewsbury and in the parish of Halifax.

Quite a lot of land which was bought by John Wheelwright was often at first the result of a mortgage. This system of property buying was a very common practice at that date and it was one way of putting money out at interest.

By whatever means John Wheelwright amassed his fortune, he was certainly "well-off" by the standards of those days and besides the lands referred to above, he was a considerable landowner in the Dewsbury District also. Most of the land towards the eastern side of the town which was not owned by the Savile family was owned by him, land on which the former Lancashire and Yorkshire Railway Market Place Station stood and which is now the site of the Longcauseway Gardens, the Crown Building and the former Lancashire and Yorkshire Railway Goods Station, now the site of the new municipal swimming baths, the former Great Northern Railway passenger and goods stations in Crackenedge Lane and Railway

Street (now British Rail), the Town Hall site and the former Ridings Colliery on the west side of Wakefield Road, formerly belonging to Messrs. Crawshaw and Warburton, as well as other property in Dewsbury Bank (i.e. the Wakefield Road area).

Because so much Wheelwright land in Dewsbury, was sold to the railway companies etc. Mr. S. J. Chadwick was able in 1886 to plead successfully to the Charity Commissioners for money to build a secondary school in the town. The Dewsbury portion of the Estates, when sold had produced quite a lot of the money which was held by the Wheelwright Trustees at Halifax and so Mr. Chadwick contended that the town was entitled to some of it back in order to provide a grammar school for the children of the town which it so badly needed at the time.

His efforts were eventually successful in that he was able to obtain £22,000 from the Wheelwright Trustees for the erection and the equipping of the buildings which now stand in Halifax Road, Dewsbury. We shall return to this again much later in this history.

There appears to be no date available when John Wheelwright was appointed a Collector of Salt Duties and it would seem that he carried on right to the time of his death.

From 1706 to 1716 John Wheelwright is referred to as of North Shields but before and after these dates he is described as of Sandal Magna.[2]

John Wheelwright was interested in so many mortgages and transactions in real estate during the last thirty years of his life, all this in addition to his work as a collector of salt duties, that it is evident that he was a very active and capable business man. Other than these details very little else is known about him. He died on 26th October, 1724 according to the inscription on his gravestone in the south aisle of the Church of St. Helen at Sandal Magna, near Wakefield and he was sixty years of age.[*]

There is also a mural tablet on the south wall of the south aisle in the same church which was erected in 1826 which also gives the date of his death and the names of the Trustees which were living at that time.

From his will we conclude that he had few or no very near relatives, for in it he leaves 5/- to the person who could prove himself heir-at-law and although there were cases of people trying to establish this, we have no evidence of it being proved. He could have had nieces and nephews, but this item in his will has led many people to believe that he had been a rover from his youth and had lost touch with his relations, particularly, as he is described as of North Shields.[2]

In the inventory made after his death, the first trustees stated that his library consisted of books and Acts of Parliament relating to the reviews of the duties upon salt and some Latin and English books, most of which were not bound. It is more than likely that these books were at Rishworth; but in his will he ordered that all his books at North Shields or anywhere in

---

[*] According to the *History of Rishworth School* by J. H. Priestley (1930) there appears reason to believe that he might have been 10 years older. His age on the gravestone is covered by a pew. W.P.

Yorkshire were to be collected to form a library for the school (at Rishworth) and this would point to the fact that he considered them to be of sufficient value to form the nucleus of a Library. This love of books and of learning was probably the driving force behind his desire to give to others the benefits of knowledge and learning.[2]

Now to the will of the Founder himself, which is to be found in the Borthwick Institute of Historical Research at York and a copy of it is held by the trustees of the Wheelwright Trust at Halifax. The will goes on to state (only the parts relating to Dewsbury are given here):—

"In the name of God, Amen. I, John Wheelwright, of North Shields in the County of Northumberland, Gentleman, being weak in body but of sound and perfect mind and memory, – praised be God – do make, publish and declare this my last will and Testament in manner and form following, (that is to say) – First and principally, I commend my soul to Almighty God in full hope of pardon of all my sins by Jesus Christ and my body to the earth to be decently interred at the direction of my Executor and Trustee hereafter named and as to my worldly estate I give, devise and bequeath as follows:— Imprimus I give, devise and bequeath all and singular messuages, houses, lands, tenements and heraditaments whatsoever situate and being in the County of York and elsewhere unto John Wheelwright of Norland in the County of York, miller, Ely Dyson of Clay House in the County of York, merchant, and Abraham Thomas of Dewsbury in the said County of York, Clothier upon trust and subject to the several uses, bequests, devises, orders, directions, intents and purposes hereinafter mentioned, expressed and declared and concerning the same. and to and for no other use intent or purpose whatever that is to say upon trust that they, the said John Wheelwright, Ely Dyson and Abraham Thomas do and shall with all convenient speed after my decease convert into a *free school* and convenient appartments for the habitation of the school master, *the house I built at Dewsbury in the said County of York* and that they, the said John Wheelwright, Ely Dyson and Abraham Thomas and the survivors of them and such other person or persons as shall hereinafter be named and appointed trustees in their steads after their or any of their deaths and decease shall and do keep the said school-house in repair and shall pay to the master of the same for the time being for ever at four equal quarterly payments in every year, the clear yearly sum of £2 *for the teaching of 2 poor boys and girls there*, the same to be chosen by my trustees for the time being and also the first and every other school master to be elected by the said John Wheelwright, Ely Dyson and Abraham Thomas and the persons succeeding them in the Trust aforesaid and the said schoolmaster shall pay to the Lord of the Manor for the said school the yearly sum of 2/6d. if demanded. And upon the further trust also that the said John Wheelwright, Ely Dyson and Abraham Thomas do and shall with all convenient speed after my decease out of my personal estate hereinafter devised to them, pay and apply the sum of £150 for the building of a school at Rishworth in the said County of Yorkshire that my said Trustees for the time being so and shall also out of my real estate pay the yearly sum of £10 to a schoolmaster for ever at four equal quarterly payments (to wit) at Candlemas, Mayday, Lammas and Martinmas in every year for the teaching and the instruction of 20 boys and girls to be chosen by my said Trustees from time to time out of the poorest tenants living on any of my Estates and so many of the said boys and girls as shall not be elected out of my said tenant's children shall be chosen by my Trustees for the time being out of the poor of the parish where the said schools stands; the said Master to teach them to read and write and to prepare as many boys for the Latin Tongue as my said Trustees shall judge to have capacities to learn the same: and I do hereby order that the said 20 children so always consist of more boys than girls.

"Item. I give, devise and bequeath unto such person or persons as shall at any time hereafter prove himself or herself to be heir or heiress-at-law to me the sum of 5/– to be paid by my Executor in full of all their or any of their claims or demands of, in and to my real and personal Estate.

"And my will further is that in case my Executors should be absent at the time of my decease, that William Nixon of South Shields in the County of Durham, Supervisor of the Salt Duties, do take care to have my corpse put into a lead coffin in order to be kept till my said Executor or Trustee or some of them shall cause my said corpse to be removed from North Shields aforesaid (in case I die there) to Sandall Magna aforesaid, there to be decently interred in the quire of the Church as near as possible to the grave of my late sister.

"I do hereby authorise the Archbishop of York for the time being to enquire and rectify all and every such abuse or default made to put the same again upon the footing hereby intended, but without further power to intermeddle therein.

"Item. And I do hereby appoint the said John Wheelwright during his natural life to manage and look after the same, and after the death of the said John Wheelwright it is my mind that the said other Trustees shall choose the son of the said John Wheelwright to manage the several trusts aforesaid, and after his decease, shall choose one of their issue male of the body of the said John Wheelwright and for default of such issue shall choose and elect another person of the surname of Wheelwright to manage and look after the trust aforesaid.

"And I also hereby will and devise that constant prayers may be read to the said schools every morning and evening by the masters thereof and that the *said children be religiously and virtuously brought up and educated according to the doctrine of the Church of England as by law established.* Item. I will and hereby order that my said Executors and trustees or any of them shall not demise or grant any part of my several estates for any term exceeding one and twenty years, nor shall they or any of them reserve any greater or other rents upon any such lands or demise than the same are now actually rented at or let for. And lastly, I do hereby make, ordain and appoint the said John Wheelwright, Ely Dyson and Abraham Thomas

joint Trustees for the managing and seeing the several uses and trusts hereinafter mentioned duly observed and performed and do hereby make and appoint the said John Wheelwright sole executor of this my last will and Testament, hereby revoking former wills by me made. In testimony whereof I have hereto set my hand and seal this fourteenth day of October in the year of our Lord one thousand, seven hundred and twenty four.
JOHN WHEELWRIGHT." [2,4]

The will was registered at Wakefield on 10th December, 1724 and we see that it was drawn up some twelve days (14th October, 1724) before John's death which was on 26th October, 1724. He was buried on 30th October, 1724 in Sandal Magna Parish Church near Wakefield in the south aisle of the nave and not in the quire as requested in the will.

Towards the end of the will is the direction that the "said children be religiously and virtuously brought up and educated according to the doctrine of the Church of England as by law established". This direction was to be the source of much trouble with the local education authority, which was at the time we are speaking of the County Council of the West Riding of Yorkshire which eventually led to a House of Lords Appeal before being finally dropped. It had its beneficient side also in that when the Daw Green Charity School affairs were wound up in 1888, the moneys received from the bequest of Mary Bedford to that school, were able to go to the Wheelwright Grammar School for Girls. By her will Miss Bedford directed that the girls at the Charity School in Daw Green should be instructed in the doctrines of the Church of England and so as the Wheelwright Grammar School for Girls was the only school other than elementary ones, in the Borough of Dewsbury, in which specific doctrinal teaching was given as directed in the Instrument of Foundation, it received the benefit of her bequest.

As stated previously, the free school in Dewsbury was already founded by John Wheelwright at the time of his death and this was for two* poor children with Richard Burnell as the master in charge.

These "Free Schools" which were set up in considerable numbers in the eighteenth century were, according to Dr. S. J. Curtis (Former Reader in Education at the University of Leeds)[5] deliberately created "free" so that they might be exempted from the operation of the Statute of Mortmain. This Statute had been enacted in 1279 in order to prevent people evading payment of taxes to the King by granting their lands to some corporate body, such as cathedral or monastery, and then receiving them back as tenants. A corporate body did not pay taxes to the King and so when lands passed to this "dead hand" (mort main) the Crown lost revenue. After the Statute of Mortmain had been implemented, the King retained the right to grant dispensation which permitted lands to be granted to a corporate body

---

* This seems a very small number; but one must realise that the population of Dewsbury would be about 400 in 1724. (It was 409 in 1761 – data from E. J. Green's Thesis *A History of Education in the Borough of Dewsbury*.)

provided the bequest was for a charitable purpose. Thus a person who left property to endow a school fulfilled the above condition if he provided that all or a considerable number of the scholars received instruction without the payment of fees. An increasing number of founders of schools were willing to make this stipulation and applied for a Licence in Mortmain.

John Wheelwright specifically states in his will that the school at Dewsbury should be set up as a free school. Having engaged in collecting taxes for the Crown he would be well acquainted with the legal aspects; but there appears to be no definite application for a "Licence in Mortmain".

It seems doubtful whether this school at Dewsbury was founded to give anything more than elementary type education i.e. the "Three R's", although there is a mention in the Reports from Commissioners in England and Wales for 1826–27 p.815 et seq.[6] in the information required by the Charity Commissioners to be submitted to the Attorney General that – "he found that the School at Dewsbury was established as a grammar school and was sufficient for the accommodation of a larger number of children but he did not find any authority in the will for maintaining a grammar school there."

Richard Burnell continued as master at the school until 1773, though it would appear that for many years past Mr. Henry Goldthorpe had performed the duties of schoolmaster.[6] Burnell by this time must have been an old man as forty-nine years previously he was in office as schoolmaster at the time when John Wheelwright died.

After John Wheelwright's death, the Trustees settled down to the administration of the Estate and for ten years they were free from troubles. By 1737 people of the surname of Wheelwright began making themselves felt by claiming to be heirs-at-law to John. The Trustees either collectively or individually began receiving claims which were bogus. The last one mentioned is one Esther Wheelwright who made such a claim in 1743.[2]

In 1737 Mr. Samuel Burroughs, one of the Masters in Chancery, at the instigation of Mr. Richard Burnell felt that he should know all the matters appertaining to the administration of the Trust. The latter felt that due to his position, he was not entitled to such information. Because of this and the claims made by people carrying the surname Wheelwright, Mr. John Wheelwright, the first Trustee, frightened that the will might be destroyed by one or other party had it presented to the Courts in 1739.[2]

Matters came to a head in 1743 when Richard Burnell and another person laid information that the Trust was not being conducted properly. The Trustees, their Attorney, Mr. Radcliffe and Rev. Joseph Thomas all went to York to attend on the Archbishop.[2]

Answers to the charges made by Mr. Burnell etc., and Mr. Wheelwright stated that the yearly value of the Estate was about £378 9s. 10d. and not £500 as set out by the informants, and the "children have been duly instructed in learning and good morals and prayers, morning and evening".[2]

John Dyson, another Trustee said "that his father died in 1743 and that he was elected a month or two later. His father assisted Mr. Wheelwright at the funeral of the Testator and in repairing and furnishing the property and the school". He also said "that the property was said to be in bad repair."[2] He believed that the estate of John Wheelwright was insufficient hitherto for the charities instituted.[2] He also said "that he never stated that he and Jonas Thomas, the third Trustee, would not elect one of the name of Wheelwright on the death of the present John Wheelwright, who had no male issue."[2]

Jonas Thomas, the third trustee, stated that he was elected a Trustee a month or two after the death of his father, Abraham Thomas, which occurred in 1729. He also stated that he had never said that he would not elect one of the Founder's name on the death of John Wheelwright and divide the salary of £100 between John Dyson and himself. The reiteration of this last statement by both trustees indicates the nature of one of the charges made by the informants.

On 7th September, 1758 a commission sat at Brighouse on these Chancery Court proceedings and George Riley, son-in-law of the Trustee, John Wheelwright, was examined and witnessed the account.[2]

There was then correspondence between Mr. Burnell and Mr. Burroughs concerning the accounts etc. and by 1759 Mr. Burnell appears to have been satisfied with the way the school was carried on but it was by no means the end of the troubles. In 1760 Mr. John Wheelwright was visited by Mr. Howarth about the accounts and again in February of the same year about payments which were not properly entered in the accounts. Later the same year there were still more troubles about payments.[2]

However, in 1761 the informants in Chancery refused to bring their case on account of expense. The Trustees, however, wanted it to go forward and to have the accounts passed, so as not to be liable to be called to account afterwards[2] as they did not wish to go through all the trouble and expense again. It had now become established as one of the annual cases and they were both to lose it. During 1768 the Trustees tried many times to get the Master to make his report but to no avail. During this time, to add to the troubles, the first Trustee, Mr. John Wheelwright died.[2]

The net result of all this litigation was that it was necessary to borrow money. By 1776, £485 had been paid out to various people in costs and this was a considerable drain on the finances of the charity.[2] It was estimated that the total cost of the law suit was £1,137 19s. 7d.[2] That was up to 1779. During this period the income from the estate was £22,384 and the expenditure £22,398. The yearly receipts from 1737 to 1756 were put down at a steady figure of £397 2s. 10d. but later they increased to as much as £500 in some years.[2] The total amount of the income received and paid up to the year 1808 amounted to £37,600.[2] From these figures we get an idea of the sums of money entailed in the transactions and allowing for the depreciation of money from that time to this, we realise that a great deal of money was involved.

It must have been with considerable relief that in 1780 the Trustees were finally able to shake off all the litigation and found themselves free once

more from its clutches. So apart from the first ten years after the death of
the Founder, the next forty-six years were ones of trouble and worry to the
Trustees. In spite of all this we find that they were able to keep going both
the school at Rishworth and the one at Dewsbury. For the full account of
the Rishworth School reference must be made to the book on its history.[2]
   There is so much overlapping of the accounts in the early years of the
trust that both schools were affected.
   In the Wheelwright Trustees Minute books from 1726 *et seq.* the greater
part of each page is devoted mainly to the accounts of Rishworth School
and a list of the scholars is given. As a footnote to each page there is a
mention of the name of the schoolmaster at Dewsbury.[7]
   The first date when a scholar's name is mentioned as being elected to a
place in the school at Dewsbury is 1744,[8] though obviously there had been
scholars there before. He was "Charles Wood, son of Abraham Wood of
Ossett, tenant on one of the Testator's farms in Ossett was elected to be a
poor scholar on the foundation". From 1743 to 1758 the only entry is the
name of the Master (Richard Burnell). From 1759 onwards the names of
the scholars are entered besides that of the Master, i.e.:—
   "14 Aug. 1760 Schoolmaster, Richard Burnell 1 Michael Kitson 2 –
Hepworth."
   The surnames of the children attending the school were very typical
West Riding ones such as Hepworth, Kitson, Webster, Senior, Ellis,
Robinson, Hemmingway, Sykes, Peel, Bradley, as well as Smith and
Jeffery. In spite of the wish of the Founder that a boy and a girl should be
educated at the school it is 1797 before a girl's name is entered in the
minutes; she was Elizabeth Healey.[13] The length of time which these
children spent at school seems to have varied considerably. One to four
years appears to have been an average stay, though one child, John
Jeffery, attended the school from 1774 until 1787, a period of thirteen
years; one wonders whether or not he was employed later as a monitor to
help Mr. Naylor who was the headmaster at the time.
   Richard Burnell carried on as headmaster until 1773, when he died. It
would appear that he had been unable to perform the duties of teacher
latterly as a minute of 2nd August, 1773 states[9] that Henry Goldthorpe had
performed the office of schoolmaster for many years for and on behalf of
Richard Burnell. Henry Goldthorpe was appointed headmaster of the
school and remained until 1777. The agreement which Goldthorpe signed
on his apointment appears to have been used repeatedly for his successors,
the main point in it being that the master was to do the teaching himself
and not through a deputy. It would seem that the trustees were anxious
that a repetition of the state of affairs towards the end of Burnell's life was
not to be repeated.
   Henry Goldthorpe remained as master of the school until 1777 when he
was ejected from his office at a cost of £8 11s. 3d.[10] In that year Robert
Naylor of Thornhill was appointed Master of the school and he had to sign
the same type of agreement as that which Goldthorpe had done. Naylor

was recommended by Rev. Isaac Thomas and Mr. John Hayle (or Hoyle) who were appointed examiners for the purpose of the appointment of the Master. They stated that "Naylor was well instructed and skilled in the English Language and in writing and arithmetic and in every respect".[11] It would seem that these meetings which were held for the appointment of the Master took place at an inn in Dewsbury, Naylor being appointed at the inn of Thomas Grimshaw and when the next appointment was made in May, 1782, it was at the inn of Joseph Gledhill. Naylor had previously been an assistant master at the Thornhill Grammar School and his candidature for the Wheelwright post was supported by the Master of the Thornhill Grammar School and dated 9th September, 1776.[11]

On 1st May, 1782 another meeting was held at Joseph Gledhill's inn for the purpose of electing another master of the school.[12] This time Thomas Greenwood was appointed Master, and he was from Brighouse. His tenure of office lasted until 1791 when on 23rd June of that year a meeting was held at the inn of Mary Gledhill and at this meeting James Pearce was elected Master. Whether this Mary Gledhill was any relation to the Joseph mentioned above, it is impossible to know, though it could easily have been so. James Pearce lived at Gomersal before his appointment to the Dewsbury school. The school was known at this time and until 1859 as "Pearce's School"; it was the common practice at this time for the school to be known by the name of the Master. When John Charles Thornes became Master in 1859 it was then known as "Thorne's School", until its dissolution in 1889.

It was during Mr. Greenwood's tenure of office that the first girl's name (mentioned earlier) appears in the list of scholars.[13] There is then, unfortunately, a gap in the minutes of the Wheelwright Trustees from 1819 to 1854 and when they recommenced in that year the scholars' names are not entered up as they were before. For the events which occurred during this period of the school's history we are obliged to turn elsewhere.

In 1826 the Court of Chancery decided to look into the matter of the administration of the Trust Fund and a report was issued by a Master in Chancery who was in charge of the enquiry.[10] Information concerning the Wheelwright Charity was filed in the Court of Chancery in the year 1816 and a report was made by the Master bearing the date 21st January, 1826.[14]

From this report we gather that it was "among other things, relating chiefly to the charity at Rishworth, in the parish of Halifax and he (the Master) found that the school at Dewsbury was established as a free grammar school and was sufficient for the accommodation of a larger number of children, but he did not find any authority in the will for maintaining a grammar school there; and upon due consideration of the several schemes and proposals brought in before him, and the evidence in support thereof, and such information as had been laid before him by the several parties, he had thought fit to adopt and approve of the following as a proper scheme for the application of the surplus funds, accumulations and increased rents, in the augmentation and extension of the charities, according to the directions contained in the Testator's will, that is to say (*inter alia*, not relating to the school at Dewsbury), that inasmuch as the Testator appeared to have intended to maintain a school-house and schoolmaster at Dewsbury, the trustees should be at liberty to expend a sum not exceeding £100 a year in maintaining the school-house there, and in paying the salaries of a master and mistress, to be employed in the education of as large a number of boys and girls, children of poor parents in Dewsbury, as the said sum would enable them to educate; such children to be educated by the trustees, and to be taught reading, writing and arithmetic, according to the National Plan of education and the girls to be taught plain work." (This is the first time that the syllabus of the school has been clearly stated.)

"At the time of this inquiry, in October, 1826, the trustees were proceeding to carry into effect the several matters found and recommended by the master's report and the scheme therein mentioned; and that no steps had then been taken in respect of the Dewsbury School.

"On August 20th, 1827, some of the Wheelwright Trustees, among whom was the Vicar of Halifax, came over to Dewsbury to view the trust estate and they stated to three of the inhabitants, who called upon them on that occasion, that they were anxious to render the school at Dewsbury as efficient as possible for the purpose of education, within the rules and meaning of the master's report; and they seemed to wish that the inhabitants of Dewsbury would point out and recommend to them a proper person or persons to be appointed by the trustees as master, or as master and mistress of the school. This recommendation has hitherto been most unaccountably neglected, though I am glad to find that there is now a reasonable prospect that the scheme adopted and approved of by the master will soon be carried into effect – meanwhile, there is too much reason to fear that the old machinery of confiscation has been in active operation, and that not deterred by the signal defeat sustained in 1807, in another quarter, it has been secretly working to draw this £100 a year within the pale of the church, and thus to eke out the miserable pittance vouchsafed to that worthy but unfortunate race of young men* – for I must ever esteem them most unfortunate – who are condemned to perform the drudgery of the ecclesiastical establishment at Dewsbury; thus furnishing another instance of that great truth that men will not learn wisdom by experience – but it is to be hoped that the committee appointed at a meeting of the inhabitants on 8th January, 1829, possess too much public spirit a not to say common honesty – to suffer this machinery, though working secretly, to have any influence on their labours."[14]

On 13th January, 1829 a petition was sent to the Wheelwright Trustees signed by twelve prominent townsmen asking that the trustees should exercise the powers vested in them for educating boys and girls, poor

---

* The surplice duties in this populous parish have, for a length of time been so heavy that Dewsbury has scarcely had a curate for many years who has not left it with impaired health, if not shattered constitution.

Leeds Mercury, 17th January 1829. Speech of Mr. Tweedale.

children in Dewsbury, in the manner pointed out in the master's report, to the full extent of the £100 per annum therein mentioned. Also "That they would appropriate the £300 being the £100 per annum since the date of the master's report, and also such further sums as may be within your power, in the erection of a new schoolroom for girls, in addition to the present boys' school, with proper walls for suitable playgrounds on the site of the charity lands adjoining the school, as in your discretion may be deemed expedient.

"That in the appointment of a master and mistress under the extended funds of the charity, Mr. John Pearce, the son of Mr. James Pearce, the late master of the school at Dewsbury, and Mrs. Pearce, his widow, as suitable persons to be continued as master and mistress of the school, at Dewsbury, under such regulations and restrictions as in your discretion may be deemed advisable.

"That in the appointment of Mr. and Mrs. Pearce, or any other future master or mistress of the said school, suggest that it would be advisable to apportion a distinct salary to each, and not to make them in any manner dependent upon each other.

"That it is recommended to you the propriety of absolutely prohibiting any master or mistress appointed to the said school from teaching any children whatever, other than those coming within the limit of the appointment to the said school.

"That a committee of six or eight persons, resident in Dewsbury to assist (as trustees at a distance) in admitting and discontinuing children to be educated at the said school subject to such regulations as you may point out."

From this time onwards for the next forty years the school ran very smoothly and the only reference in that time is to an amended scheme of the Court of Chancery in 1853 by which the annual sum granted to the school was increased from £100 to £150 and the total income of the Trust is said to have been £2,479 and the income from the Dewsbury and Ossett estates £300 4s. 1d. a (S. J. Chadwick in *The Official Programme of the Grand Bazaar of 14th, 15th and 16th November, 1895*) and it remained at this level and continued to be paid until 1888.[10]

In 1855 we find another reference to a mistress at the school for in February, 1855 the Vicar of Dewsbury (Rev. Thomas Albutt) who was the examiner of the charity schools in Dewsbury, recommended that Miss Row's (Mistress of the girls' school) salary be increased as it was inadequate. It was resolved that her salary be £50 per annum and an allowance of £10 a year be made to her in lieu of providing her with a suitable residence.[15] The last year of this decade saw another change in the mastership of the boys' school. On 8th August, 1859 John Charles Thornes was appointed the master at a salary of £50 per annum with a cottage for residence, £10 a year additional (in lieu of the beneficial occupancy of cottages underlet by the late master) and also the pence usually paid by the scholars. From this it would appear that the school was no longer a free

MR. JOHN CHARLES THORNES.
(Master of the Old Wheelwright School.)
(Courtesy of the "Dewsbury Reporter" and Central Library, Dewsbury)

school, yet Green in his thesis[18] in a footnote states that the late Mr. J. E. Tolson, a former headmaster and Freeman of Dewsbury has said "that 'Thorne's school' was always looked upon as inferior because education there was free, whereas the Board Schools charged their pupils as follows :- 3d. up to Std. iv; 5d. for Std v and 6d. for Std. vi and over (the charge was remitted if parents were in receipt of Poor Law)." It was understood on the appointment of Mr. Thornes that the proportion of the scholars' pence usually paid to the master for his own personal benefit would amount to £10.[16] Mr. Albutt (Vicar of Dewsbury) also applied for £25 towards the repair of the schools and the school premises in Dewsbury.[16]

The next year (1860) Miss Catherine Hazelwood was appointed mistress of the school in Dewsbury in place of Miss Agnes Row at a salary of £60 a year.[17] This lady must have set a precedent for she was the first of the mistresses to marry her opposite number in the boys' school. Mr. Thornes and Miss Hazelwood were married in 1876.

In the same year[19] we find in addition to applications for leases of land from the Wheelwright Trustees, land was being sold, and in that year some land at Priest Pig Hill in Ossett was sold to a Mr. Speight for £550. This was one of the earliest sales of land in the Dewsbury District and it was to be followed by the notification by the Lancashire and Yorkshire Railway Company in 1863 that under the Parliamentary compulsory powers of purchase, it was their intention to take such land belonging to the Wheelwright Charity in Dewsbury as would be required for their branch line and railway works there.[20] Though the line and the station were constructed and opened in 1867[21] (1st April) the litigation connected with it was not completed until 1869.[21]

In 1864 more land was sold at Flockton for £1,050 and land at Mapplewell (Barnsley) for £650.[22] It was not until 1869 that more land was sold in

Dewsbury and this time the sum exchanged was greater than any of these already mentioned. This was land which the Dewsbury Borough Council required at the bottom of Wakefield Road, Dewsbury, for the erection of their new Town Hall. The Town Hall was at that time in Bond Street opposite the Telephone Exchange. This plot of land between Wakefield Road and the Lancashire and Yorkshire Railway Station (part of which is now the Longcauseway Gardens) was the subject of a special meeting of the Trustees on 8th April, 1869. The site was divided into two Lots, Lot 1 comprising 3,300 sq. yds. at £2 2s. 0d. per sq. yd. and Lot 2 which was 7,000 sq. yds. in area. If the Dewsbury Corporation decided to buy both lots together and dispose of Lot 2 as they wished, the Trustees were willing to sell both lots at £1 1s. 0d. per sq. yd. However, the Council decided against this and settled for Lot No. 1 which cost them £6,930. So it would appear that the Town Hall site alone accounted for more than a quarter of the money which was eventually granted by the Wheelwright Trustees for the erection of the new schools in Halifax Road. For some reason or other, though the site was purchased, the Town Hall was not built for another seventeen years as the Foundation Stone was laid in 1886 and the completed building opened the day before the Wheelwright Grammar Schools were opened in Bond Street, namely 17th September, 1889.

The next major sale of Wheelwright land in Dewsbury was the purchase of some land adjoining the Town Hall site by the Great Northern Railway Company in 1871 and 1872. This land was sold to the railway company for £1,200. There is a relic of Wheelwright ownership of the land in this part of the town in the name of the street separating the rear of the Town Hall and the former Great Northern Railway Goods Depot (now British Rail) and continuing in front of the Crown Buildings. This is called Rishworth Road from the name of the other half of the Wheelwright Estates which are situated there.

This last sale took us rather into the future. In 1870 Forster's Education Act was passed and in preparation for it, the school at Dewsbury was inspected under the Endowed Schools Act of 1869 by Mr. Fearon, an assistant commissioner. He made a report on the school.[23] It was found that John Charles Thornes, who was an uncertified teacher, was assisted by several boys acting as monitors and together they taught 87 boys, and Mrs. Thornes with one assistant taught 57 girls. Mr. Fearon reported that the range of subjects was rather limited though the children were efficient in the subjects taught.[10] The children belonged to the poorest families and they remained at the school for only a short time before being removed to other schools in the town. There was some need and desire for secondary education in the town as "The ex-Mayor (of Dewsbury) thinks it is a most undignified position for Dewsbury to be dependent on Batley on the one side and Thornhill on the other for its secondary education."[10] Mr. Fearon decided against changing the status of the Wheelwright School and at a public meeting in Dewsbury Town Hall stated that "he's been instructed to look at the Wheelwright Charity School and a Charity School at Daw

Green and to see if either were fit for such purpose (i.e. For the purpose of a grammar school) but had come to the conclusion that they were elementary schools and as such could be very useful."[24] The Endowed Schools Commission also proposed that free education should be abolished except as a reward of merit. This caused great consternation among the people of Dewsbury and they claimed that this decision violated John Wheelwright's will.[25] In February, 1875, a petition was sent by the Trustees containing sixteen objections to the Commissioner's proposals. Objections 3, 4 and 5 in particular had special reference to the Dewsbury school. The Commissioners, under their scheme, suggested that the school at Dewsbury should be discontinued and the petitioners pointed out that under the 1869 Endowed Schools Act, they had no power to do this. Also it was claimed that the Commissioners' scheme would violate the testator's will in that children of the middle classes would benefit by the scheme instead of the children living in the parishes in which the schools were situated. Objection No. 5 was to the effect that Dewsbury was also a large and populous town and growing in size. The School Board's objection was that "In the opinion of the Board the Wheelwright School in this town is doing good service as a useful elementary day school and as such they are anxious that it should not be removed from the borough."[26] Besides this there was a petition from the Dewsbury Corporation to the same end with the added implication in their second objection "That by the 17th Section of a scheme contained in an Order of the High Court of Chancery dated 12th February, 1853, it was ordered that "inasmuch as the Founder appears to have intended to maintain a school-house and schoolmaster at Dewsbury, the Trustees shall be at liberty to expend a sum not exceeding £150 per annum in maintaining the schoolhouse there belonging to the charity and in paying the salaries of a master and mistress to be employed in the education of as large a number of boys and girls, children of poor parents, in Dewsbury as the said sum will enable them to educate, such children to be nominated by the Trustees and to be taught reading, writing and arithmetic according to the national plan of education and the girls to be taught plainwork."[26] The idea behind the scheme of the Commissioners was to establish a Higher Grade School in Dewsbury with the moneys from the Charity. However, such was the opposition that the whole scheme had to be dropped.[10]

Nothing of importance occurred again until February, 1876, when Mr. Thornes was given an increase in salary to £70 a year to be effective from the following July. At the same meeting of the Trustees, Rev. Francis Pigon (Vicar of Halifax) was elected a trustee to succeed the late Archdeacon Musgrove.[27]

The next year the Trustees were obliged to assert clearly that though they appreciated the support of the Dewsbury Town Council and the Dewsbury School Board in their opposition to the scheme of the Charity Commissioners, they found that they were bound by section 18 of the scheme which was in force at the time, under the Endowed Schools Act, so that they could not contribute to a fund to assist the establishment of a Higher Grade

School in Dewsbury. They were also precluded from doing this by the increase in the number of boys at Rishworth. At the same time Mr. Thornes was allowed £15 towards the cost of desks at Dewsbury. In August of the same year an interesting case came before the Trustees. This was the application of Mr. George Brooke of Dewsbury asking for the nomination of his daughter to the school. This was refused on the grounds that she was not eligible as he was a lessee, not a tenant, of the Wheelwright charity lands within the terms of the Founder's Trust. Lands were sold in Dewsbury to the Great Northern Railway Company for the sum of £1,125 and in Elland to the School Board for £957 8s. 9d.[28] By this time lands had been sold in the Dewsbury parish realising upwards of £24,000,[29] and this caused friends of education in the town to consider whether or not an effort should be made to obtain a new scheme for the management of the Wheelwright Trust by which some satisfactory and adequate provision might be made for the founding and endowing of a school for providing secondary education in Dewsbury.[29]

So we come to one of the most interesting periods in the history of the schools, the struggle which lasted over the next ten years or so for the establishment of a grammar school in the town and the part which the late Mr. S. J. Chadwick played in this fight to obtain money from the Wheelwright Trustees so that the grammar school could be founded, first temporarily in a warehouse in Bond Street and later in the fine buildings erected from Dewsbury's share of the Charity moneys, in Halifax Road.

In 1870 there was a growing need for secondary education in Dewsbury when Mr. Fearon (an assistant commissioner) in December of that year made his inspection of the schools. As the 1870 Education Act had not come into force at this time, Mr. Fearon held out very little hopes of assistance from the Trust and he put forward certain proposals made by the Charity Commissioners for the establishment of a grammar school in the town. A committee was formed and it endeavoured to raise funds for the erection of a school, but no really active steps were taken and nothing came of it. Nothing more was done until 1881 when the matter was taken up by an influential local committee. A memorial to the Wheelwright Trustees was drawn up by Mr. Malcolm Paterson, C.E., one of the originators of the movement and was signed by most of the gentry and leading men of the town and neighbourhood and a copy was forwarded to the Charity Commissioners with the result that on 18th August, 1882 Mr. Fearon again visited Dewsbury and met a deputation of the memorialists who urged on him the claims of Dewsbury to further assistance from the Wheelwright Trustees. These claims were constantly urged on the Charity Commissioners and the Wheelwright Trustees until 1884. The arguments were for a grammar school to be established out of the trust funds "to be erected in a central position in Dewsbury with provision for the foundation scholars to be chosen by competitive examination from children attending efficient elementary schools within the parish and district."[30]

In August, 1882, the Charity Commissioners wrote to the Wheelwright

Trustees asking them to furnish them with a report on the state of the schools at Dewsbury and from their reply we gather that John Charles Thornes was appointed on 8th August, 1859 at a salary of £70 per annum and his wife, Mrs. Catherine Thornes at a salary of £60.[31] The number of children on the books was 87 boys and 115 girls, making a total of 202 and an average attendance of 161, this low figure being caused by half-timers. These figures appear to be contradictory to those given by Bamford in his Thesis[10] in which he states there were 93 boys and 73 girls when Mr. Fearon visited the Dewsbury School in August, 1882 (Borough of Dewsbury Extensions Enquiry 1909 Vol. 1 App. ii and iv).

Also Mr. Fearon gave a summary of the syllabus in the two schools which was as follows:—

"Instruction in the Boys' School.

Reading, writing, arithmetic, grammar, geography, and religious knowledge.

Girls' School.

Reading, writing, arithmetic, religious knowledge, sewing and knitting."[31]

From this point onwards for the next few years, correspondence flows thick and fast, with the Wheelwright Trustees guarding their position. These letters are too tedious to quote fully; but enough will be given to try to give a clear picture of the state of things leading up to the Scheme of 3rd May, 1888.

At first the Wheelwright Trustees were willing to allow only £500 for the purpose of education in Dewsbury to come from the funds of the Charity, and suggested that the schools at Dewsbury should be discontinued, as was also suggested by the Charity Commissioners.[32]

In 1885 Mr. Fearon wrote to the Wheelwright Trustees to the effect that estimates had been made so as to provide an income of £500 per annum to Halifax and Dewsbury (in the former case to the Heath Grammar School which was in need of financial assistance as it was at this time closed) and this to be in addition to the £150 a year already made payable there.[33]

On 30th April, 1885, a letter from Messrs. Emmett and Walker (solicitors and clerks to the Wheelwright Trustees) was written to the Charity Commissioners to the effect that they had come to another decision; that a sum of £22,000 should be applied for the benefit of Heath Grammar School and that the amount to Dewsbury, which was a town about half the size of Halifax should be reduced, and also because the bulk of the Founder's estates were in the parish of Halifax, and that the associations of the Founder were much more closely connected with Halifax than with Dewsbury. The Trustees suggested that £15,000 or a sum not exceeding £17,000 should be appropriated to Dewsbury and that in addition the Dewsbury School site should be sold and the proceeds applied for educational purposes at Dewsbury.[34]

By this time it should be mentioned that the accumulated income of the Wheelwright Charity had amounted to about £40,000 in Consols and it was agreed to share out the moneys as follows:— Dewsbury, £15,000 (this sum in addition to the value of the school site in Dewsbury), Heath Grammar School at Halifax £18,000, Hipperholme Grammar School £3,000 and Sowerby Grammar School £3,000.[35]

All through this period the patience of the townspeople of Dewsbury was wearing thin. So much so that two very opposite factions decided to go ahead and establish schools for secondary education without waiting for the outcome of the Wheelwright struggle. These two factions were the High Church Party under the leadership of Canon Brooke (later Archdeacon of Halifax) and the Vicar of Dewsbury (Canon Lowther Clarke, who later became Archbishop of Melbourne). This party was responsible for the establishment of St. Augustine's Grammar School in Leeds Road, Dewsbury, and the High School for Girls in St. Mark's schoolroom. The other party was headed by the leading Non-Conformists who established the Dewsbury Grammar School Company and hired a warehouse in Bond Street in which building the school was carried on. This will be dealt with in greater detail later as its buildings and fittings were taken over by the Wheelwright Grammar Schools under the Scheme of 3rd May, 1888.

First, then, let us look at St. Augustine's Grammar School. This will be dealt with at some length as it was to prove a rival to the Wheelwright Grammar Schools in their early years, particularly the boys' school.

ST. AUGUSTINE'S GRAMMAR SCHOOL, DEWSBURY

On 27th January, 1883, a letter appeared in the *Dewsbury Reporter* over the signature of Mr. F. W. Reuse, a prominent Dewsbury churchman urging that something must be done to get things moving for the establishment of a "Higher Grade School" in the town for as yet nothing had been done in spite of the committee elected to encourage this move in education which was then three years old.[44] Nothing superficially appears to have been done during the next year, though some hard work had been going on, for in the same local paper for Saturday, 19th April, 1884, the first advertisement, giving the full details of St. Augustine's Grammar School appeared. This gave the name of the School's Visitor (The Bishop of Ripon), and the Provost of the Northern Division of the Woodard Trust (Rev. Canon Lowe, D.D.) and the name of the headmaster. This was a venture by the Church party into grammar school administration with the help of the Woodard Corporation. In August of that year an examination was held for the award of a scholarship and which was open to all boys under thirteen years of age who for the two years previously had attended an elementary school under church management in the Dewsbury Rural Deanery. An advertisement in December of that year gave a list of the local Committee responsible for governing the school and this included many notable churchmen in the district. It was also stated that the headmaster (Rev. W. H. Fisher) had two assistant teachers.

In May, 1885, the school had its first Prize Day at which the Dean of York presented the prizes. After the ceremony, the Dean preached in St.

Philip's Church (which is now demolished). Two boys won scholarships to Denstone College.

In 1886 Herr Hugo Schoenemann was appointed German master at the school so that at this time he had appointments at both St. Augustine's and the Dewsbury Grammar School.

A new headmaster, Rev. J. Haworth, B.A., Cambridge, was appointed in April, 1888, and details are given for the examination held to award the only scholarship from elementary schools in Dewsbury. The subjects were English, English Grammar, Arithmetic, Geography, History and Divinity.

After the first Prize Day which was held in May, the rest of the annual Prize Days were held at the end of the summer term. From 1889 onwards the new Bishop of Wakefield (Dr. W. Walsham How) took a very keen interest in the school and appears to have been the principle speaker at the Speech Days for many years. In 1889 there were 48 boys in the school as against 49 the previous year, and the report of the external examiner was also very gratifying to the governors.

The year 1890 appears to have been a trying one for the school as during that time it was short-staffed for much of the time but from January, a third assistant was appointed. Again the examiner gave a good report of the year's work even under these trying circumstances. According to the examiner's report one gets an idea of the curriculum, which was as follows:— English, Mathematics, Geography, History, Chemistry, Geology, Physical Geography, French and German.

1891 saw the death of Herr Schoenemann whilst still teaching at the school and glowing tributes were paid to his untiring work both at this school and at Wheelwright Grammar School where he was now also the German master. By this time, there was a feeling growing concerning the rivalry between St. Augustine's and the new Wheelwright School. The Rev. H. Lowther Clarke mentioned this in the vote of thanks which he proposed to the Bishop of Wakefield at that year's Speech Day. This is interesting, really, as he (Lowther Clarke) was largely responsible for any "feeling" which grew up between the two schools. Two of the masters at the school at this period appear to have been resident ones. Numbers were dwindling at this time but there is a mention in 1892 that the numbers had risen from 21 to 43 and that also one County Council Scholarship had been won. This was to the value of £60 per annum. Canon Lowther Clarke hailed the new headmaster (Rev. D. Johnson) as "one of the most successful teachers in the North of England."

When the Archbishop of York came to open the new Wheelwright Grammar Schools on 19th May, 1893, he also paid a visit to St. Augustine's and expressed delight to see boys in a school belonging to that great Foundation of Canon Woodard which he believed was one of the greatest enterprises of the century. At the Speech Day of that year the headmaster said that though the work was improving, he hoped for better things, though it was gratifying to learn that one Old Boy had obtained his Inter

B.Sc. at Victoria University (now University of Manchester) at 16 years of age.

Difficulties began to show themselves in 1894 when it was announced that the fees would have to be increased and at the Speech Day, Canon Lowther Clarke stated that he had paid more than was asked by the governors for his son who was a pupil at the school. This is very interesting as reference will be made later to Canon Clarke's position as chairman of the governors of the two grammar schools in the town. During 1894 Mr. Walton Batley, A.R.C.O. was appointed music master at the school so that he, like Herr Schoenemann had connections with more than one secondary school in the town.

Mr. Johnson remained as headmaster until 1897 when he was succeeded by Rev. H. W. Lowe, M.A. Besides being Headmaster of St. Augustine's Mr. Johnson had also occupied the position of assistant curate at St. Mark's Church in Dewsbury from 1890 to 1896.[50] This was probably due to the small salary which he received as headmaster of the school. By now a cricket and football field had been obtained by the efforts of the Old Boys of the school and was used by the present pupils.

The next year saw the first of the appeals for the churchman of the district to support the school. Even under these adverse conditions good reports were still being obtained by the school.

At the 1898 Speech Day, there were further appeals for support by the churchmen of the district by the chairman of the governors. But in spite of these the school had to close in March, 1899. On 11th April of that year the premises were re-opened as a private school under Mr. Happerfield, who had been senior master when it was run as a grammar school. Before leaving the school we find a good description of it in the *Dewsbury Reporter* for 1896. ". . . it was situated in a two-storey building in Leeds Road on a waste piece of land. The lower storey contained one moderately-sized classroom with two little classrooms off it and the upper storey was used as the gymnasium. At the time of writing (1896) there were fifty boys in the school and the fees were £4 15s. a year in the junior school and £7 10s. in the senior school. There is no endowment and the buildings were originally partly paid for by subscriptions, and there is still a debt on them now. There is some science teaching in the school, the boys taking chemistry, and selected boys doing a certain amount of a qualitative analysis, the laboratory being one of the small classrooms with a few poor fittings. The boys are not sent in for the Science and Art Examinations. Of the fifty boys, 16 are boarders who pay £39 a year inclusive. The headmaster is allowed by the governors £300 out of which he is supposed to pay the assistant masters. These masters hold no degree and receive £45 a year and their board. There are three assistant masters. The headmaster seems to be making considerable efforts under difficult circumstances, having obtained two County Scholarships, one to the Yorkshire College (now the University of Leeds) and one classical scholarship to Shrewsbury School in the past two years.[38]

"Most of the boys come from elementary schools and stay to about fifteen years of age."

"The composition of the school is somewhat deplorable, of necessity by the absence of a Conscience Clause, cut off from County Scholars and from assistance from local funds, while at the same time it is not supported properly by those responsible for bringing it into existence, so that the headmaster is in a very painful position".

By backing the St. Augustine's Grammar School the Woodard Corporation went outside its normal sphere of residential education and helped to establish a day school.[18] However, it would seem that the Woodard Corporation "has cause to congratulate itself on the fact that the struggles of its Dewsbury venture between 1889 and 1899 effectively warned it against any further experiments in the day-school field."[37]

By the closure of the St. Augustine's Grammar School in March 1899 the competition between it and the newly opened Wheelwright Grammar School for Boys was ended.

THE HIGH SCHOOL FOR GIRLS

The second of the experiments to provide secondary education for the children in Dewsbury contemporary with St. Augustine's Grammar School was the High School for Girls. The history of this school opens when in July, 1884 a secretary was sent from London to Dewsbury to help with the work of founding the High School for Girls and among other things arranged, it was decided that there should be a Conscience Clause in the Scheme for this school. A company was floated called the Church School Company Limited which had a capital of £100,000 in 20,000 shares of £5 each and in the issue of the *Dewsbury Reporter* for 13th December, 1884 the first advertisement appears stating that the school would open on 13th January, 1885 under a qualified headmistress (Miss A. M. Smallpiece) who was trained at Newnham College, Cambridge and had previously taught at the Queens School, Chester.

The school officially opened on Tuesday, 13th January, 1885 and this opening was preceded by a celebration of the Holy Communion in St. Mark's Church at eight o'clock in the morning. At half past eleven a large congregation assembled in the church to hear the sermon by the Lord Bishop of Ripon after which service there was a luncheon in the school. The Vicar of Dewsbury (Rev. Thomas Whitby) was supported by most of the leading churchmen in the district. It was emphasised that this school was in no way a competitor to any other school in the district and it was hoped that the venture would be so successful that in the near future a new building would be needed.[46] The school was held in the Sunday School room of St. Mark's Church.

Besides the headmistress only one other mistress is mentioned in 1885 and that is Miss M. A. Tatham; but by 1886 several teachers are mentioned. Besides Miss Smallpiece there are Misses Innison and Allen, Miss Wormald for the piano and two men teachers, one for Art (Mr. Stevenson)

21

and one for dancing and deportment (Mr. Harrison Taylor).

The first Prize Day of the new school was held on 21st September, 1886, the day that the school re-assembled for its second session. The examiner (Mr. F. B. Jevans, M.A., Tutor and examiner in the University of Durham) read his report of the first year's working and said that he found the younger girls more enthusiastic regarding the school than the older ones, which he thought a very encouraging sign as they were the future members of the school.[47]

In April, 1888 a new headmistress was appointed; she was Miss Barbara Foxley, B.A. (Cambridge) and in the September of that year an advertisement in the *Dewsbury Reporter* gives an idea of the nature of the syllabus of the school. The headmistress was to teach the French, German by Fraulein Von Mollin, painting by Mr. Foster and Dancing by Mr. Taylor.

A kindergarten was established in September, 1889 under the direction of Miss Herbert for both boys and girls, and the following September a further addition to the staff was made in the person of Miss Wilson (trained at the Stuttgart Conservatoire) which would seem to indicate that the music side of the school was flourishing.

By March, 1891 the school owed St. Mark's Church £26 10s. 1d.[45,49] and the school moved to new premises. When the school re-opened after Easter on 18th April, 1891 it was in Eightlands House in Ashworth Road near to what was then the London and North Western Railway Station (now the Wellington Road station of British Rail). In September the following list of assistant teachers was given in the local paper – Misses Wormald and Wilson, and Messrs. Bowling, Foster and Harrison Taylor.

In 1892 the fees for the kindergarten were given in the advertisement in the local paper for 10th September, 1892 as £2 5s. 0d. for the under sevens, £7 for the seven to twelves, and £10 for the over-twelves, and there was an extra charge of £1 1s. 0d. for those attending Mr. Harrison Taylor's dancing classes.

On Friday, 19th May, 1893 when the Archbishop of York opened the new Wheelwright Grammar Schools in Halifax Road, he also paid a visit to the Girls' High School at Eightlands House. In this year also the school carried out an experiment with boarders as well as day girls. The girl boarders were to live with Miss Smith at 18 West Park Street, Dewsbury and the same year saw another change of headmistress, the new one being Miss M. M. R. James. She stayed for three years and was replaced in 1896 by Miss Page, B.A. (London).[36]

In 1899 the title of the school was altered to "The High School, Eightlands" and in the advertisement in the *Dewsbury Reporter* for 4th January 1899 it was announced that dinners would be provided for pupils from a distance. In September 1900 Miss Gedge was appointed headmistress of the school and in the following January, the school moved again to new premises. This time it moved to Highfield House, Hill Head. From the advertisement in the local paper of 19th January, 1901 there appears to have been a headmistress and six certificated teachers and Canon Clarke was still the chairman of the governors. The stay at Highfield House was a short one, as the school closed in the Spring of 1902.

THE DEWSBURY GRAMMAR SCHOOL

Once again we return to 1884 in order to trace the history of the other contemporary secondary school in the town which was the Dewsbury Grammar School. The first move to inaugurate this school was a meeting which was held on Friday, 16th May, 1884 in the Lecture Hall of the Wesleyan Chapel, Dewsbury. Mr. Simon Crawshaw occupied the chair and Mr. Evans was elected secretary *pro. tem.* A few weeks earlier a committee had been formed which had met on four occasions and it decided that a public school limited company should be formed to carry out the wants and requirements of the scheme for the establishment of a high class school at Dewsbury and they recommended that the company be called the "Dewsbury Grammar School Company Limited."[51]

The next move was the appearance of an advertisement in the *Dewsbury Reporter* for 28th June, 1884 describing the new venture and the names of the promoters who were John Walker Esq., J.P., Mark Oldroyd, J.P., John Ingram, J.P., Mark Hirst, J.P., John Riley Robinson Esq., LL.D., and William Howroyd Esq. Premises were obtained in Bond Street, Dewsbury, in a warehouse which until lately (1971) was in the possession of Messrs. G. H. & F. Hill, wholesale tobacconists.

The *Dewsbury Reporter* for 13th September, 1884 carried the first advertisement for the new grammar school, stating that the school would be opened on Monday, 15th September, 1884 under Mr. A. Wooldridge Godby M.A. as headmaster and Miss Edith Millar, late Jodrell Scholar, as headmistress with Mr. Walter Heslop M.A. as assistant in the boys department and Miss Milnes assistant in the girls' school. The address of the girls' school is given as Grove Street, which is the street adjoining Bond Street at the corner of which two streets the school was situated. From this it would seem that there was probably a separate entrance for the girls and the boys.

The school was officially opened on Monday, 15th September, 1884 when a large number of promoters and others attended the ceremony. Mr. John Walker of Dewsbury Mills, occupied the chair and amongst others present was Prof. Bodington M.A. (Principal of the Yorkshire College, Leeds).

Mr. C. R. Evans, the secretary, gave a report concerning the origin and progress made by the scheme to found a school. He referred to the fact that though Dewsbury on the whole considered itself superior to the neighbouring town of Batley, yet it had to send its children to that town for higher education; but that now that state of affairs was to end. Boys and girls could get the higher education they asked for in their own town. Several schemes had proved abortive, but the new Dewsbury Grammar Schools were the result of the untiring efforts on the part of the promoters and particularly of Rev. C. Burbridge. The secretary went on to state that the objects of the promoters were to establish a grammar school for everyone; no religious tests whatever were to be imposed upon anyone connected with the schools beyond the very broad one "That the headmaster and the headmistress must be members of some Christian congregation."

He went on to say that all education is based or should be based on high moral principles which in turn are based on the New Testament, so that the education would be Christian but not sectarian. There was a difficulty in the fact that they had no endowment, no ancient foundation on which they could establish scholarships for the encouragement of deserving students but to provide for this they had issued Foundation Shares, the dividends from which would go to provide such scholarships. Mr. Evans went on to say that they were lucky in obtaining the services of Mr. Godby of Magdalen College, Oxford, and Mr. Walter Heslop, M.A., his assistant on the boys' side and Miss Edith Millar of Newnham College, Cambridge and Miss Milnes her assistant. The School had been or would be divided into Classical and Modern sides; the boys in the former would be prepared for the universities and examinations in which a knowledge of Greek is required. On the Modern side the instruction was to be such as to fit the boys for mercantile life, special attention being given to French and German. Also in order to meet the needs of a manufacturing district, special attention was to be given to Chemistry, and science in general, so that boys from the school could proceed without difficulty to such colleges as the Yorkshire College at Leeds. In the girls' school, the directors aimed at as inclusive a course as the boys', the only extras being music, advanced German and advanced drawing. A special feature of the girls' side was that classes of advanced students would be held for selected subjects not included in the school course. One for English was in process of being formed. The lectures would be such as to qualify the students for the Higher Cambridge Examinations.[48]

The motto of the school was to be *Semper ad lucem* – always towards the light.

The chairman said that "there was a company known as the Public Schools Company which assisted grammar schools but they had found that the claims on that company were so heavy that they decided it would be easier to establish a school on their own basis than through them."

Mr. Godby was then asked to speak and outlined the aims of the school. Once again he stressed the unsectarian character of the religious teaching and said that he would endeavour to train the boys so that they would grow up sober and busy Englishmen. He thought it important that Latin should be part of the curriculum and stressed the importance of French and German in a great centre of industry like Dewsbury and then went on to give his views on corporal punishment (but these were not stated!).[48]

In September, 1885 Mr. Heslop had been replaced by Mr. J. E. Forty, M.A. (Oxford) and Mr. Alfred Broughton had also been appointed as music master. Those pupils wishing to take music had to pay an extra fee above the standard rate; for boys under thirteen years of age it was £1 0s. 0d., and those above that age £1 6s. 9d.

The spring term of 1886 saw the appointment of a German Master (Herr Hugo Schoenemann of the University of Prague). This gentleman was also to become the German master at St. Augustine's Grammar School and he also taught privately German, French, Italian, Spanish and Dutch from his home in Oxford Road. When the Dewsbury Grammar School became defunct in 1889, he, like Miss Hovey, carried on with the newly formed Wheelwright Grammar Schools until his death in 1891.

Mr. Forty was a graduate in mathematics and when he left he was replaced by another mathematician. Miss Kay, the second headmistress, was also a graduate in mathematics.

In January, 1896 Sgt. McNally was appointed drill sergeant, as the teacher of physical education was called in those days. Both Mr. Godby and Miss Millar appear to have been very keen educationists as besides being heads of the two schools, they were also joint secretaries for the Cambridge Local Examinations. Besides these activities Mr. Godby also advertised in the local press that he would prepare people for the various examinations at his residence in Alexandra Crescent and he also taught at evening classes which were held in the Dewsbury Grammar School premises in Bond Street. In 1887 Miss E. J. Kay (Newnham College, Cambridge) was appointed headmistress in the place of Miss Millar and there was an addition to the staff in the appointment of Miss Hovey, B.A. (London). The next year Mr. Forty left and Mr. R. H. Greatorex, B.A. (Oxford) was appointed assistant master. He also was an honoursman in Mathematics and Science.

A Preparatory class was started in 1888 for boys and girls aged five years to eight years of age and also commercial subjects were added to the curriculum.

By the time that the Wheelwright Scheme received the Royal Assent on 3rd May, 1888, the Dewsbury Grammar School was finding it hard to carry on as it had no endowments and the expense of meeting the costs of maintaining the premises and school without any outside assistance made it impossible to carry on. As the newly established Wheelwright Grammar Schools had no building to go into, they were glad enough to lease the same warehouse in Bond Street until recently occupied by the Dewsbury Grammar School and purchase the equipment (desks etc.) which had belonged to that school and put it to use themselves until a new school could be built.

THE ESTABLISHMENT OF THE WHEELWRIGHT GRAMMAR SCHOOLS IN DEWSBURY

The three schools which we have just dealt with were established and in operation contemporaneously with the final years of the struggle to obtain money from the Wheelwright Trustees in order to set up a really good secondary school in the town. So back to 1885, when, in a rider to a letter from Messrs. Emmet and Walker on behalf of the Wheelwright Trustees to the Charity Commissioners on 14th May, of that year, it was suggested that the £15,000 which was to be appropriated for use in Dewsbury for the erection of a good secondary school should be divided as follows:— £10,000 to St. Augustine's Grammar School and £5,000 to the Dewsbury High School for Girls (St. Mark's) as the education given in these schools was in accordance with the principles of the Church of England. The Trustees were anxious that only schools which strictly could be called "Church Schools" should benefit from the moneys. The Trustees also felt that they had conceded so much to mixed charities and they were satisfied that they had not approached the subject in a narrow spirit in making the decision that the £15,000 should be devoted to giving the children of Churchmen higher education in the town.[38]

A personal visit to Dewsbury was made by the Trustees of Wheelwright's Charity in July, 1885 for the purpose of seeing the conditions of the schools and also to meet the Mayor and Town Clerk and they also met and had discussions with the trustees of the Dewsbury Grammar School in Bond Street, St. Augustine's and the High School for Girls and they finally received a deputation from the working men of the town. The main point at issue was whether it would be advisable to apply a portion of the funds to some central* middle class schools for boys and girls or to subsidise the present boys' and girls' schools in Dewsbury.[39]

At their meeting on 6th July, 1885 the Wheelwright Trustees decided that as a result of their visit to Dewsbury they were satisfied that a new good centrally placed Church of England Grammar School for both boys and girls such as was proposed by the Corporation of Dewsbury as well as the moderate churchmen, should receive their support and that the previous offers of help to St. Augustine's Grammar School, and the High School for Girls should no longer hold.[39]

Now we find the first moves towards the final scheme which was to culminate in that of 3rd May, 1888. Various draft schemes were sent to the Trustees for their consideration. The first one was put forward in July, 1885. A letter from the Wheelwright Trustees to the Charity Commissioners after stating that they had met the Town Clerk of Dewsbury and a committee had been appointed by the Dewsbury Corporation agreed upon headings for founding a Wheelwright Grammar School at Dewsbury. Among these headings was that a grant of £15,000 be made for a school for boys and girls at Dewsbury to be educated in the doctrines of the Church of England, the Scheme to have a Conscience Clause, the site of the present School to be sold, there to be 14 governors, nine of them co-optative Churchmen, the Wheelwright Trustees to make the first appointment, and that there should always be a majority of churchmen on the governing board; eight scholarships for boys and four for girls; that Mr. and Mrs. Thornes be paid a pension of £70 and £30 respectively for the rest of their lives and they admitted that the people of Dewsbury had claims upon the

* Meaning by this term schools in which education higher than elementary was given.

funds of the Charity as well, and that the Trustees would oppose every scheme proposed by the Charity Commissioners unless it was within the terms of John Wheelwright's will.[40]

The suggestions of the Wheelwright Trustees were considered by the Charity Commissioners and in their reply we come across the first mention of the higher figure of £22,000 as the sum which would be required for the schools at Dewsbury.[41]

This letter also goes on to discuss fees and the number of governors, co-optative and otherwise. It also objects to the suggestion made by the Wheelwright Trustees that they should have a vote on the appointment of co-optative members of the governing body.

By 5th May, 1886 copies of the draft scheme were in the hands of the Wheelwright Trustees.[42] The final year of the negotiations was mainly taken up with satisfying the Wheelwright Trustees that the Church of England character of the school would be maintained in order to fulfil the directions of the Founder. As late as 16th July, 1887 the Trustees were still making this point and insisting that "The first governors to the number of 14 of which nine should be members of the Church of England and that care be taken against the possibility of an accidental majority the other way, and having the direction in Clause 47 of the Scheme that religious instruction in accordance with the doctrines of the Church of England must be given in the school."[43] We shall have reason to refer back time and again to this clause as during the next twenty years it was to be a bone of contention between the Wheelwright Trustees and the West Riding County Council Education Committee.

During all these years one must always keep in mind the great work which the late S. J. Chadwick did in order to obtain the £22,000 from the Wheelwright Trustees so that the schools could be established, first in Bond Street and then later in Halifax Road, Dewsbury.[52] Besides the Founder, himself, S. J. Chadwick was one of three other men in the town to whom education was nearest their hearts and without whom the school would probably not have existed as we know it. The other two men were the late Dr. Matthew Hinchliffe and the late Major P. B. Walker. Mr. Chadwick was able to see where the Wheelwright Trustees had obtained so much of their money and planned to see that the town of Dewsbury from which so much had come would benefit from it.

The 3rd May, 1888 saw the Wheelwright Grammar Schools Scheme receive the Royal Assent and by this Scheme the Schools at Dewsbury were to receive £22,000 Consolidated Bank Annuities which were part of a sum of £41,276 14s. 5d. like annuities standing in the same name of the Official Trustees of Charitable Funds to the credit of the Charities created by the will of John Wheelwright. Besides that they were to receive ' The land and buildings situate in Wheelwright Road, in the borough of Dewsbury, containing by estimation 1,890 sq. yds. or thereabouts now or lately occupied or used for the purpose of Elementary Schools in Dewsbury aforesaid commonly known as the Wheelwright Schools.'[53] The site and the buildings in Wheelwright Road were sold in March, 1889 for £1,459 and by a similar Scheme of 3rd May, 1888 the Daw Green Charity School was closed and the site and the buildings were sold for a sum of £502 16s. 7d. This latter sum together with its investments formed the Daw Green Exhibition Fund. The Daw Green Scheme with its moneys (except those specifically directed to go to the Technical School), and the £22,000 from the Wheelwright Trustees and the money from the site in Wheelwright Road, constituted the whole of the endowment of the Wheelwright Grammar Schools when they were formed and this was reduced to £10,400 by the appropriation from them of the greater part of the cost (upwards of £14,000) for the new schools and playing fields in Halifax Road. This sum of £10,400 was invested in Dewsbury Corporation at $3\frac{1}{2}\%$ interest and provided an annual income of £338.[53] Mr. Holme had reason to mention the lack of substantial endowment time and again during his reign.

The temporary Wheelwright Grammar Schools were opened on 18th September, 1889 in the Bond Street warehouse formerly occupied by the Dewsbury Grammar Schools for 46 boys and 54 girls. The headmaster was Mr. A. E. Holme, M.A. (Oxon) and the headmistress Miss Ellen Huckwell (later to become Mrs. Holme). Both were to hold these positions for the next thirty years until 1919. Herr Schoenemann and Miss Hovey "went over with the premises" so to speak and did good service with the Wheelwright Grammar Schools. Mr. Godby left Dewsbury and went to a school at Ilkley as headmaster, which was in all probability the Ilkley High School.[54] Mr. and Mrs. Thornes received a small annual pension of £70 and £30 respectively and Mrs. Thornes continued to draw hers until 1903. What happened to Miss Kay appears to be unknown. The Wheelwright Grammar Schools were now safely established in Dewsbury and after attention has been paid to the histories of the other charities in the town, the foundations of which were amended so that moneys accruing could be used for scholarships at the Wheelwright Schools, we shall return again to 1889 and follow the history of the schools under Mr. Holme and Miss Huckwell until they retired in 1919.

THE MASTERS OF THE WHEELWRIGHT SCHOOLS, DEWSBURY

Burnell,	Richard	?1724–1773
Goldthorpe,	Henry	1773–1776
Naylor,	Robert	1776–1782
Expenses paid for the eviction of late master for possession of school house and croft – no name given)		1778
No name, but master definitely appointed		July, 1781–May, 1782
Greenwood,	Thomas	June, 1782 and still there in 1788

Pearce,	James	1791 (John Hoyle paid for examining the candidate in 1791)
Pearce,	James	1795 (He was definitely schoolmaster in the early 19th century)
Pearce,	John	1830–1859
Pearce,	G. C.	1859 (May to August)
Thornes,	Isaac	1859–1866*
Thornes,	John Charles	1859–1888

THE HEADMISTRESSES OF THE WHEELWRIGHT SCHOOLS

Stainforth,	Ann	1830
Knowles,	Ann	1838
Row (or Raw)	Agnes	1855 (She was teaching in that year and until 1860)
Hazelwood,	Catherine	1860–1888

(She later married John Charles Thornes)

HEADMASTERS AND STAFF OF ST. AUGUSTINE'S GRAMMAR SCHOOL, DEWSBURY

Headmasters

Fisher,	W. H. (Rev.)	1884–1888
Haworth,	J. (Rev.)	1888–1892 M.A. Cambridge
Johnson,	D. (Rev.)	1892–1897 B.A.
Lowe,	H. W. (Rev.)	1897–1899 M.A.

Assistant Masters

Only three of these are mentioned by name:—

Schoenemann,	Hugo	1886–1891 (died)
Batley,	Walton	1897–1899 A.R.C.O.
Happerfield,	F. H.	? –1899

* Isaac Thornes is given in Green's Thesis[18] but the minutes of the Wheelwright Trustees give J. C. Thornes as being appointed in 1859. There are several references to this appointment.

HEADMISTRESSES AND STAFF OF THE HIGH SCHOOL FOR GIRLS

Headmistresses

Smallpiece,	A. M. (Miss)	1885–1888 Newnham College
Foxley,	Barbara (Miss)	1888–1893 B.A. (Cambridge)
James,	M. M. R. (Miss)	1893–1896
Page,	(Miss)	1896–1900 B.A. (London)
Gedge,	(Miss)	1900–1902

Assistant teachers

Tatham,	M. A. (Miss)	1885–?
Innison,	(Miss)	1886–?
Allen,	(Miss)	1886–?
Wormald,	(Miss)	1886–?
Stevenson,	A. (Mr.)	1886–?
Taylor,	Harrison (Mr.)	1886–?
Von Mollin	(Fraulein)	1888–?
Fisher,	W. G. (Mr.)	1888–?
Wilson,	(Miss)	1890–?

No dates of termination of employment have been found

THE HEADMASTER, HEADMISTRESS AND THE STAFF OF THE DEWSBURY GRAMMAR SCHOOL

Headmaster

Godby, A. Wooldridge — 1884–1889 M.A. (Cambridge)

Assistant Masters

Heslop, Walter — 1884–1885 M.A. (Oxford)
Forty, J. R. — 1885–1888 B.A. (Oxford)
Broughton, Alfred — 1885–1889
Schoenemann, Hugo — 1886–1889 University of Prague
(Carried on with W.G.S. when formed)
McNally (Drill Sergeant) — 1886–1889
Greatorex, R. H. — 1888–1889 B.A. (Oxford)

Headmistresses

Millar, Edith (Miss) — 1884–1887 Newnham College, Cambridge
Kay, E. J. (Miss) — 1887–1889

Assistants

Milnes (Miss) — 1884–1889
Hovey, (Miss) — 1887–1889 B.A. (London)
(Carried on with W.G.S. when formed)

References
1. Correspondence with Mr. J. M. H. Wheelwright (Pateley Bridge) .. 1969
2. *A History of Rishworth School,* Priestley 1936
3. Correspondence with H.M. Customs and Excise (through R. Townend, Esq.) 1969
4. Borthwick Institute of Historical Research, York 1826
5. *A History of King James' Grammar School, Almondbury,* G. Hinchliffe p.64 1963
6. Charity Commissioners Report, House of Lords Records Office 1826
7. Wheelwright Trustees Minute Book 1742
8. Wheelwright Trustees Minute Book 1744
9. Wheelwright Trustees Minute Book 1773
10. Thesis: *An Evaluation of the part played in education at Dewsbury and Rishworth, Halifax, by the Charities of John Wheelwright, Gentleman.* Bamford, K. 1857
11. Wheelwright Trustees Minute Book 1776
12. Wheelwright Trustees Minute Book 1782
13. Wheelwright Trustees Minute Book 1797
14. Seventeenth Report of the Court of Chancery pp.815 to 822. This was republished by T. S. Brooke of Dewsbury as *Report of the Commissioners for enquiring concerning charities, respecting charities of the parishes of Batley, Mirfield, Birstall and Thornhill, with a notice of Wheelwright's Charity at Dewsbury with notes by J. B. Greenwood* 1826
15. Wheelwright Trustees Minute Book 1855
16. Wheelwright Trustees Minute Book 1859
17. Wheelwright Trustees Minute Book 1860
18. *A History of Education in the Borough of Dewsbury,* Green, J. R. .. 1953
19. Wheelwright Trustees Minute Book 1862
20. Wheelwright Trustees Minute Book 1863
21. Wheelwright Trustees Minute Book 1869
22. Wheelwright Trustees Minute Book 1864
23. Ministry of Education Archives Ed16/360
24. *The Dewsbury Reporter,* 17th December 1870
25. Wheelwright Trustees Minute Book 1871
26. Wheelwright Trustees Minute Book 1873
27. Wheelwright Trustees Minute Book 1876
28. Wheelwright Trustees Minute Book 1877
29. Programme for Grand Bazaar, November, 1895 (notes by S. J. Chadwick) 1895
30. Endowed Charities Commissioners Report (Dewsbury) 1896
31. Letter Book of the Wheelwright Trustees 1882
32. Letter Book of the Wheelwright Trustees 1883
33. Letter Book of the Wheelwright Trustees .. .. .. 3rd March 1885
34. Letter Book of the Wheelwright Trustees .. .. .. 30th March 1885
35. Letter Book of the Wheelwright Trustees .. .. .. 30th April 1885
36. *The Dewsbury Reporter* 1896
37. *The Story of the Woodard Schools,* N. E. Kirk 0000
38. Letter Book of the Wheelwright Trustees .. .. .. 14th May 1885
39. Letter Book of the Wheelwright Trustees .. .. .. 7th July 1885
40. Letter Book of the Wheelwright Trustees .. .. .. 20th July 1885
41. Letter Book of the Wheelwright Trustees .. .. 22nd February 1886
42. Letter Book of the Wheelwright Trustees .. .. .. 5th May 1886
43. The Wheelwright Trustees Minute Book 1887
44. *The Dewsbury Reporter* .. .. 2nd January 1883
45. St. Mark's Churchwardens Accounts 1885–1891
46. *The Dewsbury Reporter* .. .. 17th January 1885
47. *The Dewsbury Reporter* .. .. 25th September 1886
48. *The Dewsbury Reporter* .. .. 20th September 1884
49. St. Mark's Church Registers .. .. 3rd March 1891
50. *St. Mark's Church, Dewsbury 1865 to 1965,* R. Brown. Birkdale Books .. 1965
51. *The Dewsbury Reporter* .. .. 17th May 1884
52. *The Dewsbury Education Week Handbook* 1925
53. The Wheelwright Grammar Schools Scheme of 3rd May, 1888 1888
54. Correspondence with the Headmaster of Ilkley Grammar School .. 1969

CHAPTER II

Charities which have

benefited the children of Dewsbury

It has been said that Dewsbury was one of the most fortunate towns in England in having so many charities providing for the education of its children. These charities were founded from the seventeenth century onwards and are no longer serving their original purposes since the passing of the 1944 Education Act which abolished fees at the Wheelwright Grammar Schools and made entrance there solely dependant on passing the Selection Examination at the age of eleven.

Other charities besides the Wheelwright one, were the Thornhill Grammar School, the Daw Green Charity School, the Thornhill Walker Trust and the Dewsbury Moor Exhibition. Some children benefitted because they were the direct descendants of Grace Harrison, the sister of John Harrison of Leeds.

THE THORNHILL GRAMMAR SCHOOL
Mention is made of schools and teaching in Dewsbury from the Tudor period onwards to the seventeenth century;[1] but the only permanent educational institution in the district in that century was the Thornhill Grammar School. This was founded by the will of Rev. Charles Greenwood (Rector of Thornhill, 1612 to 1644) dated 14th July, 1642. For some reason or other Sir William Savile, Bart., owner of the land in Thornhill owed the Rector £500. In his will the Rector directed that he would be satisfied, if on his death the debt was paid by Sir William by building a grammar school, with school house and schoolmaster for the better bringing up of the youth in the town and parish of Thornhill (which included at that time Flockton, Middlestown, Whitley Lower, Overton, Netherton as well as Thornhill itself and Thornhill Lees with Savile Town). The schoolhouse was duly built with playground, garden and allotments attached[2] costing about £100. Richard Wilson was one of the earliest, if not the first schoolmaster there; he was certainly there in 1662.[1] There are some gaps in the records and unfortunately one gap until 1764 covers the peroid with tradition says that Oliver Goldsmith was an usher at the school.

The income from the school always seems to have been precarious and at least one master's wife opened a shop on the premises to augment the income.[3] This was due to the small number of children (eleven in 1829)[4] and the meagre returns from the Trust. The curriculum was Reading, Writing and Accounts for the free scholars; but Latin was taught to the boarders and seldom, if ever, applied for by the free scholars.[1]

By 1865 the school was not in use, the children having been attracted to the other newly-built schools in the district.[1] Things became so bad that rooms were hired in Dewsbury and the building at Thornhill enlarged so as to attract more children. By 1870 there were 44 children (ten were girls).[3] Soon after this the effect of the Forster Education Act of 1870 began to be felt and the school declined still further. In 1875 the school premises, land etc. were sold to the Trustees of the Thornhill National School for £585 (Green's Thesis gives £505 and the date 1875[1]). £252 12s. 1d. was paid to Mr. Henry Savile of Rufford Abbey, Notts., to settle all claims by him and his predecessors for outlay and repairs to the school, £206 7s. 0d. was claimed and paid to the schoolmaster for loss of office. The allotment was sold in 1877 for £108 18s. 0d. and there was an annual income of £96. All these moneys were invested in Consols. Nothing more was done until 1893 when the Trustees arranged for Greenwood Exhibitions to be awarded to boys and girls in Thornhill to be tenable at Wheelwright Grammar Schools, Dewsbury with tuition fees and grants of £5 per annum; the scholars must have lived in the parish of Thornhill for at least two years. The old grammar school buildings were used by the Thornhill Church of England School until 1968.

THE DAW GREEN CHARITY SCHOOL, DEWSBURY

Six years after the founding of the Wheelwright Charity, the Daw Green Charity School was founded in 1731 by the will of William Walker of Wakefield. The original site of this school is now occupied by the car park of the Textile Club in Aldams Road. William Walker left £400 for the education of 20 poor children in Dewsbury. £100 of this was spent in building the school and school house and the rest was used to buy land at Edge End in the Parish of Bradford.[5] From the farm there and the coal seams beneath it the Daw Green Charity received some of its income.

There were two other bequests to this school, one by Thomas Bedford of Crow Nest, Dewsbury, who by his will dated 15th November, 1734 left £500 and by a codicil another £200 if Mary Bedford of Thornhill Briggs, Halifax did not leave any money to the school. However, she did (£200), by her will dated 13th October, 1735 and also she stated that "five poor boys be taught reading and five poor girls be taught to read, knit and sow . . . and shall be instructed in the principles of the Religion as now taught and instructed in our churches." This is the only bequest to the charity school stipulating religious teaching, and because of it, when the charity was wound up in 1888 Wheelwright Girls Grammar School was able to benefit from the moneys. In 1754 John Turner gave some land at Revey in North Bierley (Bradford) the rents to buy "testaments with Bibles to be bound up with the Common Prayer of the Church of England . . . and for no other use, intent or purpose whatever."[6]

From the account books of the Charity School we learn a great deal of what life was like for master, dame and scholars and as conditions would be similar to those in the Wheelwright School some extracts are quoted here:—

An entry dated 5th October, 1745 states, ". . . Also that the Master shall have for his salary the yearly sum of £18 for teaching the said boys and that the Dame shall have for her salary the yearly sum of £10 for teaching the said girls.

"Also, it is ordered that there be thirty-five boys and fifteen girls immediately admitted to be taught.

"It is ordered that Thomas Gibson shall be schoolmaster of the said Charity School for one year from this day and that Susanna Moss (widow of Joseph Moss deceased and who was the first named Master of the School) shall be Dame and of the said Charity School for one year from this day.

"Also, it is ordered that neither the Master nor the Dame shall teach five scholars more than the Charity.

"Also ordered that both of them diligently attend their scholars from eight o'clock to twelve and from one to five from Lady Day to Michaelmas and from Michaelmas to Lady Day until four at night.

"Also, ordered that the school be inspected and examined once in three months by one or more of the Trustees.

"Also ordered that some short prayers be read in the school by the Master and the Dame at eight o'clock in the morning upon every school day, such as the Trustees or some of them shall think proper to appoint."[7]

The salary appears to have been insufficient as in 1748 Thomas Gibson was found guilty of taking in more scholars than was permitted and in June, 1749 he was paid £22 10s. 0d. by order of the Court which was for his salary and quitting the profession. Judith Hall's salary was very inadequate as by 1760 she was receiving part of her salary in advance.[7] This went on for a number of years.

It seems that the girls were not taught to write (only reading, knitting and sewing) at least in the middle decades of the 18th century as Rebecca Lodge (the Dame) could not sign her name on the salary receipts when appointed. They were signed with a "X". Later on she was able to write her name.[8]

In 1807 the Charity School moved from the site in Aldams Road to the site in Boothroyd Lane, bounded by that road, High Street and School Street. On the Master's House was a tablet bearing the following inscription:—

"Erected
by the aid of several leg
acies, for the free education
of poor children
During the Trust of
Rev. M. Powley, late Vicar
Rev. J. Buckworth, present Vicar } of this Town
Mr. Thomas Chaster, Maltster
Mr. Jno. Hutton, Gent. Kingston upon Hull.
Mr. George Newstead, Gent. of Wetherby.
A.D. 1807"

In 1812 the Daw Green Charity School lost £100 due to the liquidation of the local banking firm of Messrs. Ingram, Kennet, Dawson and Ingram, typical of so many small local banks operating at this time.[9]

In 1833 new desks were needed and were "to be made as the desks and seats to the Wheelwright Charity School."

In 1857 a new Master was appointed and candidates applied from as far away as Scarborough, Helmsley, Dunford Bridge and Great Ouseburn. Mr. Joseph Radcliffe in his application stated, "I am 26 years of age, married and three children, the youngest of which is two years old, without signs of more, so we hope that the family will not materially interfere with Mrs. Radcliffe's appointment and if so, not with mine."[10]

Mr. and Mrs. Rodgers were appointed and like one of their predecessors gave their name to the school. It was known as "Rodger's College". During their time and that of their successor, the efficiency of the school deteriorated so much that in 1886 Mr. Leach (Assistant Charity Commissioner) said that the school was no longer serving a useful purpose.

In 1870 the school was inspected and at that time besides the "Three R's" Dictation and Religious Knowledge, the boys were taught Geography and the girls Needlework. A fee of ½d. per week for tuition in writing was charged to the boys and ½d. per fortnight for the girls, and a shilling entrance fee, another shilling "Fire-money" was charged at the beginning of the winter, plus ½d. each week per child was collected. There were then 40 boys and 30 girls.

As a result of the above inspection it was decided that the school be devoted to primary education and the funds belonging to the school be used for secondary education.[11]

The Rodgers resigned in 1880 and the last headmaster, Mr. William Singleton was appointed; but by now there were only 29 boys and 19 girls.

By an Order in Council dated 3rd May, 1888 the Trustees of the School were directed to discontinue it and sell the site, the money to be spent in helping to erect a girls grammar school in which the teaching of religious instruction according to the doctrines of the Church of England (a direction from Mary Bedford's will) was to be carried out. The only school fitting these directions was Wheelwright Grammar School for Girls. Also

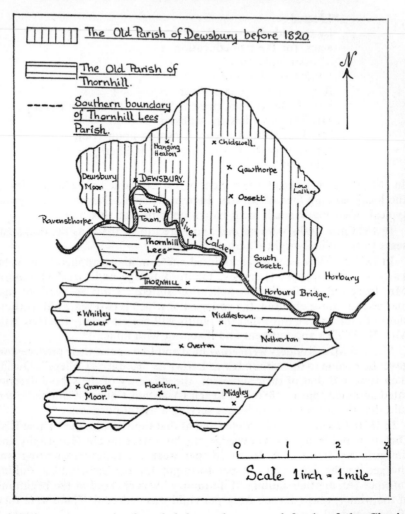

The Old Parish of Dewsbury before 1820.

The Old Parish of Thornhill.

Southern boundary of Thornhill Lees Parish.

N

Hanging Heaton
× Chidswell.
× Gawthorpe
Dewsbury Moor
★ DEWSBURY.
Low Laithes
× Ossett
Ravensthorpe.
Savile Town.
River Calder
Thornhill Lees
South Ossett
THORNHILL ×
Horbury
Horbury Bridge.
× Whitley Lower
Middlestown.
×
×
Netherton
× Overton
× Grange Moor.
Flockton.
×
Midgley
×

Scale 1 inch = 1 mile.

exhibitions were to be founded from the accrued funds of the Charity which were to be tenable at the Wheelwright Grammar Schools. These exhibitions were for boys and girls who had lived at least two years in the ancient parish of Dewsbury (this meant the parish as it was in 1820 which included Earlsheaton, Hanging Heaton, Ossett and the part of the Parish of Thornhill comprising the perpetual curacy of Thornhill Lees with Savile Town). These exhibitions covered tuition fees and £5 per annum for maintenance.

On 24th October, 1888 both sites (Aldams Road and Boothroyd Lane) were sold. St. John the Baptist Church bought the school in Boothroyd Lane and used it as its parish hall until the church became defunct in 1967.

In 1900 the Dewsbury Endowed Schools Foundation was created to administer the combined Wheelwright, Daw Green, Hinchliffe and Technical Schools Trusts.

THE DEWSBURY MOOR EXHIBITION

This exhibition was the direct result of a school founded in the eighteenth century in what is now School Lane, Dewsbury Moor and which ceased to exist in 1892 due to lack of pupils.[1] The school was sold to the Dewsbury Corporation for £160 and this money was used to provide these exhibitions tenable at the Wheelwright Grammar Schools.

THE WALKER ENDOWED SCHOOL AT THORNHILL

Children in Thornhill benefited under a charity founded by Richard Walker, a farmer of Thornhill, in 1812. An indenture founded a free school and the first school master, David Butterfield, received £40 per annum for teaching 82 scholars. The school was enlarged in 1896–97 by the Trustees.

The school was handed over to the Dewsbury Education Authority in 1915 and a trust was created to administer the moneys for the benefit of children attending institutions of higher education. Eventually under the Scheme of 1923 secondary school exhibitions tenable at any grammar school recognised by the Board of Education (the nearest being the Wheelwright), teacher training exhibitions tenable at teacher training colleges and university exhibitions assisting those who had won scholarships from the grammar school to the university were created.

HARRISON'S CHARITY

One frequently sees references to "Harrison Scholars" in the minutes of the Dewsbury Education Committee. These were children who were at the Wheelwright Grammar Schools and benefiting under the will of John Harrison of Leeds. He was born in Leeds in 1579 and was Charter Mayor in 1621. He built St. John's Church in Briggate, Leeds and as his marriage was childless[12] he founded a charity to benefit the descendants of his sister, Grace. One must be a direct descendant of Grace Harrison to benefit from this Charity which assisted pupils in schools of higher education anywhere, not specifically those attending the Wheelwright Grammar Schools.

References

1. *A History of Education in the Borough of Dewsbury* by E. J. Green. (Unpublished thesis.) 1956
2. Report of Charities, 1829 with notes by J. B. Greenwood, p.11
3. *The Dewsbury Reporter.* Article by T. Myers .. .. 7th March 1931
4. *Ecclesiastical History of Dewsbury* by J. B. Greenwood
5. Indenture of 9th March, 1750 (Daw Green Charity School Documents, Central Library, Dewsbury).
6. Daw Green Charity School Documents (Folder B/15) Central Library, Dewsbury.
7. Daw Green Charity School Documents (Bundle EE) Central Library, Dewsbury.
8. Daw Green Charity School Documents (Bundle D) Central Library, Dewsbury.
9. Daw Green Charity School Documents (Folder E) Central Library, Dewsbury.
10. Daw Green Charity School Documents (Bundle M) Central Library, Dewsbury.
11. Daw Green Charity School Documents (Bundle HH) Central Library, Dewsbury.
12. Correspondence with Harrison's Charity 1969

CHAPTER III

The Holme Regime 1889 to 1919

It has been previously stated that the Wheelwright Grammar School Scheme received the Royal Assent on 3rd May, 1888. The Scheme was an Order to build a new secondary school for boys and girls in Dewsbury. Until that could be achieved, and with the demise of the Dewsbury Grammar School in 1889, premises were available in Bond Street. These premises were gladly accepted by the newly formed Wheelwright Schools where they could stay until new premises were built. The first advertisement informing the general public that the newly formed Wheelwright Schools would open in the Dewsbury Grammar School's premises on 17th September, 1889, appeared in the *Dewsbury Reporter* on Saturday, 6th May, 1889, some weeks before the Dewsbury Grammar School became defunct, with Mr. A. E. Holme, M.A. (Oxon) and Miss E. M. Huckwell as headmaster and headmistress.

The first business was to get the school opened and functioning. Side by side with this and even before the school was opened, the Governors were looking round the district for a site on which the new schools could be built. The warehouse in Bond Street was leased from 17th June, 1889 to be taken over on 1st August of that year and leased from year to year.[1]

Sites in various parts of the district were inspected. The first one dealt with in January 1889, was the site immediately below the original technical school building in Carlton Road. The purchase of this site was gone into with considerable thoroughness. A common entrance to the Technical School and the new Wheelwright Grammar School was envisaged in Carlton Road. The land had a steep slope so that a basement storey for covered playgrounds and a gymnasium could be made,[2] but there was no room for playing fields here so that this site was abandoned.

Mr. Wm. Lipscombe, agent to the Savile Estate, in October, 1889 offered the Governors two alternative sites in Savile Town, one in Head-field Road and the other near Bottom's Farm (just north of the Cricket Field).[3] These were also turned down as were other alternative sites in Boothroyd Lane and Moorlands Road, Oxford Road and Crow Nest Park.[4] The Governors, however, failed to come to terms with the Town Council in regard to the Borough Park and this led Mr. Joe Fox, one of the deputation to the Council, to buy the Hill Head Estate and offer to the

38

Governors any portion they might select at the price he paid for it.[4] They selected the Birkdale Road portion of the estate i.e. the part occupied by the present Boys' School buildings plus the front field and the pre-fabs at the back of the building. Highfield Farm and its field (the "Top Field") and the other field reaching to Victoria Crescent were bought later.

In the meantime the Wheelwright Schools opened on 17th September, the boys under Mr. Holme, who had been for the past seven years head of the Physics Department at Manchester Grammar School. He was a double first in Mathematics and Natural Science, and was assisted at the beginning by Mr. Stafford Hayden M.A. (Cantab), Mr. C. H. Owen, M.A. (Edinburgh), Mr. T. Knowles, B.A. and Lt. Lingwood. Miss Ellen Huckwell was the headmistress of the Girls' School assisted by Misses Rosa Hovey, B.A. (London) and Miss Oakshott and the modern languages were taught in both schools by Herr Hugo Schoenemann (University of Prague).

The subjects taught in the curriculum were Religious Instruction (from which exemption could be claimed), Reading, Writing, Arithmetic, Geography, History, English Grammar, Composition, and Literature, Mathematics, Latin, French, German, Natural Science, Drawing, Vocal Music and Drill. Also Book-keeping and shorthand (both optional). The number of children on roll was 46 boys and 50 girls.

A very vivid picture of the old building in Bond Street was given in an article in the *Dewsbury Reporter* in 1932[5] by an Old Girl styling herself "Stella" (Mrs. North), ". . . I became suddenly conscious of the girls who entered that front door every morning, of the rather small and dingy, if aweinspiring headmistress's room to the right, and of the Boardroom on the left which, when not used for Governors' meetings became the assistant mistress's room, where naughty or dull children might be detained after school hours to do special tasks. But the room which intrigued my memory most was the cloak room, the gymnasium or the playroom according to the timetable and the purpose for which it might be required. Round the walls on three sides were pegs for our clothes, underneath were racks for boots or slippers. A few strong circular pillars supported the overhead structure. I remember these, as in games or drill the girls had to dodge them. The curved wide staircase leading from near the front door to the first storey was an important feature of this room. A piano and a few loose benches near the fireplace comprised the furniture. Apart from a window on the first landing which was high and remote no direct light penetrated. At the other end of the room, light streamed through a glass partition which shut off the glass-roofed lavatories.

"In this gymnasium Lt. Lingwood put the girls through drastic physical exercises with and without dumb-bells, with and without musical accompaniment. There was no other apparatus, but we lunged to the front, right and left and generally contorted our bodies in the manner as practised in all branches of Her Majesty's Army. Here also a form mistress would take her girls for a 'Scrap-drill' when dumb bells would be swung to the tune

'Dresdina', the exercise ending with a merry march, the tinkling piano setting and varying the pace.

"When the Wheelwright Trust took over the schools on the opening day there were not more than 50 girls and perhaps a few more boys (actually a few less. W.P.). These were drawn from Dewsbury, Batley, Horbury, Ossett, Thornhill, Mirfield, Heckmondwike, Liversedge, Drighlington and Luddendenfoot.

"It was found necessary to advertise the schools for the first few years and besides the Annual Speech Day held in the Town Hall in July, an entertainment was given in the Industrial Hall (now the Pioneer Cinema) in December. At the first of these the girls contributed charming items which included Greek tableaux from Homer's 'Odyssey'.

"The numbers grew and in the girls School Miss Athya and Fraulein Bever were added to the staff. Unfortunately Herr Hugo Schoenemann, a man of strong personality, a strict disciplinarian with a saving sense of humour and a born teacher, suddenly died. He had three children at Wheelwright Grammar School and with them we mourned their loss. He was succeeded by Herr L. P. Loeffler who had different qualities. A man of profound learning, gifted in many ways and especially in music, he was not a strict disciplinarian – indeed I am afraid the mildest of his pupils took advantage of his German unawareness of English Psychology. I have already stated that he was a finished musician. He had studied at Leipsig Conservatoire and had played before kings. One day when he was taking a class of older girls in a room on the top storey inharmonious tootling sounds came from the street below. Herr Loeffler hurried to the window, looked out, banged down the sash to exclude the noise and returned to the desk and ejaculated 'Och! it is a German Band. They are a disgrace to Germany. They are riff-raff, just riff-raff who come over here'. A meek voice gently piped up from the back row 'Did you come over with a German Band, Sir?' 'Oh, Miss Crabtree' was all he could reply as he subsided overwhelmed. Poor Herr Loeffler, he never understood the Yorkshire Child.

"Although we children did not realise it at the time, in Bond Street there were few amenities which would be deemed essential in a school today. The rooms were heated by old-fashioned stoves with the tin chimeys going through the ceilings. The temperature varied and the boys made great sport with the stoves, especially in Herr Loeffler's form; a few musk lozenges placed on the hottest part (the boys used India Rubber) were often a somewhat overwhelming welcome to visiting masters."[6]

From the above account we also learn that the waste strip of land between Grove Street and Bond Street was the playground for the boys and they also played football in Bond Street, the police very kindly turning a blind eye to the offences so committed.

Both Mr. and Mrs. Holme were people of distinction; repeatedly Mr. Holme is referred to by Old Scholars as a typical English Gentleman. He was sedate, dignified and he apparently never hurried, he walked a leisurely pace from his home in Marlborough Terrace to the Halifax Road entrance to School. After Miss Huckwell and Mr. Holme married in 1899, she would see him on his way to school and then lock up and follow along. They rarely came along together. He was a strict disciplinarian, mellowed by understanding of the boys.

The timetable in the boys' school in Bond Street days is interesting when compared with that of today's. School hours were 9.10 a.m. to 12.30 p.m. and in the afternoons, 2.15 p.m. to 4.15 p.m. except Friday when school ended at 4.45 p.m. Practical Chemistry was from 4.15 p.m. to 5.45 p.m. on Thursdays and 9 a.m. to 12 noon on Saturdays. There was no half-day.[7] In the Girls' School ¾ hr. was devoted to Church Catechism but in 1891 it was only attended by nine children.[8]

In those days the School had an annual examination by an external body, the Yorkshire College at Leeds. From the reports on these examinations we find that as early as 1892 the School was getting a foothold on the ladder of academic success. For in that year it had gained one Open Mathematical Scholarship to Christs' College, Cambridge, four County Scholarships of £60 per annum, one Entrance Scholarship to Ley's School, Cambridge (£50 per annum) two County Scholarships of £30 per annum, one Ackroyd Scholarship of £30 per annum at the Yorkshire College, Leeds and one County Studentship. In the previous year one boy had obtained a distinction in Chemistry in the Cambridge Senior Examination (3rd in the country) and one got 49th place out of 6,691 candidates in French.[9] There were equally good results in the Girls' School when four out of five candidates passed the Cambridge Local Examination; 15 girls entered for the South Kensington Science and Art Examination and eight got 1st Class and four 2nd Class passes. Prof. Miall (Examiner for the Yorkshire College) said that the teaching in the Girls' department was excellent in all English subjects and he had to testify to the very unusual excellence in Mathematics.[9] At this time Miss Huckwell also decided to make games a compulsory subject at a fixed charge.[8] This would seem to be in anticipation of the move from Bond Street to Halifax Road.

1892 involved Mr. Holme in a clash with the Governors. He made an interim report to the Governors defending his position due to a report on Religious Instruction made by the examiner, Rev. H. Walsham How, who was Vicar of Mirfield. He had criticised the Religious Instruction particularly in the Boys' School but Mr. Holme defended his position and that of his staff manfully. He detailed out the primary cause of the poor results in that subject which was due to the short stay of the children at school. The average stay was 1 year 10 months and this hardly enabled anyone to do much good work.[10] This was the first of continual pleas for many years to come that parents would keep their children at school longer and so gain full benefit from the grammar school education and not just use the school as a snob tab.

In 1891 definite moves were made towards building the new school in Halifax Road. In February 1891 tenders were invited for erecting the building as designed by Mr. J. Lane Fox, architect. These tenders were for the excavation of the site, for masons and bricklayers required in the erection and completion of the new Wheelwright Schools for a sum of £3,712 10s. 0d. The contract was secured by Messrs. George Horsfall of Liversedge and this was signed on 10th May, 1891.[11] The total cost of the schools including the furnishings, site etc. amounted to around £14,000 and this left £10,000 to be invested which brought in £338 per annum. Another £3,000 had to be borrowed and this was repaid by a series of bazaars.

The new schools were built and equipped by early 1893 and on Friday, 19th May, 1893 His Grace, the Archbishop of York (The Most Rev. William D. Maclagan, D.D.) opened them. There is a tablet in the main entrance hall of the school commemorating this event. Besides the Governors, the Mayors of Dewsbury and of Ossett with their members of Council were present (in view of the fact that so much of the money had come from Dewsbury and Ossett). The Archbishop entered the grounds from Halifax Road and Master G. Almond (one of the boys) standing on the steps, delivered an address of welcome in Latin to the Archbishop to which he duly replied. His Grace, after receiving an address of welcome from the Mayor and Corporation of Dewsbury, used a special silver key which was mounted with the Wheelwright coat of arms, to make the formal opening ceremony.[12]

The Schools finally left the Bond Street warehouse and entered the new buildings in Halifax Road on 7th June, 1893. Almost immediately both Mr. Holme and Miss Huckwell mention the beneficial effects of the new surroundings with the wonderful playing fields (one must remember that only the Front Field was part of the playing fields at that time). The boys occupied the ground floor of the building and the girls the upstairs; the boys entered by the main door and the girls by the side entrance. Both shared the basement for physical exercises and for dinners. There was no gymnasium at the rear of the building in those days either. Miss Huckwell on one occasion asked that the doorway between the Girls' department and the old Chemistry Laboratory be bricked up but the architect would not agree – swing doors were placed there. It was through the crack in these swing doors that notes from boys to girls and vice versa were "posted" arranging clandestine meetings. From this point in time the segregation of the two departments was more strictly enforced.

Much of the history of the school during the time that the two departments occupied the one building (now the Boys' School) is common to them both. So the history of the older building in Halifax Road will be done through to 1970 and then a return made to Miss Huckwell's days in the old building and finally the history in the new Girls' School to the same date, without repeating incidents which were common to both departments, such as the religious dispute with the West Riding County Council, etc. and much later the financial difficulties in which the schools found themselves after the First World War.

In 1894 Mr. Holme, at the Speech Day, was stressing the fact that nearly

50% of the boys stayed in the school less than one year. There were now 119 boys on roll. In the academic sphere no West Riding County Council Secondary School had done so well as Wheelwright; it obtained two County Council Scholarships, one Class A of £60 per annum which was won by the late Prof. W. G. Fearnsides who later became the first Professor of Geology at the University of Sheffield, and an international authority on minerology etc.

From 1894 onwards for a couple of years or so there was irritation about the way the religious instruction was carried out, especially in the Boys' School. It was really antagonism by the High Church Party to Mr. Holme. It all stemmed from the report on religious instruction made by Rev. H. Walsham How in that year. He adversely criticised the way the religious instruction was taught in the school. The High Church Party immediately seized on this point to try to make Mr. Holme very uncomfortable. They ". . . imagined him to be a Non-conformist (or Dissenter as they termed him) teaching at a Non-conformist Sunday School, making heterodox speeches and last, but worst of all, being about to take to himself a Dissenting wife."[13] Mr. Holme had been in the new school only eighteen months and had enough to do to get the new school on its feet without the Chairman of the Governors (The Rev. Canon Lowther Clarke) making the task harder. But this gentleman appears to have been the stooge for the late Archdeacon Brooke who was really the power behind the movement against Mr. Holme. To try to ease the situation in January, 1894 Mr. Holme wrote to Canon Clarke saying that he would be obliged if any alteration in the Scheme of Work (which at present follows the lines of most secondary schools) would meet with the Governors' approval as a body.[14]

The whole root of the trouble was the rivalry between the St. Augustine's Grammar School and the newly formed Wheelwright Grammar Schools. Canon Clarke was chairman of the Governors of both schools but was urging parents to send their children to St. Augustine's and not to the new Wheelwright Schools. Rev. H. Walsham How, the author of the report which upset Mr. Holme, was the son of the then Bishop of Wakefield, who in turn was the Visitor of St. Augustine's Grammar School. This was really the last stand of the High Church Party against the progress of non-sectarian secondary education in the Borough of Dewsbury. They knew that since 1870 work had been under way to establish a grammar school in the Borough from the Wheelwright moneys but backed by Archdeacon Brooke they were determined to have a Church of England Grammar School at all costs.

There was the debt on the new school to face and in order to help repay the £3,000 borrowed, the first of a series of bazaars was held in November, 1895. This was also a momentous year as it was the first time the annual Sports Day was held on the Front Field of the School instead of up at the Crown Flatt Rugby Field as had been the case ever since the school was opened in 1889. There were also now three boys in the Sixth Form.

In 1897 we catch a glimpse of the "gentleman" in Mr. Holme; a side of him which would not give way on a point of principle. There had been some criticism of the way German was being taught in the school; but Mr. Holme came to the defence of his staff manfully. He said, "Mr. Long is no longer with us now to explain: but in my opinion we have never had a modern language master so hard working and conscientious."[15] The modern language post had also been vacant three times in the last three years which had also helped to weaken the teaching of this subject.

Another illustration of Mr. Holme's character is seen in the fact that by 1894 the financial state of the School was such that he agreed to accept a lower salary, in order to help the school along. When he was appointed he was to be paid £160 per annum plus £2 10s. for the first 100 pupils and £2 for all above 100. This was altered to £2 5s. for all above the first 100. Not till the year 1900 did Mr. Holme take steps to ask for his original salary again. He was intent on building up the school – it was his life.

On 1st August, 1897 a local doctor died aged 74. He was Dr. Matthew Hinchliffe who in his will left nearly £50,000 for the better education of children in Dewsbury. This sum of money came at a time when the finances of the Wheelwright Grammar Schools were anything but rosy. As Mr. Holme pointed out in the article in the special edition of the *Dewsbury Reporter* to celebrate Dr. Hinchliffe's bequest, the Wheelwright Schools were very badly endowed in comparison with many grammar schools in the country such as St. Paul's, London, King Edward VI at Birmingham, Bedford, Leeds and Wakefield Grammar Schools etc., etc.

There was a mistaken idea amongst the working class people of Dewsbury that the Wheelwright moneys should be used for the education of any poor children in the Borough. In point of fact it was stipulated in John Wheelwright's will that the money was to be used for the *education of the poor children of tenants of the Wheelwright Estate, unless there were not enough to use the money and then children of the general poor could benefit.* This was a point very frequently overlooked in the arguments which were constantly being used at this time to put pressure so that one or other party would benefit by the bequest of Dr. Hinchliffe. There was a feeling that the new Wheelwright Schools had been built with Wheelwright money by the middle class people of Dewsbury for the education of their children. Mr. Holme put the matter very clearly to the people holding these views in the special "Hinchliffe Number" of the *Dewsbury Reporter* in 1899, when he stated that "more working men's children had received free secondary education at the institute than could possibly have been provided for if the whole of the £24,000 had been devoted to a free school for them and for them alone."

DR. MATTHEW HINCHLIFFE
Now to Dr. Hinchliffe, and let us see what sort of man this was who gave so much money for the education of Dewsbury's children.

Like John Wheelwright he was a bachelor and a man of frugal habits. A couplet he was very fond of quoting from his favourite song illustrates the type of man he was:—

"Let us speak of a man as we find him
And heed not what others say."[16]

Dr. Matthew Hinchliffe was born in 1823 and was the son of John Hinchliffe who was landlord of the well-known Dewsbury inn, "The Duke of Leeds" in Union Street (the premises are still standing at the junction of Union Street and Branch Road). His father was previously a grocer in Huddersfield and was a person above the average of his calling in that he was moderately well educated, had artistic tastes, could paint tolerably well and was possessed of a love of flowers with a fair knowledge of Botany and Entomology. His mother was in some respects also a superior woman and of considerable force of character and had, of course, great influence over her son. The father and son and sometimes Mrs. Hichliffe attended Ebenezer Independent Chapel (still standing in Longcauseway) but not infrequently she worshipped at Dewsbury Parish Church. When Matthew was nine years old he was sent to a Dame's School and one of the scholars of about his own age was John Spiking, afterwards a grocer in the Market Place and later in Bond Street. Between the two a friendship struck up which lasted until death brought about a severance.

When Hinchliffe (who had earned the sobriquet among his school fellows of "King Matthew") and Spiking grew old enough, they were sent to Batley Grammar School, which was situated near the old church and under the management of Dr. Senior, well known for his learning and amiability of character. That young Hinchliffe was a diligent student we learn on good authority and he remained on the list of pupils until the time came when the choice of profession had to be made. His inclination was for that of medicine. In due course he was articled to Mr. Joseph Savage, a Dewsbury practitioner and gave much satisfaction to that rather exacting gentleman. After qualifying, Matthew Hinchliffe went into partnership with Dr. Fearnley, who became the Charter Mayor of Dewsbury. Dr. Fearnley lived in a house called Grove House which stood on the site now occupied by the Dewsbury West Riding Police Offices in Grove Street. The two doctors had a large practice. Due to some private reason the partnership was dissolved and Dr. Hinchliffe removed to rooms leading off the passage in Westgate by the "Little Saddle Hotel". But before this happened Dr. Hinchliffe had gained the degree of Doctor of Medicine at Dublin University of which title he was not a little proud. Later he chose a site at the junction of Ashworth Road, Nelson Street and Wellington Road and built a commodious house in which he spent the rest of his life and ultimately died there.[16]

Like the Founder of the School he lived very frugally as the following passage from a Speech Day address by the late Miss Kirk shows:— "The only holiday I ever knew him take was one day every year when he went to Windermere and spent a day on Orrest Head enjoying the glorious view of lake and mountain."[17] She goes on to give us a word picture of him, "He had very bright blue eyes which looked at you very straightly and he always knew if you were pretending to be worse than you really were.

"Dr. Hinchliffe was a great reader and I remember him sitting in a big armchair smoking his long 'Churchwarden' pipe and surrounded by books – all round the room were shelves from floor to ceiling and every shelf was packed with books."[17] In politics he was a Liberal and supported Sergeant Simon and at one time was elected councillor for the St. John's Ward (1865) and became an alderman in 1869. His interest in education would appear to stem from his connection with the Dewsbury Mechanics Institute when it was located in a building in Northgate which was the predecessor of the present Salem Methodist Chapel.

The above gives us a picture of Dr. Hinchliffe and has been given at length with that idea in view as when he died in 1897 aged 74 it was through the will of the doctor that the education facilities of the children of Dewsbury were to benefit to the extent of nearly £50,000 which was a very, very large sum of money in those days. The will dated 15th August, 1878 occupies six pages of writing and has two codicils and the interesting point is that although he was a medical practitioner, the Dewsbury General Infirmary did not benefit by the will at all. He served the Infirmary from 1879, when that body found it difficult to fill the vacancies on the honorary medical staff, until 1882 when he resigned feeling that it "will be necessary to relinquish the duties of such a position" as he put it, and gave the Infirmary Board a cheque for £100. However, in spite of warm and sincere thanks on the part of the Infirmary authorities, the fact that he was not made an honorary consultant physician upset him and he decided that he would not leave the institution any more money.[16] Though he was touchy on this point there was nothing mean or niggardly in his character as in his will he cancelled all outstanding debts from patients owing to him at the time of his death.

One would have expected that so generous a gift as £50,000 would have pleased the people of Dewsbury. It did up to a point, but it also started off a controversy which raged for three years or so as to what was to be done with the money. In one sense we are back to the 1870 to 1888 era when opposing factions in the town wanted the money to be spent as they thought fit and the working classes were led to believe that the money was ultimately only to be used to ease the fees which the middle classes paid for their children at the grammar school.

On page three of Dr. Hinchliffe's will the bequest is stated clearly:— "To the Mayor and Corporation of Dewsbury all said last mentioned Trust fund with accumulations thereof upon Trust, the interest, dividends and annual proceeds thereof to be paid and used annually for ever for the promotion and furtherance of high class education among the young of both sexes, above the age of thirteen years and being resident in the Borough of Dewsbury. . . .".[16] Mr. Albert Kirk, Architect, and Dr. Oates of Leeds Road were appointed executors. Dr. Oates died on 15th May, 1898 and after some delay, Captain (later Major) P. B. Walker of Lees House was appointed in his place. This is the beginning of Major Walker's very long association with secondary education in the borough and with the Wheelwright Schools in particular which lasted until his death in 1941.

Many and varied were the suggestions which were put forward at a conference held in Dewsbury Town Hall on 9th May, 1899 as to how the Hinchliffe Bequest could be used. There were suggestions from more than one quarter that as both the Wheelwright Schools and the Technical School were financially very poor (the Technical School had been recently (1899) "gibbetted" in the *Daily Telegraph* for paying starvation wages[16]) the money should go to help to finance higher education as given by the Wheelwright Schools and the Technical School and that these two bodies be amalgamated with each other and the Hinchliffe Trust, and the schools be known as The Hinchliffe and Wheelwright Grammar and Technical Schools". Mr. George Harry Hirst, the then organist of Dewsbury Parish Church, was all for the creation of musical scholarships from the fund. Apart from Mr. T. L. Chadwick (Chairman of the Wheelwright Governors), this suggestion received very little support. The establishment of university scholarships had more support. Another idea was for the Hinchliffe Bequest to reduce the fees at Wheelwright Schools from £10 to £7 per annum (the working men's chief fear).

Again Clause 47 in the Scheme of 1888 came up for discussion; this is the one insisting that the children had to be instructed in the tenets of the Church of England according to the Founder's wish. Mr. W. Webb, the leader of the 'Vigilance Committee" brought the matter up at the conference just referred to, and he admitted that there appeared to be no difficulty as the parents were satisfied by the way religious knowledge was being taught at the school. "In fact," said Mr. Webb, "The only scholars who at present were being instructed in the Catechism were three children of a dissenter!" – a paradoxical situation which created a little amusement.[16]

The Vigilance Committee mentioned above was a group of people who were worried that the benefits of Dr. Hinchliffe's will would go to the middle classes instead of the working classes of the town. It had its origin in a meeting of the Dewsbury Pioneers Industrial Society (The Co-op) on 7th November, 1898 and it had a membership of about 50. The committee was composed of co-operators and representatives of various trades organisations in the Borough – the main plea in its programme being equal educational opportunity for every child in the Borough of Dewsbury irrespective of either class or creed.[16] It also supported the amalgamation of the Wheelwright, Technical, Daw Green and the Hinchliffe Trusts to achieve their ends which were (a) That in any scheme that may be devised, provision is made for free day and evening schools; (b) That equal opportunity be given to the children of all classes in the Borough of Dewsbury absolutely unfettered by any system of examination, competition, competition almost invariably giving advantage to the middle and higher classes over the children of the humbler members of the community; (c) The Wheelwright School being a sectarian foundation and as such a cause of much prejudice in the district, they urged the necessity of eliminating from the proposed

Scheme all stipulation as to sectarian teaching; (d) The Hinchliffe Bequest being almost one half of the combined trust and it also being left in trust with Dewsbury Corporation, it was suggested that the people's representatives should be such as to secure effective control in its administration. The committee therefore asked that the principle of municipal control, which was one of the cardinal principles defined in the late doctor's will, should be embodied in any scheme formulated for the future administration of these charities and give its hearty support to the proposal giving to the Corporation a clear majority of members on the new Board of Governors provided such majority were members of the Corporation.[18]

There were other suggestions that the Hinchliffe Bequest be used to enrich the Free Library Funds.

Before proceeding further it is as well to take note of the date when the will was made (15th August, 1878). It would seem from the date, a time when a great deal of work was being put in to secure support from the Wheelwright Trustees for secondary education in Dewsbury, that Dr. Hinchliffe had an idea of helping the scheme to establish a high class secondary school in Dewsbury. Little did he realise that when finally he passed away some twenty years later, the money would come in the nick of time to save the newly founded Wheelwright Grammar Schools financially.

All this discussion and uncertainty could have been avoided if Dr. Hinchliffe had consulted a solicitor in the framing of his will instead of doing it himself. He would certainly have created less trouble for his executors.[18] The moneys had been invested in Consols by the Charity Commissioners at 112. During the long discussions about the Scheme the market price had slowly depreciated and when agreement was finally reached had fallen to about 95 at which the stock was sold and re-invested in Dewsbury Corporation Stock. Mr. S. J. Chadwick, by his legal knowledge, and his long connection with the higher education of the borough, was of the greatest assistance to the members of the Corporation, who decided on his advice to ask the Charity Commissioners to draw up a scheme for the amalgamation of the Wheelwright Grammar Schools, the Technical School, the Hinchliffe Bequest and the Daw Green Charity in one foundation to be called the Dewsbury Endowed Schools Foundation and in 1900 this body came into being.[19] By its formation the Wheelwright Grammar School and the Technical School were worked by separate committees of the one governing body on which the Dewsbury Corporation had a majority of representatives, so that from before the beginning of the present century the Dewsbury Town Council has had a controlling influence in the management of the schools. This arrangement, novel at the time, was soon imitated in several other towns where secondary schools received large financial assistance from the Town Council, and was the forerunner of the modern municipalisation made possible by the Education Act of 1902 and now usual throughout the country.[19]

The Hinchliffe Bequest also enabled scholarships to be awarded at the Wheelwright Grammar Schools and at the universities.

The chief points of the Dewsbury Endowed Schools Foundation Scheme as it affected the Wheelwright Grammar Schools were that £600 should be spent on maintaining both the Wheelwright and the Technical Schools; £100 a year should be spent to maintain scholarships to be called the "Hinchliffe Scholarships"; these entitled the holder to receive not less than £5 and not more than £10 a year besides tuition, etc.; another £100 to maintain the "Wheelwright Scholarships", each holder to get £4 per annum towards the payment of the tuition fees; £300 to maintain exhibitions at a university or similar place of education each valued at £50 per annum and the rest of the income from the Hinchliffe Bequest to be used in the promotion of general educational interests at the Wheelwright and the Technical School.[25]

As well as the Dewsbury Endowed Schools Foundation being inaugurated in 1900 the Government of the time also formed the Board of Education. It was discovered that the Higher Grade Schools which had been set up by the School Boards were illegal and a brief Bill had to be put through Parliament to allow them to continue for one year.[19]

The new Bill became the Education Act of 1902 which created local education authorities which were to be responsible for elementary and higher education. The School Boards were replaced by County and County Borough Councils which were mainly concerned with Part II of the Act dealing with higher education.

The old Board Schools were now Council Schools and were known as Provided Schools. The Church Schools had a definite place in the scheme, having to provide free elementary education in these schools and in return they could give religious instruction of their own choosing, subject to a Conscience Clause. Much opposition to the giving of rate aid to these voluntary schools was raised by the Non-conformists.[19] This factor and the passing of the Local Education Authorities Default Act in 1904 by which the Board of Education could deduct from its grants to a local education authority if that authority did not make adequate grants to the voluntary schools, were the main causes of the religious clause dispute which dogged Wheelwright Grammar Schools from 1904 to 1911.

The turn of the century saw the building of the new gymnasium which was situated between the "arms" of the building and at the rear (behind the present dining hall in the basement). Its cost was defrayed largely by Major Chaley Fox. It was entered from the basement—one entrance (for the girls) through the dining hall and the other (for the boys) through a door leading off the corridor opposite the old boiler house. It had a glass roof like a greenhouse which blocked the view from the old Assembly Hall (now the library). This feature caused it to be very cold in winter and hot in summer. It was ready for use in September, 1900.[20]

Now that the Dewsbury Endowed Schools Foundation was functioning by 1901, the fees at the Wheelwright Schools were able to be reduced from £10 to £8 per annum for pupils over 12 years of age. Obviously the financial situation had eased somewhat. In the same year Mr. Holme pressed the Board of Education asking that the school should be recognised as a School of Science under that Body. One difficulty immediately presented itself and that was that there was no Physics laboratory at Wheelwright. Mr. Holme wished to obtain the use of the Physics laboratory at the Technical School and contacted the headmaster there direct and not through the Governors and that rather annoyed the Governors. It was some years (actually 1904-5) before the pressure of students at the Technical School eased and enabled an agreement to be made so that Wheelwright pupils could use the Physics laboratories at the Technical School during the day-time. This arrangement lasted until the new Physics laboratories were built as one of the additions to Wheelwright Schools in 1938. It was the best arrangement at the time but as the Technical School was half a mile from Wheelwright, it entailed quite a lot of wasted time going to and from the two buildings.[21]

In 1901 the first entrance scholarship by the school to be gained at Trinity Hall, Cambridge, was won by W. G. Fearnsides who ultimately became Professor of Geology at Sheffield University.

The new school buildings in Halifax Road were held in such esteem as being the most progressive design at the time, that in March, 1902, photographs of them were exhibited at the Cork Exhibition of that year.

In 1903 the idea of a Pupil Teachers' Centre at Wheelwright was first mooted. Mr. Holme said he was willing to assist in every way possible and also agreed on behalf of the staffs of the schools.[22] It was agreed that the salaries of both Mr. and Mrs. Holme should be increased in consequence of the extra responsibility of supervising and managing the Pupil Teachers' Centre.[23] The next year Ossett Education Authority made application to be allowed to send their pupil teachers to the Wheelwright Centre.[24]

By the passing of the Education Act of 1902 the West Riding County Council became the local education authority responsible for secondary education in the district.

THE DISPUTE ABOUT THE RELIGIOUS CLAUSE IN THE SCHEME OF 1888

As local education authority for the area, the West Riding County Council arranged that the Wheelwright Schools took 40 pupils from their area and for this the Wheelwright School received a grant of £335 per annum. As mentioned earlier, there was a growing feeling amongst Nonconformists and the Liberal element that schools giving specific sectarian teaching should not have aid from the rates levied by the local authority. The feeling came to a head at the Higher Education Sub-Committee of the West Riding County Council which was held on 17th September, 1903, when a resolution was passed that, "Grants on the proposed increased scale be made to all Secondary Schools where no conditions exist as to religious tests for the teachers or as to distinctive denominational teaching and that in all other cases the existing grants be continued with a view to enable the Governors to consider the question of amending the schemes so as to remove the conditions in question.

"If this resolution should come into force it will have the effect of depriving of the increased Grants referred to therein all Secondary Schools in the West Riding whose trust deeds or schemes contain conditions as to religious tests for teachers or as to distinctive denominational teaching notwithstanding that the districts served by these schools will have to contribute to the rate levied by the County Council for the purpose of providing the grants".[26]

This list of schools included the Wheelwright Grammar Schools.

For the next eight years or so the chief topic which occupied the minds of the Governors of the Wheelwright Schools was the reduction of the grant from the West Riding County Council in accordance with the Resolution made above.

On 3rd March, 1904, the Director of Education for the West Riding County Council (Mr. W. Loring), wrote a letter to the Clerk of the Dewsbury Endowed Schools Foundation to say that if the Governors of the School should find it possible to modify their Scheme as regards the Clause named above so as to bring it in this respect into harmony with the schemes of the great majority of schools which the County Council aids, the resolution would no longer apply and the Committee would then be in a position to consider what amount of additional aid should be offered to this school and what special conditions should be attached to it.[27]

The Clause under discussion is Clause 47 of the Wheelwright Grammar School Scheme of 1888 which states "Subject to the provisions of this scheme religious instruction in accordance with the doctrines of the Church of England shall be given in the school—". This is in compliance with the will of the Founder in which he stated that "The said children be religiously and virtuously brought up and educated according to the doctrines of the Church of England as by law established".

This was also a condition of the sharing of the Wheelwright moneys between the school at Rishworth and the Dewsbury School and was insisted upon by the Wheelwright Trustees.

Naturally the above letter from the West Riding County Council came as a shock to the Governors of the Wheelwright Schools. They were immediately placed on the horns of a dilemma. The £22,000 which the Wheelwright Grammar Schools' Governors received from the Wheelwright Trustees in 1888 was conditional upon this Clause. The Dewsbury share impoverished the Rishworth School for more than two decades and altogether the Governors were very deeply indebted to the Wheelwright Trustees on the one hand and the latter were in duty bound compelled to see that the will of John Wheelwright was not violated in any way. On the other hand children from the West Riding area were being educated at the school and this county was the Local Education Authority responsible for Secondary education in the district and was making grants to the school.

The School needed the financial help of the County Council but it was another and far more serious matter to even think of asking for the Scheme to be altered as the County Council insisted. How would the school stand then in the eyes of the Wheelwright Trustees? Unfortunately for the Governors of the Wheelwright Schools they found themselves as the pawns in a political game which was roughly Tories and Churchmen against Liberals and Non-conformists. It was the latter faction which was pushing for the deletion of the Religious Clause from the Wheelwright Scheme. Also by the time this religious controversy developed, Wheelwright was making itself felt in the academic sphere and its fame was spreading further than its immediate district. It could be that this caused some jealousy among the West Riding County Councillors, Wheelwright not being one of their County Council Secondary Schools nor one which that body had helped to resuscitate. Whether this was so or not the County Council was adamant that Clause 47 should be deleted from the Wheelwright Scheme.

Much water flowed under Savile Bridge and reams of correspondence accumulated without headway being made until in November, 1907, at the Wheelwright Governors' meeting it was moved by Councillor Waddington and seconded by Major Walker "That this meeting is of opinion that in the interest both of the Wheelwright Schools and Secondary education in the district, steps should be taken now to secure the deletion of paragraph 1 of Clause 47, from its Scheme in order to comply with the new regulations in the Board of Education and the requirements of the West Riding County Council as embodied in its resolution of 14th October, 1903".[28]

Throughout 1907 and 1908 the dispute went on and a very long letter dated 15th June, 1908, from Mr. W. Scholefield to the secretary of the Board of Education highlighted all the salient points in the dispute. These were (1) that though the Board of Education were satisfied that Wheelwright Grammar Schools had accepted Article 5a of the Education Act of 1902, the West Riding County Council would accept nothing short of the absolute deletion of the denominational clause (Clause 47) of the 1888 Scheme. "It was also intimated that unless this was done absolutely and unconditionally the West Riding County Council would not only refuse as hitherto to give any additional grants to the schools, but would also withdraw the grant which they were then making, namely the £335 per annum". [29] (2) In the same letter it is noted that the West Riding County Council intended not only to withdraw all grants, but as soon as possible to remove the Intending Teachers and Pupil Teachers' for whom they now paid the full fees.[29] (3) The letter further goes on to state that "Clause 4 of the Education Act of 1902 is equally emphatic that a Council in the application of money under Part II of the Act shall not require that any particular form of religious instruction or worship or any religious catechism or formulary which is distinctive of any particular denomination shall or *shall not* be taught, used or practised in any school—aided but not provided by the Council".

"The Governors further admit that the action of the County Council in the past with regard to these schools had been ultra vires as contrary to the express provisions of Clause 2 and 4 of the Education Act of 1902".

Another very interesting point is raised which emphasises the action of the County Council and which appeared with intent to injure the schools. This is the paragraph stating that:—

"At the same time the Governors would call attention to the fact which is well-known to the West Riding County Council that there has never at any time been any religious difficulty in these schools, that they have been attended by children of all religious denominations including Roman Catholics and Jews; that no religious tests have been ever applied in the appointment of teachers; that the same absence of tests applies in the case of the Governing Body; that in the carrying out of Clause 47 of the Scheme, the Governors in actual practice had anticipated Clause 5a of the Regulations for Secondary Schools (1907) and only provided instructions in the Catechism of the Church of England to the children of those parents who had asked for such teaching and finally that with the exception of Roman Catholics and Jews who have attended the schools no withdrawals from the general religious instruction of the School has been claimed under Clause 59 of the Wheelwright Scheme (which allowed pupils to be exempted from religious worship and attending prayers and from lessons on a religious subject without being deprived of any advantage or emolument in the school)".[29]

It would appear from the above that the action of the County Council was indeed illegal but the interesting point is that the *Board of Education was doing nothing to force the hand of the County Council. It can only be presumed that the Liberal Government of the day was in full sympathy with the County Council, though in absolute fairness, Mr. Walter Runciman, who was Liberal M.P. for Dewsbury and was at the time the President of the Board of Education, wisely did not interfere in the dispute.

The School was losing up to £1,000 a year in grants from the West Riding County Council as a result of the dispute (not including the Board of Education Grant of £5 per head).[29]

Questions were asked in the House of Commons on 19th December, 1908, by Lord Robert Cecil as to what steps the Board of Education were taking to secure obedience to the law by the West Riding County Council. To these Mr. (Later Sir) Charles Trevelyan replied that the Governors were now in the position that they had asked the Board of Education's advice as they were in honour bound to the Wheelwright Trustees to uphold the religious clause and it was up to the Governors to ask the Wheelwright Trustees to release them voluntarily from the provisions of the Scheme of 1900 drawn up by the Wheelwright Trustees, the Town Council and assented to by the Charity Commissioners. The Board of Education gave very guarded advice to the Governors when they sought it. In fact it threw the responsibility back on the Governors.[30]

*Unfortunately for Wheelwright the County Council knew they had the "whiphand".

At this time, at the end of 1908 and the beginning of 1909, there were people in Dewsbury who hoped that by staving off a decision time could be killed until the proposed County Borough of Dewsbury was an actuality. In that case it was hoped that that would be a peaceful way out of the dispute with the West Riding County Council. But as the "Dewsbury Reporter" commented on 30th January, 1909, "In Dewsbury itself as well as in the outside districts there are forces which will fight the battle which the West Riding County Council are now fighting independent of the general tendency towards complete municipalisation of such schools".[31]

At a special meeting of the Wheelwright Governors on 1st February, 1909, after very careful and considerable airing of views from both Churchmen and Non-conformists, the former thought that to apply to the Board of Education for an amendment of the Scheme was to condone the illegal action of the West Riding County Council.[32] At the vote taken at the end of the meeting there were 9 Governors for the motion (i.e. to ask the Board of Education to delete the offending Clause 47 from the Scheme), 7 against and 2 abstained from voting. So the motion was carried.

In April, 1909, we find the first intimation that the Wheelwright Trustees intended to contest the Board of Education's action. They intended to ask the Judicial Committee of the Privy Council to compel the Board of Education to show cause why the alterations (to the Scheme) should be made. Throughout the dispute with the West Riding County Council it had been known that if the Board of Governors of Wheelwright Grammar Schools made a bona-fide application to the Board of Education or the Charity Commissioners for leave to alter the Scheme, the West Riding County Council would treat the attempt, if it proved unsuccessful owing to Legal Form, as evidence of goodwill on the part of the Governors. Unfortunately the West Riding County Council was still treating the Wheelwright Schools with less generosity than it treated other schools of the same status.[33] The dispute carried on two years until April, 1911, when the Appeal of the Wheelwright Trustees against the action of the Board of Education in settling a Scheme to suit the Governors of the Wheelwright Grammar Schools went to the House of Lords.

The hearing was on 8th April, 1911. The Earl of Dartmouth moved the address praying His Majesty to withhold his consent to the Scheme settled by the Board of Education in tne matter of the Wheelwright Grammar Schools at Dewsbury.

Among those noble Lords who took part in the appeal were the Earl of Beauchamp, the Marquis of Salisbury, Viscount Haldane, Lord Halifax, the Marquis of Londonderry, the Bishop of Wakefield and the Archbishop of Canterbury. Naturally the Bishop of Wakefield hit out at the West Riding County Council saying that setting aside Clause 4 of the 1902 Education Act was "anything but a most flagrant illegal action".[34] The Lords threw out the Board of Education's Scheme by which the denominational clause would be eliminated. The local press, particularly "The Dewsbury Reporter" which had Liberal sympathies in those days, was greatly worried, went on to state, "We are greatly afraid that the action of the House of Lords places the Wheelwright Schools in an awkward position. Extensions are to be undertaken at the schools and it was hoped that the County Council would give considerable help towards the cost. But if the Council reverts to its former attitude towards the schools, there is little hope that this will be done".

By this time, of course, the spade work for the formation of the Dewsbury County Borough had been done—in fact in August of the following year (1912) the County Borough Order was received which was to become operative as from 1st April, 1913.

All this has been given in considerable detail because of its importance not only as it affected Wheelwright Grammar Schools but in showing how political factions over many decades have used education to serve their own ends.

The period 1904 to 1911 must have been a very trying time for Mr. and Mrs. Holme. Particularly, Mr. Holme seemed to have been dogged over the years by one or other religious controversy. Coupled with this latter dispute was the lack of grants from the County Council.

In spite of the cloud, Wheelwright Schools appear to have had the power to attract teachers who were prepared to stay at the school over a long period of time. Right from the very beginning, along with Mr. Holme came Mr. Walton Batley who stayed thirty years (1889—1919); Mr. James Gledhill who came to the school in 1893 and stayed until 1919; Mr. Geoffrey Hawkes who became Senior Assistant stayed 10 years and he was followed in that post by Mr. J. H. Evans who stayed from 1906 to 1920. These were the first of quite a long line of masters who stayed for periods far in excess of 10 years. The tradition is still with us as quite a few of the present staff have been there well over ten years and some over twenty. Also came Albert Peel—a man with a shock of carrotty red hair who quickly earned the by-name of "Orange". He had also a very violent temper. He stayed eight years and then entered military service during the First World War.

In 1909 the headship of the Technical School became vacant and it was decided to appoint a head under the title of "Organising Master". There was considerable discussion as to whether or not Mr. Holme should hold the position as well as that of headmaster of the Wheelwright Grammar School. However, the Board of Education would not agree to this appointment—it considered that the two buildings were too far apart for the efficiency of both not to suffer and so a separate appointment was made to the Technical School in Mr. Herbert J. Taylor who had been for some years science master at Wheelwright and also science teacher to the Pupil Teachers' Centre also held at Wheelwright.

In 1910 we find the first mention of possible major additions to the schools since the gymnasium was erected in 1900. It was decided to build some new classrooms to accommodate the extra pupils. In November of the same year arrangements were entered into to purchase the field which was used as a football field and belonged to Hill Head Farm (the Top Field). One must remember that up to this time the only playing fields were still the front field and the tennis courts behind the main building. Also in this year the West Riding County Council recognised Wheelwright Grammar Schools as two separate schools—up to now they had been classed as one school.

The next year, Dr. Dufton, H.M.I., proposed alterations to the school— these were estimated at £1,500 but he really preferred a new school for the girls—a separate building to be used as a girls' school only. This was estimated to cost £5,000. This was the first mention of the need for a new girls' school by officialdom but it was twenty-four years before the girls were finally settled in their new school. Immediately after Dr. Dufton's announcement, a letter was received from Mr. Hallam, the Director of Education for the West Riding County Council, stating that the Board of Education proposed that a new girls' school should be built and the existing building be utilised altogether for the Boys' School.[35]

This same H.M.I. requested that a wooden floor be placed in the gymnasium to replace the concrete one there! One can hardly imagine this state of affairs today. At this time also Mr. Sidney Diggery Nicholas was appointed chemistry master. Legend has it that he was sent a postcard to school one day and unwittingly left it on his desk. Someone read it! From thence he was known as "Dickery-Dock". During the First World War he was called up for military service and entered a Government munitions works at Liverpool. Later he became a lecturer in Chemistry at the University of Birmingham.

In March, 1912, things seemed to be moving regarding the building of a new Girls' School and the Governors advertised for competitive plans for a new school to accommodate 200 girls, the building to be not more than two storeys high, and to be built on the site recently purchased from Mr. Fox, i.e. the Top Field.[36]

A final settlement of the religious trouble was reached in April, 1913, when it was decided by the Governors "That instruction in the Doctrines, Catechism and Formularies of the Church of England shall be given to pupils whose parents or guardians have, in writing, requested the Governors to provide such instructions for them and that a notice to that effect be inserted in the School Prospectus". At last all the trouble was over!

In July, 1913, there was one of the many periodic applications which Mr. and Mrs. Holme made throughout their headships for increases of salaries for their assistant staffs.[37]

The following February (1914), very determined efforts were made by Messrs. Chadwick, Son & Nicholson, to gain possession of Hill Head Farm so that work could be started on the new Girls' School. Possession was gained a few weeks later.

The following month trees were planted on the two sides of the School grounds (Halifax Road and Birkdale Road) at an estimated cost of £10.

These trees have certainly proved a great amenity in that part of the town.

This brings us to the period of the First World War which, of course, naturally put a stop to the plans for the building of the new Girls' School. The school had had a few years respite after the religious dispute and now there was further trouble ahead; though this was common to all schools and not just to Wheelwright as had been the other trouble. With the typical optimism which prevailed at the beginning of the First World War that it would be over by Christmas, 1914, the Board of Education in December of that year asked for the plans to be formulated and submitted so that as soon as hostilities finished, the Governors would be in a position to carry them out without any undue delay.[38] In retrospect this was ironical as by the time the War was over, inflation and financial difficulties placed the Governors in such a position that instead of building the new Girls' School they had to relinquish what they had to the Local Authority. (See below).

In November, 1914, arrangements were made for the older boys to have rifle practice. This was the first sign that the school was becoming aware of the War; but it was another year before the harsher effects of the hostilities began to be felt.

In January, 1915, Mr. Peel was released from his teaching appointment as he had been called up for military service; he was the first member of staff to go to the War. At the same time the Wheelwright Grammar School Committee were called upon to pay £40 a year for the use of the Physics Laboratories and Woodwork Rooms at the Technical Schools. Even in the midst of War-time complications both Mr. and Mrs. Holme applied for permission to engage a teacher of Commercial subjects.[39] These subjects had not received attention since the early days at Bond Street when Mr. Owen took shorthand, etc. there.

The Board of Education informed the Wheelwright Governors as to the procedure to be adopted if and when the military authorities found it necessary to use the schools for the purpose of billetting troops.[40] Luckily this exigency never occurred, but it had an unsettling effect on the schools.

By 1916 more applications were made for increases of salaries to offset the increase in prices caused by the War. Mr. Nicholas left to become a chemist at a Government munition factory in Liverpool and Mr. Evans was exempted for the time being under the Lord Derby Scheme.

Later that year the H.M.I. (Dr. Dufton) met the Governors "to consider what means could be devised to accommodate the existing patients at the Staincliffe Institute so as to enable the Board of Guardians to place the infirmary there at the disposal of the military Authorities for the treatment of wounded soldiers".[41] The Governors were very much against the use of the school for this purpose as the idea was to scatter the pupils among the town's Council schools for the duration of the War. It was impossible to teach subjects like the sciences, in schools without laboratories and so for the time being, the proposals were dropped and Boothroyd Lane School was to be used for this purpose instead of the Wheelwright.

In April, 1917, it was decided to form a Cadet Corps and £100 was granted towards the cost of its formation—the remainder of the cost to be raised by subscription.[42] The corps was finally founded in May of that year with two officers and 73 Cadets (old and present boys). The first Commanding Officer was Cadet-Capt. J. H. Evans and they were drilled once every two weeks by an N.C.O. of the 2nd/4th K.O.Y.L.I. Capt. Evans held command until taken over in 1919 by Cadet-Capt. P. A. Lewis who had command until 1922.[43] The latter was assisted for a time by Mr. M. I. Hemstead.

Once more the military authorities had their eyes on the school. This was in December, 1917. Major Russell (Commandant of the Dewsbury War Hospital) met the Governors and informed them that he had had urgent demands for further accommodation at Staincliffe and wished to utilise the Wheelwright Schools as a hospital for wounded soldiers. Again the Governors pointed out the difficulties of accommodating a grammar school in other schools. Eventually Major Russell looked elsewhere.[44] From that time onwards the school was left in peace from military intervention.

The middle of 1918 found the schools very overcrowded, so much so that it was imperative that some building be found to house the Kindergarten and the 1st Form Girls and so ease the situation in the main building.

The first thought in the minds of the Governors was to use the old farm buildings belonging to Hill Head Farm, suitably modified for the accommodation of the Kindergarten, etc. The Borough Surveyor (Mr. H. Dearden) prepared plans which were submitted to the H.M.I. (Dr. Dufton).[45] At the same time the Governors were looking round for accommodation in other directions and this was offered at St. Mark's Schoolroom. This was not proceeded with as they decided to use rooms at the Technical School, Mr. Taylor (Headmaster there) to have disciplinary powers over all Wheelwright pupils at the Technical School.[46]

Details required by the Board of Education in connection with the modification of the old farm buildings, made it impossible to carry out the work. So nothing was done and several generations of Wheelwright boys will bring back to mind the happy though clandestine adventures which were indulged in in the old buildings. The temporary easing of the overcrowding problem was not forthcoming until the army huts were purchased and also the Marlborough House Estate—the former for the junior forms of both boys' and girls' schools and the latter for the accommodation of the Kindergarten.

The employment of additional staff was also granted to both head-teachers.

In February, 1919, Mr. and Mrs. Holme tendered their resignations to the Governors to be effective from 31st July, 1919. The last important things which Mr. Holme was able to see through were first the War

Memorial to the 50 Old Boys who lost their lives in that War, out of 450 who served their country.[19] The War Memorial itself was a Fund to provide two University Scholarships for boys at Wheelwright. Having explained the proposals, Major P. B. Walker made a gift of £500 to the und as a beginning.[47] A tablet was also set up in the main entrance to the oys' School to record the names of the Fallen later on. On Sunday, 22nd June, 1919, a special service was held in Dewsbury Parish Church in memory of all the Old Boys who had fallen in the War.

Mr. Holme had also the satisfaction of having the school recognised by the Board of Education to run advanced courses in Science.[48] He was unable to see the easing of the overcrowding problem as the Army huts were not erected until after he retired.

Having opened a very small grammar school in a warehouse in Bond Street, Mr. Holme steered it through the upheavals of competition from a sectarian grammar school in the same town, built up almost from scratch an entirely new school in Halifax Road, from 1893 onwards, faced the opposition of religious troubles again over a period of seven to eight years, at the same time facing financial troubles due to this dispute. When money did appear unexpectedly there were further squabbles (The Hinchliffe Bequest) and then quickly following the religious dispute came the Great War and with it increased inflation. Both Mr. and Mrs. Holme, over the years, appear to have spent considerable time asking for advances in salaries for their staffs. Many epithets have been used to describe Mr. Holme but one of the best is probably that of an Old Boy who gained the first Ph.D. the University of Cambridge ever awarded in aeronautics. He says, "He seems now to have been almost a re-incarnation of Pythagoras or Archimedes".

Soon after the Great War ended it was time for both Mr. and Mrs. Holme to say goodbye. In spite of all the opposition (or could it be because of it?) Mr. Holme had fought to make his school the best in the district and very early on it had gained more than a purely local reputation. It grew and grew in spite of the establishment of new grammar schools and the resuscitation of old ones within its catchment area and even the veiled threat by the West Riding County Council to establish a County Council Grammar School in Dewsbury in direct opposition to it. It is entirely due to Mr. and Mrs. Holme that Wheelwright Grammar Schools became not only the grammar schools serving the Dewsbury District but became "THE WHEELWRIGHT"—something far more important. When people asked residents to be directed to the grammar schools, even the most uncultured would reply "You mean The Wheelwright".

Mr. Holme was known as "The Keph" a title which his successor inherited. He was firm, understanding and gained discipline through respect though if need be he did not hesitate to use the cane. The chief punishment was the "Punishment School" after school hours and there are some humorous entries in one of the Punishment School books still extant. Some of the reasons given for putting a boy in Punishment School are fascinating to say the least, such as "Going down" (i.e. going to the toilet) "Stopping 'down' " "Rushing out of school", "Loitering", "Disorderly entry into 'Puni' " (Punishment School), "Indicative of DORMER. He didn't know it", "Ungentlemanly behaviour" and two superb ones "Abysmal ignorance" and "General idiocy"![49]

Although Mr. Holme was a science man he believed in the Classics as well—one feels that when the newly formed Wheelwright Grammar Schools needed a headmaster that shrewd educationist and organiser, Dr. Boddington (the Principal of the Yorkshire College) saw immediately the man for the post in Mr. Holme as Boddington had been at Manchester Grammar School also before going to the Yorkshire College. If that was so, then the choice was well made. Mr. Holme built up Wheelwright and Mr. Sadler, Mr. Bolton and the present headmaster have carried on the good work.

The recognition of the Advanced Course in Science by the Board of Education in the last six months of Holme's time, would seem to have influenced the Governors in the appointment of his successor. Mr. Sadler was appointed because he was a Mathematics and Physics man and so could carry on a continuity of effort. As one looks back to Mr. Godby's days at the Bond Street School when mathematics and science graduates were prominent, there is a continuity of Mathematics and Science at the schools covering a period of nearly 70 years.

The 31st July, 1919, saw the end of the reign of Mr. Holme—an Englishman in the best tradition—and the end of an era as well. But it was also the beginning of a period of expansion under the succeeding headmasters. Holme laid the foundations and the others built on them.

References

1. Daw Green Charity School Papers (Bundle P) Dewsbury Central Library 1889
2. Daw Green Charity School Papers (Bundle B) Dewsbury Central Library 1889
3. Daw Green Charity School Papers (Bundle P) Dewsbury Central Library Oct. 1889
4. The Dewsbury Education Week Handbook 1925
5. *The Dewsbury Reporter* .. .. 3rd Sept. 1932
6. *The Dewsbury Reporter* .. .. 18th Jan. 1941
7. *The Dewsbury Reporter* .. .. 24th Oct. 1936
8. Headmaster's and Headmistress's Reports 1891
9. *The Dewsbury Reporter* .. ..
10. Headmaster's and Headmistress's Reports .. .. 1st Aug. 1891
11. Daw Green Charity School Papers (Bundle G) Central Library 1891
12. *The Dewsbury Reporter* 1893
13. *The Dewsbury Reporter* .. .. 27th May 1896
14. The Scrap Book in the Dewsbury Central Library 1896
15. Headmaster's and Headmistress's Reports 1897
16. *The Dewsbury Reporter* Hinchliffe Number 1899
17. *The Dewsbury Reporter* .. .. June 1944
18. The Dewsbury Education Week Booklet 1925
19. Bamford, K. *An Evaluation of the Part played by Education at Dewsbury and Rishworth by the Charities of John Wheelwright, Gentleman* 1957
20 *The Dewsbury Reporter* .. .. 28th July 1900
21. Minutes of Dewsbury Endowed Schools Foundation 1901
22. Minutes of Dewsbury Endowed Schools Foundation .. .. March 1903
23. Minutes of Dewsbury Endowed Schools Foundation .. .. .. Dec. 1903
24. Minutes of Dewsbury Endowed Schools Foundation .. .. .. Jan. 1904
25. Daw Green Charity School Papers (Bundle N) Central Library 1900

26. Wheelwright Trustees Letter Book .. .. May 1908
27. Wheelwright Trustees Letter Book 1904
28. Minutes of Dewsbury Endowed Schools Foundation .. .. 25th Mar. 1907
29. Wheelwright Trustees Letter Book .. .. 15th June 1908
30. Wheelwright Trustees Letter Book .. .. 13th Nov. 1908
31. *The Dewsbury Reporter* .. .. 30th June 1909
32. *The Dewsbury Reporter* .. .. 6th Feb. 1909
33. *The Dewsbury Reporter* .. .. 23rd April 1909
34. *The Dewsbury Reporter* .. .. 8th April 1911
35. Minutes of the Dewsbury Endowed Schools Foundation .. 20th Mar. 1911
36. Minutes of the Dewsbury Endowed Schools Foundation .. 11th Mar. 1912
37. Minutes of the Dewsbury Endowed Schools Foundation .. 10th July 1913
38. Minutes of the Dewsbury Endowed Schools Foundation .. 4th Dec. 1914
39. Minutes of the Dewsbury Endowed Schools Foundation .. 8th Mar. 1915
40. Minutes of the Dewsbury Endowed Schools Foundation .. 12th April 1915
41. Minutes of the Dewsbury Endowed Schools Foundation .. 13th Nov. 1916
42. Minutes of the Dewsbury Endowed Schools Foundation .. 2nd April 1917
43. Correspondence with H.M. Docton .. .. 16th April 1917
44. Minutes of the Dewsbury Endowed Schools Foundation .. 18th Dec. 1917
45. Minutes of the Dewsbury Endowed Schools Foundation .. 17th July 1918
46. Minutes of the Dewsbury Endowed Schools Foundation .. 14th Oct. 1918
47. Minutes of the Dewsbury Endowed Schools Foundation .. 13th Jan. 1919
48. Minutes of the Dewsbury Endowed Schools Foundation .. 10th Feb. 1919
49. Mr. Holme's Punishment Book.

CHAPTER IV

Mr. Sadler's Reign at Wheelwright (1919 to 1950)

On 18th February, 1919, the Governors of the Wheelwright Grammar Schools convened a special meeting to receive the resignation of both Mr. and Mrs. Holme to take effect from 31st July, 1919. A month later advertisements were inserted in the various scholastic journals for a headmaster and a headmistress.

Immediately there was an outcry from the Assistant Masters' Association because of the wording of the advertisement for the headmaster. Obviously with a view to retaining continuity in the teaching, the Governors had advertised for candidates to be honours graduates in mathematics or science of one of the older universities and not to be over forty years of age. This annoyed the Assistant Masters' Association and a letter[1] signed by the secretary of the York branch, L. H. Leadley, vented the indignation that this body felt, namely, that the candidates should be limited to men from the older universities. In spite of all this only one honoursman of the older universities was among the candidates and that was Leslie Sadler.

He was a double first (Mathematics and Physics) of Oxford. He was educated at Worcester Grammar School and went up to Hertford College with a Hastings Scholarship. He came to Wheelwright from Bradford Grammar School where he had held the post of head of the Physics Department. He was 36 years of age when he was appointed.

A very shy man (it was said that he paced the corridor at Bradford Grammar School at morning break, coffee in hand, rather than face the sea of faces in the staff room), and often misunderstood, as shy people so frequently are. He took over the reins at Wheelwright at a very critical time. He was immediately post-war and had a staff of eleven (six men and three women on the permanent staff and two part-time assistants). Two of the permanent staff were men of experience and had been at the school quite a long time; J. H. Evans who was senior master had been there since 1905 and W. Morgan (English) since 1910. With this staff Sadler undertook to teach just over 200 boys on the ground floor of the present building with part use of the basement and joint use of the chemistry laboratory in the upper storey or girls' school and the use of the physics laboratory at the Technical School. For nearly ten years there had been talk of a new girls' school but the advent of the War put that back and by now costs were rising and so the new girls' school was still a long way off. It was under crowded and adverse conditions that Sadler commenced work there. To add to the difficulties in the building, there were staff shortages and a general shortage of teachers; so much was this the case that he was given a free hand to get what staff he could by offering more than the recognised salary of the day. This state of affairs led to at least one infamous appointment. After Mr. Evans left in 1920 to take up a post at Leamington Spa, Joseph Kirwan was appointed physics master. This position was a cover up for his real activities, the reason for his being in England at all, which was the smuggling of arms for the I.R.A. (Independent Republican Army of Ireland). He was subsequently caught at Birmingham and put off for the Assizes in that city, and made his get-away to Ireland and made a farce of the proposed trial at Birmingham Assizes by not turning up!*

Owing to inflationary tendencies the first three years of Sadler's reign were marked by the Governors of the Dewsbury Endowed Schools' Foundation getting more and more into the red. So much was this the case that it is understood from a high authority that but for the beneficence of the Chairman of the Governors (Major Walker) the teaching staff would have been without their salaries.

In such cramped conditions and under the adverse conditions of the state of the Dewsbury Endowed Schools' Foundation, it was obvious to Sadler that he could take one of two courses; he could adopt a policy of "Laissez-faire" or as he could teach mathematics himself, and knew he could, by means of following a fairly narrow syllabus, make a name for the school along a specialised line. He took the latter course, so that whoever shone in mathematics were literally pounced upon and schooled and coached to scholarship standard so that in his thirty years at the school he had about eighty open university scholarships to his credit.

This line of action by Sadler is the usual criticism levelled at him by people without all the facts at their command. Though he was a shy man and scarcely known in Dewsbury, as he did not enter public life at all, he certainly put Wheelwright, and because of this Dewsbury, as well, on the map.†

Besides the continuance of the mathematical and science successes it must be stressed that once the new girls' school premises were occupied, he at once widened his syllabus and fought for the new laboratories, etc. which were ultimately opened in 1938.

He was a man of very stately bearing—who can forge this slow, dignified walk up Birkdale Road in navy blue suit, bowler hat and with black walking stick? He had a habit, being a tall man, of bending at the hips over small boys when talking to them and putting the fear of the Lord into them. It is said that he could not remember names unless the owner was famous as a

---

* *Dewsbury Reporter* 15th July, 1922.

†Students taking scholarship examinations at either of the older universities were often asked by the Master of the College, "And how is Mr. Sadler?" so well-known was he among the academics.

mathematician or "infamous" as a miscreant. He remembered the author's name and he was not a mathematician! But he never forgot a face. He would enter a classroom and excuse himself to the teacher-in-charge remarking that he was looking for a face; guilty ones would cringe until he had passed them by. If the culprit deserved the cane, or "Twang" as it was called, he would say in a soft voice, "I think a little stick (pronounced "leetle steek") will help you". From this remark one must not get the idea that he was a frequent user of that adjunct to education. He used it rarely and so it was all the more effective when used. When it was administered he would intersperse the strokes with a little discourse on the delinquent's particular "crime". Another side of this remarkable memory of his was that he was able to stand up at assembly and re-arrange the whole of the time-table, if this was necessary due to absences, without recourse to notes and paper. He was a strong disciplinarian—the mere appearance of his person brought quietude to the assembled masses in the Assembly Hall (now the library). He never shouted; to raise his voice, even slightly, was evidence of his ire and that punishment was just round the corner. He had the habit of walking, when inside school, with his arms bent at the elbow or standing arms akimbo with half-closed eyes looking down the hall spotting would-be wrong-doers.

Being an honoursman in both physics and mathematics, he was able to continue the good work which Mr. Holme had done; there was in other words continuity in the science tradition.

As was to be expected Sadler made several changes in the running of the school, one being that the silver cap-badge bearing the Wheelwright Coat of Arms was discontinued. This badge was sewn on to a plain navy-blue cap. Some reports say this this was because of the cuts received by boys using their caps as fighting weapons. In its place came the navy-blue cap with the letters W.G.S. embroidered in red on the front. This was not very pleasing, really, and entitled the wearer to be dubbed "Wheelwright Gutter Snipe".

The other big change was in the time-table. During Sadler's first year the school sessions were 9 a.m. to 12.15 p.m. and 2 p.m. to 4 p.m. with a half-day on Wednesday afternoon, and Saturday morning school as on other mornings. In September, 1920, Sadler introduced his new time-table which lasted more or less until the 1960's with minor modifications. This was a school week of three full days and three half-days on Tuesdays, Thursdays and Saturdays. The afternoons of these days were so that the boys could indulge in voluntary games. Although a keen sportsman himself and a player at both football and cricket, he did not introduce compulsory games into the school until after there were complaints by the Inspectors in 1939[2] when they thought that the bad posture they saw in the boys was due to lack of compulsory games. He yielded a point, but only so far, as the compulsory games were limited to the first forms only. The school sessions were now in the mornings from 9 a.m. to 12.25 p.m. and 2.15 p.m. to 4.15 p.m. in the afternoons, detentions being held after afternoon school from

4.15 p.m. to 5 p.m. Three detentions in one week "earned" the culprit a "Thursday afternoon" or "Thursday" as the boys knew it. This was a normal school session in which written work was set to fill the two hours and the boys were supervised by the "Detention Master" on duty.

It wasn't until the early years of Mr. Lancaster's reign that the Ministry of Education complained that the school was not fulfilling the requirements of the New Regulations of 1959 which stated that a school working a six-day week should have two half days. Wheelwright was enjoying three, Tuesday, Thursday and Saturday afternoons.

As an immediate and temporary relief to the over-crowding problem, two ex-Army huts[3] were erected to the north of the main school in 1920 and these were linked by a covered way between them. One half of the hut accommodation was for the boys and the other half for the girls and to maintain the separation of the two sexes which was in force in the main building, there was a brick partition in the covered way betwen the two huts. These huts were a painful necessity as in winter they were very cold and in summer tropical. For quite a time after their erection, they were lit by oil lamps before the mains were connected; they were indeed very miserable in the depth of winter, cold and lit by storm lanterns!

During the first few years of Sadler's regime, the nucleus of the old "Holme staff" left, some for delayed promotion due to the war and others for different reasons. The first to go was Mr. Hemstead, the mathematics teacher, and he was followed by Mr. Evans and Mr. Morgan (both mature teachers and worthy of promotion). Mr. C. Williams ("Docker" to thousands of Wheelwright boys) came as junior mathematics master as Sadler himself was the Senior Mathematics Master. He was the first of a batch of teachers who came here at this time and stayed for a long number of years. Williams stayed for 39 years and in the years up to 1926 others who joined the staff and remained there until retirement or death broke their connection with the school were Browne (35 years) until his unfortunate death whilst still "in harness' and known to generations of boys as "Bruno", H. Perkins ("Pete") who put in 42 years for the school; Franklin 37 years ("Father"); Chester with his 41 years ("Conk"), and W. Seed with 31 years of service ("Walt"). Their total years of service came to 225 years.

Before proceeding further it might be as well to note that when the school had its full inspection in 1920 there were 14 on the staff, 9 regulars and five occasional teachers. The teachers which were recruited during the 1920 to 1926 period formed the nucleus around which many other teachers revolved during the next thirty to forty years. They gave stabliity to the school which it would otherwise have lacked. Some stayed a few months and others a few years and others topped the twenty year mark. Since the first World War one thing has stood out, looking at the staff list (see appendix) and that is the number of teachers who have stayed at the school quite a number of years besides the main nucleus. One must conclude that in spite of everything, Wheelwright must be a pleasant place to work in.

Even after the erection of the huts there was still overcrowding. The proposal to convert the old farm buildings at Hill Head into suitable school premises to ease the situation came to nothing[4] and steps were also being taken to find a suitable building to house the Kindergarten.[5] The huts, when in commission, housed the junior schools of both the boys' and the girls' departments.[6] They were only a make-shift and no one was sorry when they were no longer used for classes and converted into changing rooms; but that was many years ahead.

The Governors themselves were in a cleft stick. Besides the general increase in the cost of running the schools after the war, there was the added expense of buying the huts to ease the overcrowding and finally in February, 1920,[7] the Marlborough Estate on the opposite side of Halifax Road to the school came into the market and the Governors bought it for £8,625. All this put the Governor's account deeper and deeper into the red, so much so that they decided in March, 1920,[8] to appoint a deputation to meet the Local Education Authority with a view to obtaining financial support in connection with the purchase of the huts and the Marlborough Estate and the proposed extension in the shape of a Physics laboratory. Later the same month it was suggested[9] that the Stock which was invested by the Dewsbury Endowed Schools Foundation in Dewsbury Corporation should be sold to help meet these difficulties. These were all attempts by the Governors to stave off the inevitable financial embarrassment. Even knowing the predicament that the Governors were in they went forward with tenders for the electric wiring of the school[10] and Sadler made application for the payment of the Burnham Scales for secondary masters and mistresses to be applied to the Wheelwright staff.[11] These were adopted from 1st September, 1920, and this caused the Governors to again approach the Local Education Authority for assistance towards paying the Burnham Scales.[15]

Things seemed to be falling on to the Governors thick and fast when in November, 1920, a request came from the Technical School Committee[12] that in view of the urgent need by the Technical School classes for the use of the physics laboratory there, the Wheelwright Governors' Committee be asked to go forward as quickly as possible with the provisions of a new physics laboratory at Wheelwright Grammar Schools especially as by now the plans had been approved by the Board of Education.

The same month the Governors discussed and agreed to the proposal contained in the Education Act of 1918 that a Scheme be mooted to co-ordinate all secondary education in the county borough under one directive authority, and at the same time provide a pupil teachers' centre so that all intending teachers attended full time at the secondary (grammar) school and then proceeded to university or training college.[13]

By January, 1921, it was deemed necessary to call a special meeting of the Governors of the Dewsbury Endowed Schools' Foundation to get an interim report on the state of affairs,[14] as they were by now some £10,000 or so in the red. To back-date the payment of the Burnham Scales to 1st September, 1920, meant more financial strain and this finally brought the Governors to the decision to ask the Board of Education for a Scheme for the transfer of the whole affairs of the Dewsbury Endowed Schools' Foundation to the Local Education Authority.[16] The Wheelwright Trust was also very worried about its representation on the new governing body for secondary education which was proposed under the 1918 Education Act.[18] It is not surprising, therefore, that because of all this the plans for the proposed physics laboratory had been shelved. The purchase of the Marlborough Estate had been proceeded with and Marlborough House was then made into the home for the kindergarten, thus easing the pressure in the main school building. To help to get extra money, the governors suggested raising the school fees from £9 to £10 for the over-twelves and from £6 to £8 for the under-twelves and the kindergarten from £6 12s. to £8 for full-time attenders and from £3 3s. to £6 6s. for half-time attenders.[17] These latter increases were purely nominal really, as they could do little to off-set the large financial deficiency.

Mr. Sadler had the whole school wired for a system of electric bells, so that classes far away from the Assembly Hall such as the chemistry lecture theatre and laboratory and the gymnasium would know when the bell rang for change of lessons as under the old system, which was worked by means of the clock in the hall and a series of Leclanché cells in the bottom locker near the main door, the bells could not be heard in those distant parts of the school. The old bell system seemed to be Mr. Evans' special "toy".

As will be remembered, from the very early reports given by Mr. Holme, there were complaints of pupils leaving before the completion of the secondary course, i.e. at sixteen, so in November, 1921, agreements were drawn up between parents and the Governors that children would be kept at school until the secondary course was completed at the age of sixteen plus. After this move forward, the full secondary course could be confidently embarked upon. The following year was fettered by the negotiations necessary in drawing up the Scheme by the Board of Education so that the Dewsbury Education Authority could take over the affairs of the Dewsbury Endowed Schools' Foundation and meanwhile the monetary deficit grew and grew to around £20,000 by July, 1922.[19]

By this time a Bill had been placed before Parliament to enable the affairs of the Dewsbury Endowed Schools' Foundation to be transferred to the Local Education Authority and on 20th July, 1922, the Board of Education Scheme (Dewsbury Endowed Schools' Foundation Confirmation Act 1922)[20] received the Royal Assent and thus Wheelwright Grammar Schools, Dewsbury, became municipal grammar schools under the direct control of the Local Education Authority, with one member of the Wheelwright Trust still represented on the Board of Governors.

Under the 1922 Scheme the Wheelwright Grammar Schools regulated by the various schemes already mentioned, the Daw Green Exhibition Fund also regulated by its various schemes, the Charity of Dr. Matthew Hinchliffe regulated by its Scheme and the Dewsbury and District Technical School regulated by its scheme of 29th August, 1900, were to be administered by the Dewsbury County Borough Council. Under section 5 two yearly sums of £150 each were to be used for maintaining scholarships at Wheelwright for boys and girls who had attended schools in the ancient parish of Dewsbury for not less than two years—these were the Foundation Scholarships, and Clause 13 enabled parents to claim exemption from religious instruction and/or attending prayers or religious worship.

The final meeting of the Dewsbury Endowed Schools' Foundation was held on 11th September, 1922. This was merely a formal winding up of the Foundation. We must see Sadler's early years against this background of instability in the very roots of the school. This state of affairs together with the prevailing slump conditions of the immediate post-war years postponed the erection of the very much needed girls' school and the physics laboratory, so that the physics laboratories at the Technical school were still being used by Wheelwright pupils even though they were feeling the effects of extra pupils there.

When Mr. Sadler took over from Mr. Holme in 1919 there were three school societies and the Cadet Corps. The three societies were the Debating Society which held four of five meetings per term on the average, the Chess Club which had to meet in the Master's Room (staff room) because of lack of accommodation and incidentally even this room was pressed into use for class teaching. Up to July, 1920, there was an Esperanto class run by Mr. Hemstead.

By the end of the first decade of Sadler's Reign there were six societies together with the Cadet Corps. These were the Debating Society, Scientific Society, League of Nations Union founded by Mr. Franklin, the Boxing Club founded by Mr. H. C. Hamilton, the Orchestral Society and a School Savings Club founded by Mr. Perkins.

Mention has been made earlier to Harrison Scholars at the school. They were children holding scholarships granted by the Charity of John Harrison of Leeds for the direct descendants of his sister. Some of these attended Wheelwright but in 1924 difficulties arose concerning keeping certain Harrison Scholars at the school due to the financial state of the times. At first it was decided not to continue paying the fees of the scholars but after a meeting with the Local Education Authority, it was decided to continue paying the fees till the children were 16 years of age but that there would be no payment for books, etc.

At the Board of Education inspection in 1927 the effects of Sadler's concentration on Mathematics were beginning to be noticeable. By that time 15 open scholarships or exhibitions in Mathematics had been secured by 13 pupils; six of these were at Cambridge and seven at Durham, London and Manchester Universities as well as two State Scholarships.[21] There were now 251 boys in the school and the staff had increased to 18 (13 regulars and 5 occasional).[21] In 1926 the pace was really set for mathematical successes with 4 distinctions (2 out of the 41 awarded in Pure Mathematics, one out of eleven awarded in Applied Mathematics and one of the four only awarded in Higher Mathematics). Of the 391 schools taking part in the examination only one school gained 6 distinctions in Mathematics and one five and Wheelwright was the only one with four.[22] Even so there were signs of modern trends in education which showed themselves in 1925 when arrangements were made for a party of boys and two masters to attend a vacation course at Calais organised by the University of Lille.[23] Also in 1925 due to the pressure on the available space at the Technical School the subject of the proposed physics laboratories was re-opened.[24] At this time the old lockers which had lined the walls of the hall (now Library) and the Entrance Hall were transferred to the Technical School.[24] Pressure was also being put on the L.E.A. after the report of the 1927 inspection was released, to hasten the erection of the new girls' school and so relieve the over-crowding in the main building.

THE CADET CORPS*

At this juncture it is a good point to review the growth and fluctuations of the fortunes of the Cadet Corps. Mention has already been made of the founding of the Cadet Corps in 1917. They were a product of the First World War and unlike the Officers Training Corps there was no War Office grant. Cadet Captain Evans was the first C.O. and retained the office until 1919 when Cadet Captain P. A. Lewis became the C.O. When he left in 1922, for a few months, his successor in the French Department became the C.O. He was Mr. R. H. G. Byrne. Later in 1922 Mr. H. C. Hamilton became the C.O. of the Corps and held the office until 1929 when he left to take a post in Rhodesia. His successor as C.O. was Cadet Captain R. J. W. Bodenham who held the office for only a short time, Mr. H. M. Docton becoming C.O. in 1929.

By the time Mr. Docton took charge of the Corps in 1929 it was at a time when Cadet Corps throughout the country were having a very lean time. In fact the few survivors were those in some of the grammar schools. At the financial crisis of 1931 the £10 honorarium which was the reward for running the Cadet Corps was cut and never again revived.

Soon after the coming to power of the Second Labour Government in 1929 Government recognition of School Cadet Corps was withdrawn. This meant that boys could not be taught to shoot or even drill with rifles or indeed engage in any sort of military exercise. Many schools decided to abandon the Cadet Corps but Wheelwright decided to carry on as best it could. Boys were taught First Aid by the assistance of the St. John Ambulance Brigade. Talks were also given by various local people including two Old Boys of the School, Lt-Col. E. W. Pickering, D.S.O. and Captain L. Shaw, M.C., and Sgt. W. Ormsby, V.C. also taught the boys some boxing.

When the National Government was returned to office in 1931 once

*Material supplied by Mr. H. M. Docton and Mr. C. V. Chester.

again official recognition of Cadet Corps was restored and the Wheelwright Corps was able to resume proper military training and to wear uniform again.

A fund which was started in 1917, and which was under the control of the Headmaster, paid for all we needed. Mr. Sadler never at any time raised any queries about the use of this fund by the Officer Commanding.

In 1931 also it was felt that a Regular Army Instructor was needed to assist in the training and so one afternoon a week one such officer attached to the Dewsbury Company of the 4th Batt. K.O.Y.L.I. came to school for the main weekly parade at 4.15 p.m. on Fridays. Sometimes the Corps went down to the Drill Hall. The miniature rifle range at the Drill Hall was used on Tuesday afternoons as well.

Two or three times a year there were whole day training marches in the country, Bretton Park being a popular rendezvous. Short marches were also indulged in in company with the Bradford Grammar School Cadet Corps.

Early in the 1930's a drum and bugle band was raised under the direction of the Caretaker, Mr. Wilson, who had been Drum-Major in the Northumberland Fusiliers.

The outbreak of War in September, 1939, led to a great revival of interest in the Cadet Corps and by now it was the oldest Cadet Corps in the West Riding. By 1942 its strength was 120 and this led to the appointment of a second officer, Mr. C. V. Chester, who became Cadet Lieutenant. The services of the officer from the K.O.Y.L.I. were lost on the outbreak of War and so Cadet Lieut. L. W. Temlett from the 41st West Riding Battallion Home Guard came up to school each week to help.

An annual camp was run every year but after 1942 on the reorganisation of the Army Cadet Force, these camps were run by the Army and were composed of many units. Some of these big camps were held at Ilkley, Strensall and at Addingham. In 1942 also the Wheelwright Corps was issued with proper rifles and not "Drill Purposes Only" type, battle dress and signalling equipment. By this time also, there was some activity each day of the week; Mondays signalling, Tuesdays shooting (an hour and a half on the miniature range); Wednesdays Certificate A Class for map reading and weapon training; Thursdays Band practice; Fridays Company parade besides Certificate A training. A number of boys who passed Certificate A went on to Officer Cadet Training Units and gained commissions in both the British and Indian Armies.

Cadet Captain Docton resigned his command in September, 1945, when Mr. Chester took over for the rest of the time the Cadet Corps existed. He took charge of the Corps temporarily until someone else was found to be C.O. After the War ended interest in the Cadet Corps declined and the numbers fell until they were between 25 and 30 strong. No one was enthusiastic enough to take charge in Capt. Chester's place. The local territorial unit was also finding that interest was waning and it was even suggested that the Wheelwright Corps could join the town unit. About

1951-2 the unit was disbanded after almost 34 years of military training at the School.

In Dewsbury, as elsewhere in the early years of the 1930's, unemployment was rife and as a scheme to assist these unfortunate men, the Wheelwright Governors decided to level and relay the "Top field" at an estimated cost of £8,862 12s. 4d.[25] This was regarded as too expensive by the Board of Education[26] and so it was decided to change the gradient from 1 in 233 to 1 in 82 and in this way make a saving of £1,267.[27] This work was completed in February, 1932, and the northern boundary was fenced with iron railings to coincide with the boundary of the approach road to the new girls' school.

As soon as the girls were transferred from the upper storey of the Old building in May, 1933, changes at once were manifest there. With more space at his disposal, Sadler abandoned the huts as classrooms and they were converted into changing rooms for sports.[28] Before going on to deal with things as they happened after the girls took over their new school, it would be as well to recall what H.M.I. Whitmore said at the Laying of the Foundation Stone of the new girls' school in 1931. Mr. Whitmore said, "The girls' school was a remarkable one; but the boys' school was something quite out of the ordinary, and one that Dewsbury should really be very proud of indeed. He did not think he was exaggerating when he said that for its size, it was unique in this country. There were schools, possibly with a larger honours list than that boys' school, but they had in some cases a thousand boys. Taking that school boy for boy it was second to none in the country".[29] That was praise indeed.

Now a Geographical Society and Rambler's Society had been added to those already mentioned. Of all these societies the Scientific one remained the most popular.[30]

Cruises abroad were now being organised and Easter of 1933 saw one such cruise to North Africa and the Balearic Islands.[31] Throughout the 1930's the high standard of attainment was maintained in Mathematics and also in other subjects. To take but two examples, 1932 and 1935. In the former year 18 boys entered for the Higher School Certificate and 14 passed (77·7%). At School Certificate 41 boys entered and 30 passed (73%) —the average for the whole country being 70%—and of these 15 matriculated (50%). In 1935, 18 boys entered for Higher School Certificate and 16 passed (89%). The average for the whole country was 70%. At School Certificate 35 were entered and 33 passed (94%)—the average for the whole country being 73%. Of the 33 passes 23 matriculated (70%)[32] Again in 1938 comes the same story; 10 were entered for Higher School Certificate and 10 passed (100%). At School Certificate level 43 entered and 36 passed (84%).

During 1936 an investigation was made generally by the Board of Education into the question of homework and in the Spring Term of that year the school had a surprise visit by one of the H.M.I's, who made a complete investigation into the conditions governing homework, going round every form in the school and obtaining information direct from the boys themselves. In less than two hours the H.M.I. was pleased to report that everything was as represented on the time table and that the school compared favourably with other schools and that he had no criticism to offer.[33]

The same year saw the establishment by the late Mrs. E. M. Holme (formerly headmistress of the girls' school) of the "Holme Scholarships", one for the girls' school and one for the boys'. These were to be established by the interest from the bequests of £2,000 in memory of herself and the late Mr. Holme.

In 1937 quite a few structural alterations were made in the school to enlarge classrooms, i.e. rooms old B6 and old B7 were made into one room and the old Masters' Room and B10 were combined[34] and the following year two classrooms were thrown together to form the library. The books from the various subject libraries were then gathered together making a total of nearly 3,000 in all.

1938 was the greatest year in the history of the school in Halifax Road since it was built, for during that year the first major extensions to the original school building of 1893 were erected, that is excluding the building of the gymnasium at the back of the school which served both girls' school until 1934 and the boys' school until this year.

These new buildings erected on the south side of the original school building comprised new chemistry laboratories and lecture room, physics laboratories, physical training gymnasium and handicrafts department, additional form rooms, library, art room, geography room and additional cloak rooms and lavatory accommodation.[35]

These extensions costing nearly £12,000 for the structure and £3,000 for equipment were formally opened on Wednesday, 5th October, 1938[36] by the late Prof. W. G. Fearnsides, M.A. (Cantab), F.R.S., etc., who was the first of a very long line of distinguished Old Boys. Professor Fearnsides held the Chair of Geology at the University of Sheffield from 1913 to 1945, when he retired. The honours conferred upon him make a most impressive list and include the *Fellowship of the Royal Society in 1932.[37] Besides being a geologist he was a prodigious walker and his students often wondered whether they had gone geologising or simply to be tired out when they followed him on an excursion. He also had a very remarkable memory. He is the first listed winner of a West Riding County Major Scholarship for the School and this took him to Cambridge in 1895 where he went to Sidney Sussex College to read Natural Science with a view to qualifying in Chemistry; but he came under the influence of F. H. Newell, McKenny Hughes and J. E. Marr and changed to Geology.[37]

Prior to the actual opening ceremony there were speeches in the school

---

*Fearnsides was our first F.R.S. At the present time one Old Boy holds this, the highest scientific honour.

Assembly Hall which was crowded with parents and other guests; such a concourse was there that speeches had to be relayed into the side class-rooms and other parts of the premises where the pupils were assembled.

Miss Kirk (vice-chairman of the governors) presided and she was supported by Prof. Fearnsides, the Mayor and Mayoress of Dewsbury (Ald. F. W. Tong), Crs. Mrs. Stewart Watts, J.P. (Chairman of the Dewsbury Education Committee), Cr. Harold France, the Mayor and Mayoress of Ossett (Cr. and Mrs. W. E. Bickle), the Headmaster, the Governors of the school and Members of the Education Committee together with Mr. L. Emmerson (Education Officer). Unfortunately Major Walker was unable to attend owing to indisposition.[38] Miss Kirk summarised the history of the schools from the time of the schools moving from Bond Street to those buildings in 1893.

Mr. Sadler followed and in the course of his remarks said that he could now claim to be the first headmaster of a complete Wheelwright Grammar Schools[38] (laughter). He also remarked that Prof. Fearnsides had told him that he was present at the opening ceremony of the old chemistry laboratory but that that was not a formal occasion like this one, for some members of the sixth form had got hold of some T.N.T. and had blown out all the windows.[38] Mr. Sadler also went on to say that some people thought that some of the new equipment was too luxurious and it would seem that the Board of Education thought likewise as when they were asked to approve the plans, they stated that they were far in advance of what was usually allowed for a school of that size but in view of the work done at the school they would approve them.[38]

Prof. Fearnsides in his address took the audience back to the old school in Bond Street, for it was there that he first knew the school. He referred especially to the influence that two of the masters had had on him, Mr. Owens and Mr. Knowles. He made a plea for the introduction of Biology into the school curriculum. He said he was at Cambridge when he was 17 largely because there should have been that which could have kept him longer at school.

After the speeches came the procession led by Prof. Fearnsides to the new extension which he formally opened with the key provided.

For the benefit of the old Old Boys and Girls who remember the chemistry laboratory upstairs with such figures as Misses Harrison and Blamires and Messrs. Reynold, Griffin, Nicholas and Sorrell flitting about and around the island bench and upon the dais behind the demonstration bench, a brief resume of the new laboratories will be given. They consist of an elementary and an advanced laboratory, a lecture room and a preparation room and a small room to house the stock of chemicals. The laboratories are roomy and particularly light and pleasant to work in. The elementary laboratory has seven large windows and four small ones which not only let in light, but when opened let out fumes—a very important consideration in a chemistry laboratory.

Mr. C. M. Jones in the write-up of the laboratories in "The Wheel"[38]

73

says that "modern research is showing increasingly the alliance between chemistry and electricity. Future generations of pupils will, no doubt, find more uses for the many electric plugs dotted about the laboratories than the present generation and will be grateful for the foresight of those who planned the equipment of these laboratories".

The physics department consists of a main laboratory, and an electrical laboratory for advanced work besides an optical laboratory, together with a small dark room. Dark blinds have been fitted in the main laboratory, the optical room and the previously existing lecture room so that experiments in light can be carried out much more effectively. Ample cupboard and storage accommodation has been provided.

Seven suitably tapped 250 VA transformers supply A.C. to points on all benches at voltages up to 14 volts while 230 volts A.C. is available at a number of points. Direct Current is from a 30 volt battery of nickel-cadmium cells, the circuits being completed through a plug board, which has been designed so as to give different voltages up to 12 volts at any point. In this way it has been found possible for boys on each of the four benches in the main laboratory to use 6 volts without interfering with each other.

Mr. Boyer, who wrote the above, concluded his remarks by referring to the efforts which used to be made to get a dark corner to do optical experiments when the time taken to erect and dismantle the equipment took up most of the lessons and hoped that those older scholars may feel a little superior when they quote the old adage: "To become a true craftsman, you must be able to file with a saw and saw with a file". Even the H.M.I's in 1939 described the laboratories as excellent.[39]

The gymnasium is a great improvement on the old glass roofed one hemmed in on three sides by the walls of the old building and which was like a refrigerator in winter and hardly ever got any sun except after school hours in summer. It compares favourably with most gymnasia in the country. Even so the ghost of J. A. Pickles (no relation to the author) will haunt even this new gym; one can hear him now, "Running in a circle— GO!" and as each boy passed him he would receive a smart thwack on the rump with a gym-shoe to help to warm him up!

Lastly we come to the handicraft department. This consisted of a self-contained unit of two rooms with connecting door and ample storage room. In the main work room are the benches, tool cupboards and an electric lathe (for wood and metal). The walls have power points for electric glue kettles or any other electrical tools in use. This was a great improvement on the old "dungeon" in the basement of the main building. In spite of the fact that there was some overcrowding at the time of writing (1971), it would seem that though the laboratories are now over 32 years old, they are still very good ones and can compare favourably with those of other schools. In fact they are better than most.[39] This is certainly of importance when considering the advances made during the last 20 years or so.

The following year the school had another full inspection by the Board of

Education Inspectors (1939). This time the Chief Inspector for England paid a visit. This is most unusual, but such was the record of the school that he wished to see for himself what sort of a place it was. This was indeed a great honour for the school. The report which was subsequently issued, was to the effect that "This was a very thorough and hard working school".[40] By now the school population was 283. Towards the end of 1938 a new art room had been opened but this had not been in operation long enough at the time of the Inspection for the H.M.I's to form any opinion.

1939 brings us to another milestone in the history of the school. In September of that year the second World War broke out and immediately steps had to be taken to protect staff and pupils from enemy action. A.R.P. (Air Raid Precaution) shelters were dug in the banking at the west end of the top field at the Victoria Crescent end for 300 boys.[42] Also for a short time the basement of the school was used as an A.R.P. Post—later this was transferred into a vacant cottage in Halifax Road.[41]

As though to offset the depression of the opening days of the War, Miss Kirk invested a sum of £25 at 4% interest to be used for the purpose of providing annual prizes.[43] She invested a similar amount for the benefit of the girls' school.

Throughout this war Old Boys of Wheelwright showed their mettle as they did in the First World War; the Rolls of Honour are witness to these facts.

The side of school life which suffered most in the early days of the War were the various school societies. Until efficient black-out was obtained one could not have meetings in a blazing glare of light. The regular school work did not suffer as the school was not evacuated and so the high standard of attainment was continued undiminished. The 1940 results of the Higher School Certificate once more placed the school in the seat of honour. Two Wheelwright boys were the only two candidates to get 5 distinctions in all the country and of seven distinctions awarded in Higher Mathematics three came to the School.[44]

By February, 1941, some 60 boys were receiving school meals on three days per week[45] as against the dozen or so who used to buy dinners before the outbreak of hostilities. Later, as in all schools, this mid-day meal grew and became a permanent feature of school life.

In 1941 also Dr. Down, the History master, left after thirteen years at the school. It might be said that history was established in the School by H. C. Hamilton (1922 to 1928) and Dr. Down carried on and expanded the good work, which was further consolidated under Mr. Docton when he became history master.[46]

In spite of all the difficulties of the early years of the war, in 1942 only five candidates in the Higher School Certificate examination gained distinction in Higher Mathematics from 555 schools and Wheelwright obtained two of these five.

The year before the war ended brought the biggest change in the educational system since the 1870 Act. That was the abolition of fee-paying pupils.

The only entry to the school after the passing of the 1944 Act became operative was by passing the selective examination at the age of eleven plus. This made the school purely a secondary grammar school as the junior school was abolished. Specially bright boys could sit for the "under-age" examination and those who failed first time could sit again at an "Over-age" examination. Also a few boys each year sat for an examination at the age of thirteen for transfer to the Technical School in Dewsbury.

Besides all this, there was a big change in the way the school was governed under the 1944 Act. A new Instrument of Government was set up in which all the secondary education in the county borough came under one committee of governors. This committee was responsible for governing the following schools:—besides Wheelwright Grammar Schools, Earlsheaton Modern, the Junior Technical School, Ravensthorpe Modern, Temple-field Modern School for Girls, Thornhill Modern and Victoria Modern School for Boys.[47] This was a committee of twenty members and of these there was still one representative from the Wheelwright Trustees.

Besides the abolition of fees and the abolition of the junior school, another effect of the 1944 Act was that there were fewer West Riding pupils admitted. Before 1939 there were about 7% of the pupils at Wheelwright from the West Riding County Council area but since 1945 this percentage has dwindled.[48]

From 1940-41 onwards Mr. Sadler took parties of boys potato-picking during the October break. He also took with them the School Cook, Mrs. Ellis, to do the catering. This eventually led to the establishment of a full week's holiday for the October half-term. In 1946 two masters and a group of boys were granted two weeks leave of absence so that they could help with potato harvest in October of that year.[49] These activities were part of the School's War Effort.

The staff of the boys' school found the new arrangement of Wheelwright being but one of the secondary schools governed by one committee some-what frustrating and they feared that the general equalisation of holidays, etc. and administration which this would create might upset the efficient running of the school. A deputation which was led by Messrs. Franklin, Jones and Seed met the sub-committee and put their case. Another of their grumbles was that there was no machinery for the assistant masters and mistresses to air their views. It would appear that nothing came of all this.

In October of 1946 the County Borough Council decided to hold a "Civic Week". Mr. Sadler rather annoyed the governors because he would not agree to have an "Open Day" for the benefit of parents and visitors. Here we still see something of the old Sadler, the shy man that avoided the public gaze. He realised that a good school did not require any of this "Shop-window-dressing". He knew he had a good school and that other people whose opinions he valued, i.e. the academics at the older univer-sities, also knew it, so that what the locals thought hardly mattered to him. He was also getting towards the end of his time at Wheelwright and as this time approached he became more and more introverted, sometimes to the point of being awkward. Stories are repeated that he would not ring the bell for change of lessons nor allow the secretary to do so either and morning session has dragged on to 12.40 p.m. But we must forgive him these eccentricities and remember that he gave his life for Wheelwright to the extent that he had no outside interests other than a passing enthusiasm for railways. So much was this the case that he dreaded retirement. In spite of 79 open scholarships and Exhibitions at the various universities chiefly Oxford, Cambridge, and Durham and later at the "red bricks", 136 distinctions at Higher School Certificate examinations, 19 State Scholarships and some 60 of these going on to gain first class honours degrees, of which eleven went on to take higher degrees, Ph.D's, etc., when the author visited him in the July before his retirement, all he could say was "Nobody wants me". I brought to his notice these tangible evidences of his work but he shrugged his shoulders rather pathetically.

Then came a side of Sadler few, I think, have seen. He was well-known to have a remarkable memory better for a face than a name; but in the interview just mentioned, he suddenly turned round on his heels and drew himself up to his full height (I'd seen this done so often and knew something was coming)—"Pickles", he said, "I've an apology to make". I was quite taken aback and replied "Good heavens, why?" Then he quoted the time when he gave me a rollicking shortly before I took matric because of my interest in archaeology. "Don't you realise that you have an exam. to pass?" he growled. Now he apologised for this as he said that he had no out-of-school interests beyond railways. Peering at me in the old way, eyes almost closed, he said, "I envy you and your interests now". This shows a side of the man few have seen or known. The man who had done so much to put Dewsbury on the map[50] and who had saved the ratepayers of Dewsbury so much, as Mr. Crowther put it in his appreciation in "The Wheel",[50] now envied me! He was an academic and undoubtedly one of the most outstandingly successful mathematics coaches of his day. There was a legend that in the little room which was behind the platform in the old Assembly Hall there were stacked piles of papers with written solutions to all known problems in mathematics. Certainly just before he left there was a great bonfire of papers, etc. from there.

In 1919 he inherited the title of "Keph" presumably from the importance placed on Classics as well as the sciences by his predecessor. This remained his title to the end in the lower school. To the sixth form he was known as the "Boss" or "Johnny Boss". So we must leave him, perhaps remembering him bending at the hips over some miscreant or standing and swaying arms akimbo as he gazed out of the sixth form room when he was stumped for a solution.[50]

Mr. Holme had the task of making a school out of a warehouse and Sadler the difficult task of organising a crowded school after World War I, guiding it through a second world conflagration at a time when things should have been easier, due to more space and finally seeing the school change from a charity school to become a municipal grammar school.

References

1. *The Dewsbury Reporter* .. .. 22nd March 1919
2. H.M.I. Report on Wheelwright Grammar School for Boys 1939
3. Wheelwright Governors' Committee .. .. 1st Jan. 1920
4. Minutes of the Dewsbury Education Committee (W.G.S.) .. 8th July 1918
5. Minutes of the Dewsbury Education Committee (W.G.S.) .. 13th May 1918
6. Minutes of the Wheelwright Governors' Committee .. 1st March 1920
7. Minutes of the Wheelwright Governors' (Special meeting) .. 2nd Feb. 1920
8. Minutes of the Wheelwright Governors' Committee (Ordinary meeting) 1st March 1920
9. Minutes of the Wheelwright Governors' Committee (Ordinary meeting) 8th March 1920
10. Minutes of the Wheelwright Governors' Committee (Ordinary meeting) 11th October 1920
11. Minutes of the Wheelwright Governors' Committee (Ordinary meeting) 8th November 1920
12. Minutes of the Technical School Committee .. .. 8th November 1920
13. Schemes Sub-Committee .. .. 17th November 1920
14. Schemes (Special meeting) .. .. 7th January 1921
15. Wheelwright Grammar School Salaries Committee .. 8th February 1921
16. Dewsbury Endowed Schools Foundation Committee .. 28th February 1921
17. Wheelwright Grammar Schools Salaries Sub-Committee .. 30th May 1921
18. Minutes of Governors of Wheelwright Grammar Schools 28th November 1921
19. Building and Estates Committee .. .. 19th July 1922
20. Board of Education (Dewsbury Endowed Schools Foundation (Confirmation Act)) .. .. 20th July 1922
21. Board of Education Report of H.M.I. Inspection of W.G.S. Boys' School 3rd February 1928
22. Minites of W.G.S. Governors .. .. 10th July 1926
23. Minutes of W.G.S. Governors .. .. 10th May 1925
24. W.G.S. Governors .. .. 12th October 1925
25. W.G.S. Governors .. .. 13th October 1930
26. School Management and General Purposes Committee 27th November 1930
27. School Management and General Purposes Committee 12th December 1930
28. Wheelwright Grammar School Governors .. .. 19th January 1933
29. Brochure for the Laying of the Foundation Stone of the Girls' High School, 11th July 1931
30. *The Wheel* .. .. Summer 1932
31. *The Wheel* .. .. Winter 1933
32. Wheelwright Grammar School Governors .. .. .. July 1935
33. *The Wheel* .. .. Summer Term 1936
34. Wheelwright Grammar School Governors .. .. 8th February 1937
35. *The Wheel* .. .. Christmas Term 1938
36. Wheelwright Grammar School Governors .. .. .. September 1938
37. Biographical Memoirs of Fellows of the Royal Society Vol. 15, pp. 83 to 98, Nov. 1969
38. *The Wheel* .. .. Christmas Term 1938
39. Correspondence. with S. G. Hamilton
40. *The Wheel* .. .. Summer Term 1940
41. Wheelwright Grammar School Governors (special meeting) 11th September 1939
42. Wheelwright Grammar School Governors (ordinary meeting) 12th September 1939
43. Wheelwright Grammar School Governors (ordinary meeting) 9th October 1939
44. Wheelwright Grammar School Governors (ordinary meeting) 9th September 1940
45. Wheelwright Grammar School Governors (ordinary meeting) 10th February 1942
46. *The Wheel* .. .. Summer Term 1941
47. School Management and General Purposes Committee .. 13th July 1945
48. H.M.I's Report .. .. May 1956
49. Governors of Secondary Schools Sub-Committee .. 15th January 1946
50. *The Wheel* .. .. Vol. viii, No. 2, p. 44 1955

CHAPTER V

The Boys' School in Modern Times

(*Mr. W. Bolton, Headmaster* 1950-1964)

Mr. Sadler retired in July, 1950, and his resignation was more than just a change of headmastership, it was really the end of an era in which science and particularly Mathematics had dominated the curriculum of the school for more than thirty years. When Mr. Sadler was appointed Headmaster in 1919 he continued the science and mathematical tradition which had grown up in the school under Mr. Holme; in fact it would seem that Mr. Sadler was appointed so that this tradition should be maintained. The degree of his success has been referred to elsewhere and it was such that H.M.I. Whitmore was able to praise so highly the achievements of the Boys' School when speaking at the Laying of the Foundation Stone of the new Girls' School on 11th July, 1931.[1]

With the appointment of Mr. Winfield Bolton, M.A. (Cambridge), and later J.P., a new era was to develop. Mr. Bolton came to Wheelwright from Loughborough Grammar School where he was second master and before that he had been at Chesterfield Grammar School and Hulme Grammar School in Oldham.[2]

Mr. Bolton was educated at Barrow-in-Furness Grammar School and from there he proceeded to Peterhouse College, Cambridge, where he took a second class honours degree in Modern Languages and he gained a Distinction in the Oral Examination. Now for the first time in its history Wheelwright had an Arts Headmaster which broke what would seem to be the beginning of a tradition in Science and Mathematics.

We have seen that Mr. Holme made a grammar School out of a warehouse and Mr. Sadler made the School famous as a Mathematics school throughout the country, so that now with an Arts man at the helm there was the opportunity further to consolidate the school and with that a challenge presented itself to broaden the curriculum with all the possibilities that that would open up.

One of the first projects was the formation of a genuine Arts Sixth Form which previously had been in a very tenuous form living an almost weed-like existence! More than this, Mr. Bolton can be said to have created the Arts side of the curriculum of the school altogether and this was a side of the school curriculum which had been neglected over the years. He created a more balanced school and gave the chance for the non-scientific pupils to have the same opportunities as the science ones had enjoyed for thirty years, at least. It really was a big step forward which is perhaps not fully understood except by staff and pupils who were at the school at the time. What foresight and work this entailed can only be fully appreciated when it is realised that it was accomplished during another of the great crises which have appeared at various times in the history of the school. This was one of severe over-crowding, in fact it was the greatest one which the school has ever experienced and was due to the post-war explosion in the child population, the "Post-War Bulge". So great was the over-crowding that eventually the lower forms had to be accommodated in the premises of the Batley Carr Council School which at that time were vacant.

Before Mr. Bolton's headship, Geography had always been one of the Cinderella subjects (Music was another). Geography had been confined to the lower forms only, but now it was raised to a major school subject and finally extended into the Sixth Form.[3]

By the time Mr. Bolton took over the school, the Junior School had practically vanished. The 1944 Education Act was responsible for this, for it made admission to the school depend solely on passing the "Eleven Plus" Examination. The fee-paying pupils who were already in the school at the time of the passing of this Act were able to remain but no new ones were admitted, so that the Junior School gradually worked itself out.

At the other end of the School the School Certificate Examination and the Higher School Certificate one had been replaced by the General Certificate of Education at Ordinary and Advanced levels. The age limit for the ordinary or "O" Level Examination was 16 and immediately there was a need to cater for between 16 and 20 boys who had been barred (because of age) from taking the examination in 1949. A "Lower VI" Form was created to solve this problem.[3]

At the same time new and somewhat unstable University Admission Regulations were formulated in which six subjects, two at "A" Level, plus English Language, one Foreign Language, Mathematics or a Science subject had to be taken, or alternatively five subjects as above with two at "A" Level and one "Unrelated subject" had to be passed simultaneously.[3] Added to these problems was that of "National Service". At this time boys on reaching the age of eighteen were called up to serve in one of the three branches of H.M. Forces for a minimum period of two years. "Deferment Forms" were created in School to admit boys to take or re-take the University examinations and those of the Professional Bodies whilst deferred from doing their National Service.[3] Deferment was the concession which boys at grammar schools, etc. could apply for so that their studies were not interrupted. After their university career, or professional training was completed they could then serve their time in the Forces.

One of the first aspects of school life which claimed Mr. Bolton's attention was the re-creation of the School Magazine "The Wheel" which had lapsed during the War years and was still not under publication again. The senior boys made a request for the Magazine to re-appear and Mr. Bolton readily agreed. It was published under the guidance of Mr. H. M. Docton with C. L. Grace as the editor and D. H. Oxley and D. Raine sub-editors.[3]

When Mr. Bolton took over the school in September, 1950, there were 338 boys on roll. Quite soon this number began to increase until at the peak of the "Post-War Bulge" there were 515 boys in school in 1960.[3] In spite of this enormous difficulty and with the disappearance of the Junior School, the first year timetable was made more genuinely "grammar school" with the addition of Algebra, Geometry and French.

When the numbers began to increase in 1953 a "Quick Stream" was introduced to give abler boys opportunity of reaching the G.C.E. "O" Level in four years instead of five.[3] This appears to have met with the approval of the H.M.I's.[4]

As mentioned briefly earlier, Mr. Bolton was really responsible for the creation of the Arts side in the school and in particular the Arts Sixth Form. Here in addition to the English and History which were already taken to "A" Levels, French, German, Latin and Geography were added to benefit the non-scientific boys. The introduction of German in 1953 (or should it be the re-introduction of this subject? It was already in the curriculum in the old Bond Street Warehouse) made Mr. Benton the first German master the school had had since Dr. Leumann left in 1895-6.

During the period that Wheelwright has existed as a grammar school it appears that only three masters have died "in harness". Herr Schoenemann was the first, that was when the school was in the old Bond Street premises and Mr. B. Browne ("with an 'e', boy!") was the next in 1955. He was a great loss to the school. Mr. Browne was appointed in 1920 as Latin Master and after the resignation of Mr. Morgan, he took over the duties of Stationery Master. He became First Assistant Master (as Deputy Heads were called in those days) in 1923 and retained this position until his death in 1955. He was known to the boys as "Bruno" and not without cause! He had a stentorian voice and could growl like a bear. Woe betide any boys caught in the act of forgetting to get a new exercise book before the next class assembled; he would bellow with a fury which must have been heard in Halifax Road; certainly it was heard in Birkdale Road. He could be sarcastic; but lovably so. At one time there were two boys named Smith in the same form (Smith, M. and Smith, B. A.). Turning to the latter he would bellow, "Get those letters after your name as well as in front, boy". (He did, and became Canon Treasurer of York Minister). Looking at Smith, B. A. he would quietly say, "Go on translating (pause) SMITH—" (pause) both boys expectant, then with a mighty roar, "M". When giving out marked homework he was wont to indulge in sarcastic remarks. On one occasion the author of this little work having received 6 out of 20 for his Latin effort, Browne, paternally and quietly said, "Pickles, my boy, I can see a future at Cambridge for you, even possibly a fellowship". Then with a terrific roar, "Six out of twenty, boy". Educationists have written long diatribes on the effects of sarcasm on children but I doubt very much if Browne's had any adverse effect on anyone; I think it endeared him to his boys. He was a great teacher and it was painfully distressing to see him in his later years, suffering from asthma and bearing his cross stoically—nay heroically, when refusing a lift by another member of the staff whilst resting on the wall of St. Mark's churchyard hardly able to get his breath.

The death of Mr. Browne caused a hectic summer holiday for Mr. Bolton as during that period the latter spent much time trying to get a master at any cost to take over Latin. Eventually Mr. T. Staynes was appointed to the post which he has filled with great credit and also the editorship of "The Wheel" after the retirement of Mr. Docton.

Mr. Williams ("Docker" to generations of boys) followed Mr. Browne as Deputy Head in 1955. A Welshman, he could let his emotions run away with him. Who can forget a blow dealt from his stiff right arm? This arm had been shattered in the First World War and had had a stainless steel plate fitted in it. This deformity also made him very self-conscious and probably influenced his complete outlook to life. To assist him in maintaining order with some of the more unruly forms he occasionally used a cricket-bat "stump" (a sawn-off cricket bat!). He was the junior Mathematics Master and one can see and hear him even now drilling home some point of Geometry, banging the black-board and shouting at some unfortunate boy who could not go all the way with him, "N'arkue with me, boy!" (Don't argue with me). In spite of his ebullient temperament he liked his boys and many have enjoyed cycle tours with him on the Continent and through the Alps to Italy. He was a bachelor and an excellent chef. He would entertain parties of boys to elaborate meals at his house in Track Road.

Mr. Williams was a small man and especially when he first came to Wheelwright very slightly built, so that the Upper School boys were taller than he was and he had to look up to them. During his stay at Wheelwright from 1920 to 1959 he must have swept up a considerable pile of dust, etc. from the floor as it was characteristic of him that he always wore his gown so that it fell off his shoulders and the hem trailed behind him on the floor in the manner of an archbishop's train!

He was Deputy Head for the last four years of his time at Wheelwright until he retired in 1959.

He was a likeable man. Most people liked him in spite of or even because of his irrascible temper and the fact that he could only teach Mathematics to the Mathematicians! Mr. Williams' by-name of "Docker", from Caradoc, his Christian name, often led to confusion after Mr. Docton joined the staff in 1929. There was more confusion still during the time Dr. Down was at School. He was known as "Doc". So there was "Docker", "Doc" and "Docton". The latter eventually became "Jimmy".

The other member of staff to pass away whilst still in active service was Mr. R. Williamson (the woodwork master). He was one of a considerable

82

number of Old Boys of the School who have returned to it in the capacity of a teacher after qualifying as such. Mr. Williamson was a pupil under Mr. Holme from 1904 to 1910 and then returned to Wheelwright to teach Junior School Arithmetic and Woodwork from 1944 to 1957.[3]

The effect of the "Post-War Bulge" on the numbers caused two of the old wooden army huts, which were erected after the First World War as "temporary accommodation" and which had been for years used only as games changing rooms, to be re-floored and fitted with new furniture and lighting and brought back again into use as classrooms in 1954.[3],[5] These huts had not improved their climatic conditions; they still suffered from their initial disadvantages, the greatest of these being their complete lack of insulation, so that they were arctic in winter and torrid in summer, a temperature of 93° F. being recorded on one occasion.[3] During the same year the old hard tennis courts were enlarged, re-surfaced and re-equipped.[3]

Besides having to cope with the "Bulge" there were many upheavals in the old part of the building. The Dining Hall (Basement) had its stone-flagged floor replaced and new lighting and furniture fitted in 1954. The woodwork room (Manual Room) became a multi-purpose room, class-room, "Assembly Hall" (the original school Assembly Hall was now far too small to accommodate all the boys at one and the same time), so Junior Assembly was held there with Mr. Bolton taking it once a week. Other uses for this room were as music room, besides its legitimate one for woodwork. The teachers of this subject (Mr. Evans and Mr. Barry) produced remarkably good results in spite of all the upheavals in that room.

Later in 1960 with the establishment of the "Fearnsides Trust" which was endowed by the late Prof. W. G. Fearnsides, F.R.S. to encourage and help the study of Nature out of doors, Geography also received consider-able stimulus. The Modern Languages also received comparable stimulus from the Governors who helped students to follow Sixth Form and University courses in France and Germany.[3]

At this time also, a few boys presented "A" Level Scripture, helped by Mr. Spencer sacrificing his limited "free' time. A few boys presented Art by great personal effort and the use of the Tuesday afternoon class and still a few more boys presented Biology both at "O" and "A" Levels with the co-operation (despite many difficulties) of the Headmistress and Biology Mistress of the Girls' School (Miss Smith).[12] In Mr. Bolton's early days a small group of girls from Wheelwright Girls' School joined Mr. Hamilton's Sixth Form Chemistry class and likewise Mr. Harrap helped a few girls with their Advanced Level Geography.[3]

1953 was also noted for the presentation by the Old Boys' Association of the Island Bookcase to the Library, which is now used as a School Trophy showcase.

In 1954 the old Assembly Hall was re-floored and graciously panelled in wood and given new lighting by the Central Works Department of the Corporation.[3] In the same year an Old Boy of the School (the late F. C.

White of Leeds) gave to the School a reed organ to replace the old harmonium in the Hall. Several very promising and competent musicians, encouraged by Mr. J. M. C. Spencer, have from time to time been Wheelwright organists, one of which (D. N. Nunns) later became Organ Scholar at St. Luke's College, Exeter.

In 1956 the School had its first general inspection by Her Majesty's Inspectors since 1939. One of the differences which was noted by them was the complete disappearance of the Junior School which in 1939 accounted for 12 % of the total number of boys in the School.[4] The School was now fully "grammar" in its curriculum. The report of the H.M.I's was very gratifying and stress was laid on the benefits derived from broadening the syllabus whilst at the same time maintaining the standards achieved in the old subjects.

In 1956, also, the Annual Speech Day in Dewsbury Town Hall was revived after a lapse of several years, when Lord Morris of Grasmere (then Sir Charles Morris and Vice-Chancellor of the University of Leeds) distributed the prizes and certificates and was the guest speaker.

In 1957 the "Sadler-Browne Memorial Library" was created by the Old Boys of the School and their friends in memory of Mr. Sadler, the second Headmaster of the Grammar School, and Mr. B. Browne who was second Master and later Deputy Head for 32 years. Mention has already been made previously that long service has characterised teachers at Wheelwright. In the staff photograph of 1955 there were six teachers on the front row who gave a total of 225 years of service to the School before retiring or leaving or dying in harness; this was an average of 37½ years of teaching service each.

The controversy regarding Saturday morning School came to a head in 1956. Most of the grammar schools in the surrounding district worked a five-day week except Queen Elizabeth's at Wakefield. The system of having Tuesday and Thursday afternoons free for voluntary games with Saturday morning school had held sway since 1921. Mr. Bolton decided to test the opinion of the parents in a memorandum.[6] The result was a triumph for the status quo, there being 5 to 1 in favour of the Saturday morning school (323 for and 61 against).[7]

Organised visits to works, etc. were increasing in number as were the visits abroad by the pupils at this time.

By 1958 the "Bulge" was expanding rapidly and to accommodate the extra pupils four "Airey" Hut Classrooms were built on the site of the old and now disused grass tennis courts. One of these huts was later taken over for use by the Handicrafts Department. The Chemistry Lecture Room (C7) was also re-fitted so as to be available for use for junior science. Later still it was further put to use by the Biology Department in 1965.

The "Bulge" reached its peak in 1960. The school was then really overcrowded and to add to this difficulty soon afterwards (1963 onwards) there was the major re-modelling of the School. Even with 450 boys in the school there was still not room for everybody.[8]

This major re-modelling of the School building was done at a cost of £86,000.[3] It fulfilled a long cherished ambition of Mr. Bolton's to see the school with a really adequate library and an Assembly Hall able to house the whole school with dignity. Besides these two amenities, effective changing facilities for games, a new boiler house capable of heating the entire premises were added and the kitchens were greatly improved.[3] The suggestions made by Mr. Bolton received ready and sympathetic support from the Chief Education Officer for Dewsbury (Mr. J. D. Ridge) and suggestions made by the Ministry of Education and numerous other constructional modifications were incorporated by the Borough Architect (Mr. A. G. Beckett).

This period in the history of the School Mr. Bolton describes as a period of "mountains of yellow clay, gaping walls and floors; stumbling through the rubble in the basement . . ."[3]

For the second time in the history of the School the premises during these alterations were unable to accommodate all the pupils that were on roll. So part of the School had to occupy other premises. Luckily for Wheelwright the old Batley Carr Council School premises were not in use at this time and so the lower school was accommodated there for a period, under the direction of Mr. H. Kaye. During this period the change of Headship from Mr. Bolton to Mr. Lancaster took place. In 1964 Forms 2b, 2a and 3 were down there permanently and later in 1965 Forms 2b, 2a, 3, 3a and 3b were permanently there and all the other forms from 3b to the Sixth trekked there for Divinity. Mr. Kaye was helped all the time at Batley Carr by Mr. H. Richards who also played the organ for the morning assembly.[9] The rest of the staff at Batley Carr was somewhat peripatetic. There were also traffic problems with pupils crossing the main Halifax Road en route to and from the main school to Batley Carr. Even so Mr. Bolton kept an eye on things down there by frequent, if irregular, visits.[3]

In 1963 the "Hinchliffe Scholarships" were created by the Governors at the suggestion of the Chief Education Officer at that time (Mr. J. D. Ridge) with the ready approval of the heads of both the Boys' and the Girls' Schools to commemorate the former Benefactor of the Schools (the late Dr. Matthew Hinchliffe). The Hinchliffe Awards as originally granted were to children in the elementary schools in the town so as to enable them to attend the Wheelwright Grammar Schools. These were rendered no longer necessary by the Education Act of 1944 but still the moneys in the trust had accumulated and were still doing so. This suggestion by Mr. Ridge enabled the accumulated funds to be used to reward outstanding academic achievement such as would formerly have earned for the pupil a State Scholarship.[3] This also encouraged healthy competition amongst the pupils at School.

An "Amenities Fund" of £75 per annum, a sum which may be allowed to accumulate, was also set aside from the Endowment Fund at the suggestion of the Ministry of Education to provide items of furniture and equipment such as the film projector and the piano in the Hall, that were not normally provided by the Local Education Committee.

On the social and lighter side of school life there were many developments during Mr. Bolton's time. Mention has already been made of the re-creation of the School Magazine, "The Wheel", in 1950. The following year the Annual Sports Day was revived, largely due to the initiative of the Physical Education Master (Mr. D. Evans). This development was not confined just to the Annual Sports Day. Wheelwright Boys now competed regularly in the Dewsbury Schools' Sports, the Woollen District and the County Sports competitions. Mr. Evans also developed the water polo team and started the Swimming Gala helped by Mr. Witham (Baths Superintendent), Mr. Grimes (Sports Instructor) and Miss Gray (Physical Education Organiser). The school produced several outstanding swimmers at this time.[3]

In 1954 the Prefects' Christmas Party and Dance was inaugurated which was attended by many masters and their wives; but this was brought to a halt by the building operations in the 1960's.[3]

From 1951 the Annual Cricket Match against the Old Boys and the lunch which goes with it together with the presentation of the "Colours" by the President on behalf of the Old Boys' Association has been a tradition.[3]

Another "Tradition" was Mr. Perkins. Besides being an almost permanent "fixture" on the Front Field, he served the school for 42 years and his name became almost synonymous with the Old Boys' Annual Cricket Tour. These tours took place at Whitsuntide and were organised by Mr. Perkins. A typical one was that for 1936. Some members of the team left Dewsbury on the Friday night and others on the Saturday morning en route for Northampton. After lunch the first match was played against Northampton St. Andrews. After the game was concluded, the journey to Chesham was made. The following morning after several delays, a start was made for Hounslow with the customary call at Langley (Bucks.) for the game against the Old Latymerians (Mr. Perkins' old school). On Whit-Monday the journey was made to Epping Forest where another match was played. After the match the party returned to Chesham. The last day (Tuesday) was a free and easy morning and the return journey to Dewsbury began about 2 p.m.[10]

In 1959 Mr. Williams retired from teaching and Mr. C. V. Chester was appointed Deputy Head in his place. Charles Vincent Chester came to Wheelwright in September, 1926 as junior Science Master. When Mr. Thomas Boyer left to take a post at Bromsgrove School, Mr. Chester became the Senior Physics Master and it was to him that the honour fell of first using the new Physics Laboratories in 1938.

For many years he was also responsible for running the Cadet Corps after Mr. Docton left. He ranks second to Mr. Perkins for total length of service at the School (41 years). He held the post of Deputy Head from 1959 to 1967 when he retired.

He was known to generations of Wheelwright boys as "Conk". The Keystone Cop films on the old silent screen were at the height of their fame when he came to Wheelwright and so what more natural than that the boys should dub him "Conk" after one of the more famous of those comedians, Chester Conklin.

Who does not remember being regaled by stories of Old Boys by Mr. Chester until the class knew them almost as well as he did himself? He would pause during the telling of these stories for the class to fill in the necessary details. He loved to quote some famous Old Boy,—"For example, so-and-so (brilliant Old Boy) said that the most important aspect of present day Physics is—pause—(hand cupped to one ear awaiting response from the class). All the class would then chant the answer, "Wave mechanics" or something like that. Whilst waiting for the response he would wink and lick his prominent front teeth. This was followed up by, "And he sat right there where you are sitting—(Smith, Jones or some other boy's name) only (pause), I'll say this for him that he had a capacity for hard work". At other times he would regale them with, "I was talking to the Professor of Computer Science at Manchester University, who is—?" One hand to ear and a wink! Then the class would chant, "An Old Boy of this School". Many such stories surround Mr. Chester, though his complaints about money being spent on "less important subjects" such as Divinity, etc. instead of laboratory equipment would not be heard these days when the sciences are more liberally financed.

The following year (1960) saw the retirement of Mr. J. D. Franklin. Here was a colourful character, in fact he may be said to be the second most colourful one the School has had, the other one being Mr. Joseph Kirwan of I.R.A. fame.

John Dingley Franklin came to Wheelwright in September, 1923, as Junior French and English Master. He become Senior English Master later. Mr. Franklin, or "Bill" to the staff and "Ben" and "Father" to the many generations of boys, was a somewhat contradictory character. Though he believed to a large degree in personal liberty, he maintained discipline in school with old-fashioned rigidity.

He was far and away the best known member of the Wheelwright staff by the people of Dewsbury, His views on Socialism and Communism were well-known in the Dewsbury district. He was an addicted writer of letters to the local press and the "Dewsbury Reporter" reckoned that he had written more letters to that paper than any other correspondent.

His fight for the liberty of the individual was manifested very practically. He fought a very successful fight to keep open the public footpaths within the County Borough area of Dewsbury, often going on his walks armed with wire-cutters so as to make his way through barbed wire, etc. which had been erected to stop a footpath. The green finger-posts to be seen in the Thornhill, Whitley and Briestfield areas are memorials to him and to his fight for freedom.

It has been said that his teaching of French was so good that Old Boys of the School have later in life, when in France, been asked in which part of that country they had been taught their French. This could have been a "rub-off" from Richard Byrne who was the Senior French Master when Franklin came in 1923. He was also a character but of a very different type from Franklin, being very tall and thin and teaching French with a rasping voice (which had to be imitated accurately by the boys). So good was his discipline that this could be achieved without any disorder in the slightest in class. Because of this rasping voice he was known to the boys as "Ratcher".

The Dramatic Society was re-created in 1960. Plays were staged at this time in the Parish Hall belonging to St. Mark's Church nearby by the kind permission of the Vicar and Parochial Church Council.[3] The inspirer of the revival was Mr. E. D. Smith who had much vigorous help from boys and masters (Messrs. J. R. H. Lyne, D. Evans, P. Tattersall, K. Bamford and D. Swain), from master's wives, parents and from Messrs. Ward, furnishers, in Daisy Hill, for kind and willing loan of properties. The productions began with three one-act plays to give scope to the actors of varying ages and we shall see later that far more ambitious productions were possible especially after the School got its new Hall and stage.

As can be gathered from the H.M.I's Report in 1956[4] and "The Wheel"[2] Mr. Bolton did not reside permanently in the ivory tower of administration, indeed, he must have spent, over a considerable period, the bulk of his time in the classroom teaching meticulous French at all levels. He also speaks with pride of the occasion in 1961 when the Mathematics staff at the beginning of the School Year was reduced to one member.[2] Mr. Bolton spent much of the summer holiday seeking a mathematician, approaching people, personally known or unknown, experienced or inexperienced, active or retired, male or female, for full or part-time classes. With many misgivings on his part and doubtless on Mr. Crowther's, the Head ventured to take five classes of Third and Fourth Formers in Mathematics. To the Head's surprise all survived![3]

Mr. Walter Seed retired from the position of Senior French Master in 1957 and Mr. J. S. Crompton was appointed to the post. Naturally with the Headmaster being a French specialist, modern methods of teaching the language were encouraged. Mr. Crompton was the master in charge of these innovations which took the form of audio-visual aids, a special course in these was run and a mobile language laboratory constructed. These changes were introduced towards the end of Mr. Bolton's time and it was Mr. Crompton's honour to have full charge of these after Mr. Bolton retired in 1964. It was also at this time that the first French Assistante was appointed. She was Mlle. Macé who came to Wheelwright from Marseille and was shared with the Girls' School. She was the first of seven who have served the School up to 1970. These French Assistantes were appointed annual for one year.

The Governors received Mr. Bolton's resignation with deep regret in December, 1963[11] to take effect on August 31st, 1964. Before leaving Mr.

Bolton's regime at the School it must be stressed that the chief influence
he had upon it was that of broadening the curriculum, changing what was
to all intents and purposes a purely Science (really Mathematics) School to
one in which all subjects were treated on an equal footing. He was a strong
disciplinarian, firm, but with understanding. He stood firm on the opinions
he believed in as when he was interviewed by a press representative for a
feature article on the School, and the vexed question of corporal punishment was mooted, Mr. Bolton's reply was, "I claim the right to administer
corporal punishment if I judge it necessary. I use it very sparingly, but I
won't have parents saying 'You can't cane my boy' ". He understood
boys as boys, whereas his predecessor tended to regard them more as
immature adults. Like his two predecessors he was confronted by great
difficulties—the greatest one being the "Post-War Bulge" which created
gross overcrowding just at a time when the School was also being re-
modelled. Towards the end of his time at Wheelwright work was started on
the new Assembly Hall. Both this and the new Library Mr. Bolton had
looked forward to seeing completed; but alas that was not to be for him
as he retired before everything was again ship-shape. He was the third
Headmaster to triumph over great difficulties and leave the school richer
for his having been there.

Many of his acts went unnoticed by the majority of people such as his
private generosity to the various teams and societies, in financing parties,
theatre trips and so forth. The inauguration of the Annual Lunch on the
occasion of the Old Boys' Cricket Match is just one other example of this
generosity.

Before finally taking our leave of Mr. Bolton, it is as well to realise that
he was responsible for the increase in the number of after-school activities
and societies. The Debating Society had existed from "time immemorial",
so to speak, and with it the Chess Club. The League of Nations Union (due
to Mr. Franklin) and the Scientific Society had all held their own during
Mr. Sadler's time. With the coming of Mr. Bolton we find a Music Society,
Film Society, Gymnastic Club, Camera Club, French Club, Rambling
Club, Archaeological Society, Dramatic Society in addition to the ones
which were already active before he came.

When the time came for Mr. Bolton's retirement, he stayed on at his old
home in Alexandra Crescent, so that he can, in fact, be said to be within
earshot of the School he did so much to shape. Just before his retirement
he was honoured by being made a Justice of the Peace. Mr. Bolton never
lived the severely cloistered life which characterised his predecessor: in all
ways he had a wider concept of life.

References
1. Brochure published to Celebrate the Laying of the Foundation Stone of the
   New Wheelwright Grammar School for Girls .. .. .. 11th July 1931
2. *The Wheel* .. .. Volume ix 1964
3. Correspondence with Mr. W. Bolton 1969

4. Ministry of Education H.M.I's Report on Wheelwright Grammar School for
   Boys 1956
5. Minutes of the Governors of Secondary Education .. .. 14th June 1955
6. Minutes of the Governors of Secondary Education (Governors of
   Secondary Schools) Sub-Committee .. .. .. 17th September 1957
7. Minutes of the Governors of Secondary Education (Governors of
   Secondary Schools) Sub-Committee .. .. .. 19th November 1957
8. Welfare Services Sub-Committee 1963
9. Correspondence from H. Kaye 1971
10. Scrap book belonging to C. L. Spurr
11. Minutes of Governors of Secondary Education (Governors of
    Secondary Schools) Sub-Committee .. .. .. 17th December 1963
12. Correspondence with P. Biggin 1971

CHAPTER VI

Mr. Lancaster's Headship (1964 to ——)

At the end of the Summer Term of 1964 the School said "Goodbye" to Mr. Bolton and wished him a long and very happy retirement. In September of that year Mr. Lancaster was welcomed to the School as its new and fourth Headmaster. He is the third Oxonian to hold this post since the school was re-founded as a grammar school in 1888.

Mr. William Bernard Lancaster, M.A.(Oxon.) is a native of Blackburn (Lancs.) and he attended the Queen Elizabeth Grammar School there. After four years of army service with the Infantry (1943 to 1947) he resumed his studies at Exeter College, Oxford, taking an Honours degree in English Language and Literature and subsequently the Teachers' Diploma of the same university.[1]

On leaving the university, his first appointment was at Kent College, Canterbury; in 1952 he was appointed head of the English Department at Monmouth School and in 1956 he went to Bromsgrove School. Here he met Mr. T. Boyer who was head of the Physics Department and who had previously been Senior Physics Master at Wheelwright from 1923 to 1940 when he left to go to Bromsgrove.

Amongst other activities, Mr. Lancaster has not only taken a great interest in amateur dramatics, as one would expect, producing both staff and school plays; but was also in charge of the Scout Troup at Kent College and at Monmouth.

In the field of education Mr. Lancaster had already shown himself to be a man of ideas and many of these were to be seen soon after he came to Wheelwright. When appointed Mr. Lancaster was 38 years of age and so he has the chance to stand at the helm of the School for a very long period of time, though he will not be able to equal either Mr. Holme's or Mr. Sadler's record of service. Unlike his predecessor, Mr. Lancaster is a family man with a wife and two children.[1]

It was obvious from the beginning that Mr. Lancaster intended to carry on the good work started by Mr. Bolton in broadening the curriculum. This was shown in the appointment of Mr. P. Biggin as the first Biology Master of the School in September, 1965.[2] For the first time boys could do all the Biology course without having to resort to help from the Wheelwright Girls' School and the Technical College. Biology is now taught throughout the School including the Sixth Form. There are two laboratories, a junior one and a small "A" Level one.[3]

91

Mr. Bolton was behind the transformation of the old Assembly Hall into the present Library and the building of the new Assembly Hall. He did not see the work completed before retiring and so Mr. Lancaster inherited these two incompleted amenities when he was appointed to the Headship.

In September, 1965, the reed organ was replaced by a two-manual Compton organ supplied by Messrs. J. Wood of Bradford for £1,659.[4] The suppliers gave the school £67 10s. 0d. in return for the old organ and this money was used in converting the island bookcase (War Memorial Gift from the Old Boys' Association) into a display case for the School Trophies. The same year the headmaster made suggestions for modifications to the School uniform and at the same time made the wearing of it compulsory. Caps were on the way out and Sixth Form Scarves were introduced the following year.[5]

In 1966 an additional classroom was made over the Entrance Hall and a meteorological station was equipped for a sum of £2,233.[6] This year Mr. Lancaster really began to make his influence felt. He requested the Governors that a full-time Art Master be appointed [7,8] and he introduced a scheme of Sixth Form General Studies to be taken by the boys and organised by Mr. Woodrow.[9] This is a scheme of work which runs side by side with the purely academic work in order to broaden the pupils' attitude to life in general. All boys take the common core of the Scheme, spending three periods per week over two or three years. It includes a general survey of some of the important relationships between Man and the World in which he lives. Group activities on specific topics are included such as Politics and Government, Religion and Culture, Race, Population, Space, Art, Music, just to name a few. In addition a boy has a choice of languages or Classical, European or Scientific Studies, the former lasting for one year and the latter for two terms. To make the Scheme broad, it is insisted that Mathematicians do not take Mathematics or Science; Arts Sixth must do Science or Mathematics at some stage in the two year course.[10] To date this system of options and the introduction of a Careers Department in 1965 with a full-time careers master, John Stansfield being the first official one, have been Mr. Lancaster's main impact on the School.

During Mr. Bolton's time the Prefects had their own room; Mr. Lancaster made this into a proper Prefects' Common Room where they can make their own coffee, tea, etc.

Mr. Lancaster has been responsible for far greater co-operation with the Girls' School in such activities as dances, tennis matches, hockey, conferences at Cliffe House, and from 1967 the Archaeological Society has invited pupils and staff from the Girls' School to all their meetings.

In October, 1967, the Secondary Education Committee further amended the Hinchliffe Awards to further encourage higher attainments at "A" Levels, etc. Major and Minor Awards were instituted amounting to £25 and £10 respectively to pupils passing at certain grades in the "A" Level Examinations.[11]

1967 also saw the departure of Mr. C. V. Chester, the Deputy Head of the School. He was succeeded as Deputy Head by Mr. J. S. Crompton. Mr. Crompton was appointed as French Master to the School in 1957. He it was who steered the French teaching in the School from the older type of instruction to the modern methods using language laboratories, etc. Mr. Crompton has already been at the School fourteen years and though he may not put in the extremely long service of his immediate predecessor as Deputy Head, he is, along with Mr. Spencer, Mr. Benton, Mr. Harrap, Mr. Staynes, Mr. Lyne and Mr. Crowther part of the stable nucleus of long-serving teachers for which this School has had a reputation throughout its existence. It would seem a good thing to have this stable nucleus with the rest of the staff coming and going and bringing with them fresh ideas and new life to the school. Mr. Crompton admits that there is something about Wheelwright which attracts and keeps its teachers. Mr. Crompton's other talents have made him well-known in the Dewsbury District as a Methodist Local Preacher and after the decease of Mr. J. E. Brown he occupied the organ stool at Moorlands Methodist Church until it closed.

At a meeting of the Old Boys' Committee in 1967 it was suggested that some permanent memorial to Mr. L. Sadler, the School's second Headmaster was lacking since the room housing the Sadler-Browne Library had disappeared in the re-building of the School. A connection with Mathematics seemed obvious and it was arranged to circularise as many of Sadler's ex-Sixth Formers as possible with a view to forming a fund to provide a special prize for outstanding performance in Mathematics.

Surprisingly enough, many people were located eventually, and with very few exceptions all seemed heartily in favour of the idea. Money came in in sums varying from ten shillings to fifty pounds, many accompanied by very appreciative letters about "Keph". The response was such that the interest on the fund's money at current rates would produce a very handsome sum of money each year. So, since a recipient was not likely to be forthcoming every year and there was little point in letting the capital accumulate, it was decided that such sums could be used to further mathematical interests in the school at the discretion of the trustees. The positions held by so many of Sadler's ex-pupils is some indication of the contribution which this man, the virtually unknown headmaster of a small grammar school in a small town, has made to national and international progress.[12]

Early in 1968 for the first time a laboratory technician was appointed to be shared by all the laboratories in the school.[13] This year also saw the first school exchange connected with sailing activities. An exchange was made with Taunton's School, Southampton, the latter to benefit by a course on walking and climbing at Cliffe House and Wheelwright by a course on sailing.[14]

This brings us to the greatest change in the School routine since 1920. In March, 1968, the Chief Education Officer stated to the Committee that as

Wheelwright Boys' School worked on Saturday mornings and had two afternoons free, it was not complying with the regulations of the Department of Education and Science. It was recommended that from 1st September, 1968, the School should be in session for a five-day week, Monday to Friday.[14] The suggested and later implemented change of hours was received by both staff and boys with mixed feelings. Up to now games had not been included in the time-table; they were played on the half-days. Also there was more time for the staff to do their marking and preparation. Under the new regulations school hours are from 8.55 a.m. to 4 p.m. with a dinner break from 12.25 p.m. to 1.55 p.m. Games are now included in the time-table (whereas previously they were voluntary) and so all the boys must have full games kit. School and House matches and practices are played after school hours and matches against other schools are often played on Saturdays mornings. Each soccer team is now coached by a member of staff, the coaching not being solely in the hands of the games master. Golf has been introduced and is played on the Hanging Heaton Golf Course.[19] School detention is now only held on Fridays from 4 p m. to 5 p.m. and the Prefects' detention is held on Wednesdays.[15] The new system also allows two more afternoons for society meetings.[16] These latter have increased in number considerably, there being sixteen of them by 1968, Model Railway, Automobile, Sixty, Debating, Music, Archaeological, Photographic, Dramatic, Scientific societies; Badminton, Basket-ball, Cross-Country, Stamp, Investigators, Sailing, Tennis, Fencing Clubs (the latter was short-lived).[17] Six of these societies are now run jointly with the Girls' School.[18]

Besides the change in the school hours in 1968, an impetus to the School Fund (used to spend on School activities and special amenities) was created to offset the financial cuts imposed upon educational spending at that time by asking each boy to contribute 10/- (50p) at the beginning of the Christmas term which would supplement the money already raised by the sale of crisps, etc. at the morning break. These boys also received the School Magazine.[15]

In 1968 the first full-time Music Master was appointed. He is Mr. R. H. Wood. Now this most Cinderella of subjects has taken its rightful place in the curriculum. This has resulted in greater co-operation with the Girls' School and particularly with Mrs. Waller, the Music Mistress there. So much has this been the case that by 1970 it was possible to produce Gilbert and Sullivan's comic opera "Iolanthe" in the Boys' Assembly Hall. Besides this side, there is much greater co-operation between the two schools in the academic field. Latin is now taught jointly in the Sixth Forms and Music, Religious Education and Biology are linked so that where either school does not fully suit the choice of subjects or where very small numbers taking a particular subject do not justify separate groups operating, then the two can be combined.

The Boys' Fund already referred to which is under the care of Mr. Harrap has eventually resulted, with the help and co-operation of the parents, in the purchase of a mini-bus. In the past few years there has been increasing co-operation between School and parents. Parents' evenings have been arranged, one for each School Year.

All the expansion and the modernisation which has taken place in the School life has proceeded very smoothly in spite of the uncertain future role of the School. In 1966 the Report of the Working Committee of the Dewsbury Education Committee which was set up to discuss secondary education in the County Borough of Dewsbury was published. The recommendations put forward in this report are that gradually the Selection Examination at the age of eleven plus will be abolished. Thornhill and Earlsheaton Secondary Modern Schools and the Secondary Technical School will become comprehensive schools as far as "O" Level standard. The two Wheelwright Schools have comparatively small Sixth Forms and to these would be added pupils of Sixth Form age from the Secondary Technical School and Thornhill and Earlsheaton Modern Schools. In that way Wheelwright Schools would become the town's first Sixth Form College.[20]

Since that report was produced there has been put forward the Scheme for the reorganisation of local government into a two-tier system with Dewsbury and Huddersfield as the largest entities in the new area. Just how this will affect Wheelwright it is hard to say at this stage. Suggestions have also been made that Wheelwright could become a comprehensive school.

Whatever happens in the future one hopes that the name of the Founder will always be incorporated in the title of the school.

References

1. *The Wheel* .. .. Vol. ix, No. 6 1965
2. Minutes of the Secondary Education (Governors of Secondary
   Schools) Sub-Committee .. .. 6th April 1965
3. Correspondence with P. Biggin 1971
4. Minutes of Secondary Education (Governors of Secondary
   Schools) Sub-Committee .. .. 14th September 1965
5. *The Wheel* .. .. Vol. ix, No. 7 1966
6. School Management and General Purposes Committee 25th October 1966
7. Minutes of Secondary Education (Governors of Secondary
   Schools) Sub-Committee .. .. 15th March 1966
8. Minutes of Secondary Education (Governors of Secondary
   Schools) Sub-Committee .. .. 19th July 1966
9. Information from Mr. Crompton 1971
10. General Studies Syllabus 1971
11. Minutes of Secondary Education (Governors of Secondary
    Schools) Sub-Committee .. .. 17th October 1967
12. Correspondence with R. B. Crowther, Esq. 1971
13. Minutes of Secondary Education (Governors of Secondary
    Schools) Sub-Committee .. .. 16th January 1968
14. Minutes of Secondary Education (Governors of Secondary
    Schools) Sub-Committee .. .. 19th March 1968
15. Letter to Parents from the Headmaster .. .. Summer 1968
16. *The Dewsbury Reporter* .. .. 13th April 1968
17. *The Wheel* .. .. Vol. ix, No. 9 1968
18. *The Dewsbury Reporter* .. .. 8th April 1971
19. Notes from Mr. Crompton 1971
20. The Report of the Working Party Established by the Dewsbury Education
    Committee, to Study Secondary Education .. .. .. October 1966

Mr. A. E. Holme, M.A. (Oxon.), F.C.S. The first Headmaster of the Wheelwright Grammar School for Boys (1889 to 1919)
(*Photo: Albert Lyles.*
Photo-copy by J. Lister)

The staff of the Boys' School in July, 1919
Back row: H. Graham, H. Orgill, H. T. Sorrell, M. I. Hempstead, P. A. Lewis.
Front row: Miss E. M. Gilbert, W. Morgan, W. Batley, A. E. Holme (Headmaster), J. H. Evans, Miss P. M. Budd, Mrs. Pearson
(*Photo: Courtesy Albert Lyles and loaned by Mrs. N. Senior*)

Mr. L. Sadler, M.A. (Oxon),
the second Headmaster of the Wheelwright Boys' School, 1919 to 1950.
(*Photo: Courtesy of Walter Scott, Bradford,
and photo-copied by J. Lister, Esq.*)

Mr. W. Bolton, M.A.
(Cantab), J.P.,
Headmaster of the School,
1950 to 1964
(*Photo: R. B. Crowther*)

The staff of the Boys' School in 1955.
Back row: R. B. Crowther, G. M. Harrap, E. Dickens, J. M. C. Spencer, H. Benton, C. Saxton; *Middle row:* H. Kaye, H. M. Docton, C. M. Stansfield, S. G. Hamilton, H. Richards, D. Evans, R. Williamson.
Front row: C. V. Chester, W. Seed, J. D. Franklin, W. Bolton (Headmaster), B. Browne, C. Williams, H. Perkins. The total number of years of service put in by the front row of assistants amounted to 225 years.
(*Photo: Courtesy of H. V. Richards and loaned by H. Perkins, Esq.*)

Mr. W. B. Lancaster, M.A. ▶
(Oxon), Headmaster 1964 to
present time.
(*Photo: R. B. Crowther, Esq.*)

The staff of the Boys' School, July, 1970.
Back row: R. Donald, R. T. Hubbard, D. S. Craven, J. M. Throp, R. Womack,
M. E. Heard: Middle row: R. H. Wood, J. M. S. Stansfield, G. A. O.
Dunning, P. Biggins, G. Morris, D. Butterfield, J. R. M. Lyne, Mrs. D. M.
Stephenson. *Front row:* T. Staynes, G. M. Harrap, R. B. Crowther, J. S.
Crompton, W. B. Lancaster (Headmaster), J. M. Spencer, S. G. Hamilton,
H. Benton, K. J. Woodrow.
(*Photo: Courtesy of R. Newbury, Batley*) ▼

The signature of the Founder, John Wheelwright, on his Will which really
founded the Schools.
(*Photo: Courtesy of the Borthwick Institute of Historical Research, York.
Prerogative Court, November, 1724*) ▶

he Dischardg of the Sevrall

...nt manner as my said ...
...giously and vertuously bro...
...or Graut any part of my ...
... Rented at or Lett for A...
...fore mentioned duely Ob...
of I have hereunto Sett my

Jo: Wheelwright

The Old Wheelwright School in Wellington Road, Dewsbury (on the site of the ▲
present Central Library). The Boys' department is on the left and the Girls'
on the right of the master's house which is in the centre of the photograph.
(*Photo of original drawing in the Central Library by courtesy of the Library
Committee and the photo-copy by the Borough Librarian, F. Smith*)

The Laying of the Foundation Stone of the new Wheelwright Grammar School
for Girls on 11th July, 1931, by Major P. B. Walker, V.D., J.P. (Chairman of
the Governors) watched by the Mayor of Dewsbury (Ald. Kitson Oldroyd) and
the Mayoress, Ald. W. H. Shaw, The Rt. Rev. J. B. Seaton, D.D., (Bishop of
Wakefield), Sir Percy Jackson, L. Emmerson and others.
(*Photo: Courtesy of Mrs. P. M. Gee*) ▼

▲ Wheelwright Grammar School for Boys in 1970. The main building of 1893 is the dark central portion, with the extensions of 1938 to the left and the new Assembly Hall on the right.
(*Photo: W. Pickles*)

The Wheelwright Grammar School for Girls from the south-east showing the eastern facade and the dome of the Assembly Hall to the left of centre. This was the new school opened in 1933.
▼ (*Photo: W. Pickles*)

Mrs. E. Holme ▶
(née Huckwell), Headmistress
of the Wheelwright Grammar
School for Girls (1889 to
1919)
(*Photo: Courtesy of Albert
Lyles, Dewsbury. Copy-photo
by J. Lister, Esq. and photo
loaned by Miss E. Saynor*)

The Staff of the Girls' School
in July, 1919
Back row: Misses Audsley,
Pownall, Turner, Blamires,
Mr. W. Batley, Misses
Crankshaw, Jenkins, Giles,
Oates.
Front row: Misses Head,
Brady, Abbs, Mrs. Holme,
Misses Pickersgill, Fordham,
Parnell
(*Photo: Albert Lyles:
Copy photo: J. Lister*)
(*loaned by Mrs. W. Senior*) ▼

Miss A. D. Baker, M.A. (London)
Headmistress of the Wheelwright Grammar School for Girls (1919 to 1922)
(*Photo: Courtest of Miss Levitt and photo-copied by J. Lister, Esq*)

Miss I. Thwaites, M.A. (Cantab.)
Headmistress of the Wheelwright Grammar School for Girls, 1922 to 1948
(*Photo: Courtesy of Miss Levitt and photo-copied by J. Lister, Esq.*)

Miss N. W. Truelove, M.A. (Cantab.)
Headmistress of the Wheelwright Grammar School for Girls 1948 to 1963
(*Photo: Courtesy of J. Cocks*)

Miss D. M. Levitt, B.A. (Leeds). ▲
Headmistress of the Wheelwright Grammar School for Girls,
1963 to present time.
(*Photo: J. Lister, Esq.*)

The Staff of the Wheelwright Grammar School for Girls in 1970
Back row: Mr. Butts, Miss Ingham, Mrs. Robinson, Mrs. Killey, Mrs. Ashton,
Mr. Robinson, Mrs. Harrison, Mrs. Beckwith, Miss Sykes (Sec.), Mr. Lister.
Front row: Mrs. Andrassy, Mrs. Waller, Miss Secker, Mrs. Tuxford, Miss Levitt
(Headmistress), Miss Smith, Miss Galloway, Miss Dawson, Miss Benfell.
(*Photo: J. Lister*) ▼

SECTION II
THE GIRLS' SCHOOL

CHAPTER VII

Miss Huckwell *(later Mrs. Holme)*
Headmistress (1889 to 1919)

Now we come to the section of the history dealing with the Wheelwright Grammar School for Girls. The whole of its history from 1724 to 1889 is covered in the story of the Boys' School and will not be repeated here.

When the Dewsbury Grammar School became defunct in 1889 Mrs. Holme opened the Wheelwright Grammar School for Girls in Bond Street alongside Mr. Holme's one for boys. She was then of course, Miss Huckwell, marrying Mr. Holme some ten years later. Although the Girls' School was in the same building as the Boys' School, each was conducted as a separate entity. The fact that they were also under the same roof in Halifax Road made no difference to the separate conduct of the two schools.

Miss E. Huckwell, who was educated at a private school and later at Bedford College, Liverpool, opened the school in September, 1889 in the Bond Street warehouse with Miss R. Hovey, B.A., Miss F. Oakshott, Miss L. Mitchell, Fraulein J. Beever, Mr. Walton Batley, Herr H. Schoenemann and Lt. Lingwood.[1] The three last named were shared with the Boys' School.[2]

The curriculum in the Girls' School was quite broad and it included Scripture, English, History, Literature, Geography, Physical Geography, Mathematics, Physiology, Zoology, Greek History, French, German, Drawing, Needlework, Physical Exercises and Singing.[2]

It would appear that Miss Huckwell was quite young, about twenty-eight years of age, when she became Headmistress but the girls didn't think so[3]—they never do!

Mrs. North says of Miss Huckwell, in the "Dewsbury Reporter" of 24th October, 1934, "We could not imagine her to be other than the headmistress, as in those early days she seemed very remote from her staff and the girls, all of whom regarded her with a certain amount of awe—at once the high tone which Miss Huckwell and her staff gave to the school permeated the work and play. While we were not made to feel any undue

97

pressure, the educational attainment was steady and definite. The head-mistress taught the older girls Scripture, Greek History, Arithmetic and Algebra—her Scripture lessons were memorable for their thoroughness.

"She was slight, graceful and fair-haired, the eye-glasses she wore had a somewhat austere effect. In dress she struck an individual note, as her gowns were always cut in Classical lines, smooth materials, beautiful subdued colours with touches of pretty embroidery".

"The Greek History lessons proved enchanting. The Law-givers, warriors, artists and poets of Sparta and Athens lived again in the Bond Street warehouse and lodged in our minds for evermore. At the School entertainments in the Industrial Hall we displayed 'Tableaux vivants' of scenes from Homer's Odyssey' when girls impersonated Hector, Andro-mache, Ullyses, Penelope and other Greek maidens. Gold paper on art muslin achieved wonders in designs supplied by the headmistress. She trained any English dramatic performances given by older girls. Always she inspired the girls to be the characters they played and to declaim audibly and correctly. In her third term Wheelwright Scholars arrived to be followed by the County Minor Scholars. She welcomed with enthusiasm the advent of an educational democracy and in every way helped to break down the blind prejudice of social divisions. She had no favourites. Her fair-mindedness was unquestioned. Her reports at the annual Speech Day were models of their kind and as a public speaker she excelled, never using notes; the words ably expressed her thoughts".[4]

Miss Huckwell had a tremendous influence over the School, just how much may never really be estimated, with her well-balanced mind, her sane commonsense, and utter absence of anything snobbish, mean or unlovely.[6]

"Almost immediately Miss Huckwell commenced training her charges in good citizenship and to share their lives with others less fortunate than themselves by holding the first of many bazaars in the Bond Street premises in aid of the Dewsbury and District General Infirmary.[5] At first this was a small gathering but year by year it grew until it became an important School function. Miss Huckwell was anxious that girls should learn to be good citizens and encouraged them to do as much as they could for the town and its infirmary".[5]

Miss Huckwell was always forward-looking and there are many many instances of this, she was never prepared to just make do. In 1891 in her annual report to the Governors, she grumbled that there was no playground and concluded, "I trust that next year, even before buildings are completed, the Governors will be able to provide good tennis courts for the girls".[7] The next year Mr. Joe Fox loaned a field for athletics.[8]

The annual entertainment in the Industrial Hall by both Boys' and Girls' Schools was always very popular with the Townspeople and was often performed before an audience of a thousand people.[7]

Miss Huckwell was a strong and determined character. As late as October, 1892, just six months before the new school was opened in Halifax Road, she wanted the north classroom of the Girls' School changing into a lecture theatre[9] and she also applied unsuccessfully for the swing doors near the Chemistry Laboratory to be removed and the whole bricked-up so as to make the Girls' School more segregated from the Boys'!

Miss Huckwell opened the Bond Street School with about fifty girls, and by 1892 they had grown to eighty-two. It was with these girls that she opened the new school in Halifax Road in June, 1893. Miss Abbs records that when the removal took place some of the girls asked Miss Huckwell why they still had to mount stairs to an upper storey and why the boys should be on the ground floor and enter by the imposing front door. She did not answer the question directly, but comforted them by saying, "Some day there will be a new girls' school all for ourselves".[5] Unfortunately the girls had to wait forty-one years for this to become an accomplished fact.

By the time the new buildings were opened in Halifax Road, there were twelve free scholarship girls in the school. It was also in this year that the External Examiner (Rev. H. Walsham How) angered the Boys' School in his report and commended the Girls' School by saying, "The Girls' School is as satisfactory as the Boys' School was disappointing—I was surprised to find Church Catechism had been taught to only three girls and not to a single boy".[10] This was at the time when there was the considerable opposition to Mr. Holme mentioned earlier.

In 1897 Miss Huckwell again showed that she would not bow to authority if that authority wasn't acting fairly in her opinion. Geometry was adversely reported on by the External Examiner and so Miss Huckwell wrote to the Governors saying, "Last year the same examiner's report upon that subject in the lower forms was especially favourable, I therefore do not think that his remarks this year can be correct, especially as he only set and corrected one of the sets of papers for the lower forms".[11]

During the year (1897) to celebrate Queen Victoria's Diamond Jubilee the Jubilee League Girls' Tennis Tournament was formed by eight girls' grammar schools. Wheelwright Girls' was one of the original members and the first annual tournament was played at Wheelwright. The League has continued to function with more members, and still meets annually for a days' tennis tournament.[12]

By 1899 the School had made a name for itself as a School of Classics.

The history of the Girls' School in the first decade of the twentieth century contains no outstanding events other than the religious controversy which dogged it equally as well as the Boys' School and which has been fully discussed early in this work.

Some interesting rules which governed the pupils at the Girls' School in 1901 make interesting reading especially when compared with modern times. Rules 7 and 8 of those days read:—

7. No conversation is permitted during school hours.
8. No talking whatever is allowed in the Cloak Room or on the stairs without special permission.[13]

One very important development in the Girls' School was in the modernisation of the Physical Education. This was made possible by the appointment of Miss Mildred Marsh as gym. mistress who also had charge of games, swimming, and Hygiene. Miss Marsh was a pioneer of Physical Education for girls in Dewsbury. She was trained at the Liverpool Gymnasium and College (now the I.M. Marsh College of Physical Education of which her sister was the Founder and the Principal). Miss Marsh came to Dewsbury Wheelwright Grammar School for Girls in 1908. Before this time the girls had had "Drill lessons" from the Boys' School Instructor. For these lessons the girls wore quite long navy-blue serge tunics over red jerseys and long black stockings. Miss Marsh soon began to change this uniform. Tunics had to be shortened, a change not very favourably accepted by the older girls of the school, particularly by those who played a gentle type of hockey and who invariably stopped the ball with their skirts! The younger and more adaptable older girls, however, soon conformed to her new ideas.

Although only nineteen years of age when appointed, a fact of which her colleagues were unaware until after she had left the school, her influence was indeed remarkable. She was unsparing in her efforts to put the school "on the map". Gymnastic demonstrations were given biennially in the Town Hall and the School took its place in the West Riding Schools Hockey and Tennis Tournaments with considerable success.

In hockey there were not only 1st and 2nd elevens, but eventually 3rd, 4th and 5th teams with a high standard of achievement on the field. The West Riding Schools' Hockey Shield was won twice in her time in 1912 and 1914, only one match being lost in three years and that the final match in 1913.

The Governors were so gratified by these successes that silver brooches suitably inscribed, were given by them to the players and team badges were introduced and presented by them. Form "Gym" competitions were started and to get into the "School Gym. Eight" was a great achievement. A medal was awarded to the best gymnast. Once a year the girls who had obtained 1st and 2nd places in these competitions were taken to Liverpool "Gym." and then to the College for tea with Miss Irene Marsh herself.[14]

After ten years at School, Miss Marsh married Mr. Geoffrey Hawkes from the Boys' School and as he had obtained a post at Leeds Grammar School, they made their home in Leeds. She continued to keep in touch with school, even returning to teach for a term, during the absence of the Physical Education mistress.

She never lost her affection for the School, on which she had had undoubtedly great influence; the girls and boys in the Kindergarten who were taught by her when she assisted Miss Abbs, remember her with gratitude and affection.

In 1910 Mr. S. J. Chadwick reported that the Trustees of the late Mr. Joe Fox had intimated their willingness to accept £1,500 for the field in Halifax Road adjoining the playing field of the School (what has been

100

known to generations of Wheelwright pupils as "The Top Field"). One must keep in mind that up to this time the "Front Field" was the only playing field which the Schools possessed.[15]

In 1911 Dr. Dufton, His Majesty's Inspector of Schools suggested various alterations to the main school building to meet the current needs; but he expressed a definite preference for a separate Girls' School for this purpose.[16]

It is interesting to note that in March, 1911, proposals for the new Girls' School were invited from the Governors so that details could be supplied to Mr. Hallam, the Education Officer of the West Riding County Council, in order that that Education Committee could discuss them before they were forwarded to the Board of Education.[17] Here we come across one possible reason for the long delay in the building of the new Girls' School.

Part of the responsibility for the erection of the new school would normally have fallen upon the West Riding County Council Education Committee which was the Local Education Authority for Higher Education. Shortly afterwards Dewsbury attained County Borough Status in August, 1913, and so became the L.E.A. for Higher Education. All the schemes for the change-over were planned and so it was hardly to be expected that the West Riding were really interested in a new school which would soon pass to another authority. Also almost immediately on the heels of this change over came the First World War which was the greatest set-back the scheme for the new school ever had.

In May, 1912, the Buildings Sub-Committee decided that a new Girls' School to accommodate 200 girls and not to be more than two storeys in height be erected on the "Top Field".[18] The Governors were recommended to advertise for competitive designs for the school and so it looked for the moment as if things were really moving.[18]

The next year (1913), was taken up with active preparations on the part of the Governors for the Girls' School; but certain events thwarted progress. The tenant of Hill Head Farm proved rather difficult and a court order had to served upon him to obtain possession.[19] In the meantime Mr. J. Lane Fox had drawn plans for the new school.[20] To get ideas as to the lay-out of a modern girls' grammar school members of the Buildings Committee visited Settle Girls' Secondary School in June, 1913.[21] and several new secondary schools at Pontefract, Selby and Barnsley.[22] The Governors were very impressed with the Settle School especially as it had been built at a much lower cost than had hitherto been found possible in the West Riding, and they decided that a school on the lines of the Settle one would best serve the needs of Dewsbury. These views were placed before Dr. Dufton, H.M.I., who undertook to prepare sketch plans embodying suggestions put forward by the Committee.[22]

One must remember that at the same time all the worry brought about by the decision of the West Riding Education Committee not to pay their grant to the School as they deemed it a denominational school, which led to the House of Lords Appeal, was going on simultaneously so that at this particular period the Governors of the Wheelwright Grammar Schools were in the very unenviable position that they hoped for financial assistance from the very body they were fighting or had recently fought in the House of Lords! A somewhat ironical situation to say the least.

Both the Boys' and the Girls' Schools were by the end of 1913 increasing their numbers and along with the Headmaster, Mrs. Holme applied for another assistant teacher. Quite an interesting light is shed here on the view taken of education of boys and girls at that time. In the case of the Boys' School Mr. Holme was given authority to engage a permanent assistant master on the proviso that the numbers were maintained; but Mrs. Holme was to engage a temporary assistant teacher.[23]

There were further delays in getting the scheme for the new school under way, such as correspondence with the Board of Education, etc. and also it was not until March, 1914, that the tenant of the farm was finally evicted and the way seemed clear for getting on with the building of the school.

Five months later the country was plunged into the First World War and this was the penultimate blow to the scheme for the new school. The final blow which it received was the financial embarrassment in which the Governors found themselves after this war ended, and which has previously been discussed at length. In early December, 1914, the Board of Education were still encouraging the Governors to proceed with their plans to undertake building operations. It advised that plans should be formulated and submitted at once in order that the Governors could be in a position to carry them out without any undue delay when future circumstances permitted.[24] When the First World War started in 1914 this sort of optimism was rampant, there being a general belief that the War would be over by the Christmas of that year.

As the new Girls' Grammar School would be the girls' secondary school for the County Borough of Dewsbury, a deputation was appointed to wait on the Dewsbury County Borough Council to lay before it the plans and proposals for the new school and ascertain that body's views on the matter. The scheme was duly considered by the Town Council and the Governors were encouraged to proceed with the preparation of the plans and estimates for the new school.[25]

In March, 1915, an application was made by both Mr. and Mrs. Holme to engage a teacher of Commercial subjects. The reason for this is rather obscure. Commercial subjects are not normally part of a grammar school curriculum and there were facilities at the Technical School for anyone needing these subjects.[26] It took almost a year before Mr. Ernest Harrison, a local Chartered Account, and also an Old Boy of the School and still very much alive (1971) was appointed as part-time teacher. This appeared to have amounted to no more than one hour a week in which some book-keeping was taught.[27] When this matter was discussed with Mr. Harrison, he was unable to say exactly why this subject was needed and to the best of his knowledge the classes were taken after school, which makes it all the more puzzling.

In 1916 Mr. Hawkes, the senior master in the Boys' School, left to take up an appointment at Leeds Grammar School and the following year Miss Marsh left to become Mrs. Hawkes. This was the third occasion when a member of the staff of one of the schools had married his or her opposite number in the other.

The whole question of the Halifax Road buildings (both Boys' and Girls') being used as a military hospital in 1916 and 1917 has been discussed elsewhere. Luckily for both schools, the difficulties proved too great, mainly because of the problem of the science teaching and the need for laboratories, that eventually the idea was dropped and the schools allowed to get on with their scholastic work undisturbed.

In the Autumn of 1917 Mrs. Holme applied to the Board of Education asking that it would recognise an advanced course in Modern Studies; but unfortunately the Board were not prepared to do so on the grounds that the course proposed did not appear to be an advanced course in modern studies within the meaning of the Regulations for Secondary Schools.[28] It was arranged that the whole matter be discussed with the H.M.I's, the Governors and the Local Education Committee.

The Advanced Course in Modern Studies was finally approved by the Board of Education in September, 1918.[29] Unfortunately by this time gross overcrowding of both schools was serious and more accommodation was needed.

The Governors were still toying with the idea of adapting the old farm buildings at Hill Head to the needs of the school; but the need for more room was now very urgent.

In 1918 it was finally agreed that the old farm buildings could not be converted into school uses[30] and so that way for easing the overcrowding was blocked. The idea was for the Kindergarten and Form 1 to go there and this would give considerable room in the Girls' School.

Mr. and Mrs. Holme must have talked over their impending retirement at this time and one wonders whether in view of this (which actually took place at the end of this school session), Mrs. Holme did not put her usual pressure on the need for additional space in the School.

In February of 1919 both Mrs. Holme and her husband tendered their resignations to take effect from the following 31st of August.[31] In the advertisement for the new headmistress there was no special stress on any particular qualification as was the case for the new head in the Boys' School. Mrs. Holme had given an all round education to her pupils without any specific bias so that the Governors did not feel that there was a tradition to maintain as in the Boys' School.

Like her husband, Mrs. Holme had had the task of building up two schools, first the temporary one in the Bond Street warehouse and from 1893 the new school in Halifax Road. She had one member of staff whom she had taken from Bond Street and who was with her when she retired and that was Mr. Batley, the Music Master.

Mrs. Holme ended her career in a struggle against over-crowding and staffing difficulties due to the First World War. It would seem that at the time of her retirement, it was very difficult for teachers to find accommodation in Dewsbury and the possibility of providing a hostel for them to live in was discussed.[32] This lack of accommodation had an adverse effect on teachers wishing to come to Dewsbury. In the day to day working of the school, the Chemistry Laboratory was also shared by the Boys' School, the Chemistry Mistress being responsible for the actual teaching etc. and like the Boys' School, the girls had to walk down to the Technical School for their practical Physics. Theoretical Physics could be taught at School but naturally the whole of the Physics teaching suffered because of the fact that the laboratory was some distance away.

When Mrs. Holme left there were plans for a Physics Laboratory to be equipped in the Boys' School[33] The room suggested was the Chemistry Lecture Theatre. This would have probably improved the Chemistry teaching as this would then have all been done in the laboratory. Plans were also drawn up to erect a Physics laboratory on either the west side or on the south side of the School.[34] Unfortunately due to the financial embarrassment in which the Governors found themselves after the war, these plans came to nothing.

Mrs. Holme by her manner, and by her teaching laid the foundations for a really good school. Like her husband she belonged to a more leisurely age than that which was to follow the First World War; conduct and manner of life mattered to her equally with academic attainment.

She was an excellent organiser and certainly knew where she was going, educationally speaking, and got there if at all possible. She brooked no opposition unless it was out of her power to remove it. Both she and her husband were leaders and certainly they led Wheelwright from a warehouse to be a school worthy of note.

In July, 1919, ended that thirty years of Mrs. Holme's Headship, one of which one cannot speak too highly. Besides the loss of a great headmistress it was also a time of great change—the wind of radicalism was blowing through the educational world and with Mrs. Holme went the old-world school, though she herself was never conservative where education was concerned. In her day pupils were brought up to be "ladies" as well as scholars. Somehow the First World War altered all this and things were never quite the same again. So it was to a much younger Headmistress that the task of guiding the school through the post-War period fell, Miss A. D. Baker.

References

1. The Dewsbury Endowed Schools Ledger	..	..	..	..	1888-1900	
2. *The Dewsbury Reporter*	..	..	..	..	17th Oct.	1936
3. *The Dewsbury Reporter*	..	..	..	..	15th Jan.	1938
4. *The Dewsbury Reporter*	..	..	..	..	24th Oct.	1936

5. *The Dewsbury Reporter* .. .. 18th Jan. 1941
6. Mrs. Wither's Scrap Book
7. The Headmaster's and Headmistress's Reports to the Governors 1891
8. The Headmaster's and Headmistress's Reports to the Governors 1892
9. Daw Green Charity School Documents (Bundle FF) Central Library,
   Dewsbury .. .. 17th Oct. 1892
10. The Headmaster's and Headmistress's Reports to the Governors 1893
11. The Headmaster's and Headmistress's Reports to the Governors 1897
12. Correspondence with Miss Truelove 1970
13. Wheelwright Grammar School for Girls: School Rules 1901
14. *The Dial* 1963
15. Minutes of the Dewsbury Endowed Schools Foundation .. 17th Nov. 1910
16. Minutes of the Dewsbury Endowed Schools Foundation .. 13th Feb. 1911
17. Minutes of the Dewsbury Endowed Schools Foundation .. 20th Mar. 1911
18. Minutes of the Dewsbury Endowed Schools Foundation .. 11th May 1912
19. Minutes of the Dewsbury Endowed Schools Foundation .. 14th July 1913
20. Minutes of the Dewsbury Endowed Schools Foundation .. 28th May 1913
21. Minutes of the Dewsbury Endowed Schools Foundation
    (Buildings Committee) .. .. 9th June 1913
22. Minutes of the Dewsbury Endowed Schools Foundation
    (Governors' Special Meeting) .. .. 11th Nov. 1913
23. Minutes of the Dewsbury Endowed Schools Foundation
    W.G.S. Committee .. .. 11th Nov. 1913
24. Minutes of the Dewsbury Endowed Schools Foundation
    Governors' Minutes .. .. 4th Dec. 1914
25. Minutes of the Dewsbury Endowed Schools Foundation
    Governors' Special Meeting .. .. 8th Feb. 1915
26. Minutes of the Dewsbury Endowed Schools Foundation
    W.G.S. Committee .. .. 8th Mar. 1915
27. Conversation with Mr. Ernest Harrison 1971
28. Minutes of Dewsbury Endowed Schools Foundation
    (W.G.S. Committee) .. .. 8th Oct. 1917
29. Minutes of Dewsbury Endowed Schools Foundation
    (W.G.S. Committee) .. .. 2nd Sept. 1918
30. Minutes of Dewsbury Endowed Schools Foundation
    (W.G.S. Committee) .. .. 4th Oct. 1918
31. Minutes of Dewsbury Endowed Schools Foundation
    (Governors' Special Meeting) .. .. 18th Feb. 1919
32. Minutes of Dewsbury Endowed Schools Foundation
    (W.G.S. Committee) .. .. 10th Mar. 1919
33. Minutes of Dewsbury Endowed Schools Foundation
    (W.G.S. Committee) .. .. 16th June 1919
34. Minutes of Dewsbury Endowed Schools Foundation
    (Buildings Committee) .. .. 20th Aug. 1919

CHAPTER VIII

Miss A. D. Baker Headmistress (1919 to 1922)

At the same time that Mr. Sadler was appointed Headmaster of the Boys' School, Miss Annie Dorma Baker, M.A. (London) was appointed Headmistress of the Girls' School to take up her appointment in September, 1919.

Miss Baker was thirty-three years of age when she was appointed. She was educated at Bedford College, London, taking an Honours degree in Classics in 1909 and an education degree in 1915. She also held the Teachers' Certificate of the University of Cambridge. She came to Wheelwright from the County School for Girls at Chatham where she had held the posts of Senior Mistress and Classics Mistress. She was before that at Milham Ford Secondary School, Oxford.[1]

Miss Baker was a scholarly woman, perhaps more a scholar than a teacher, as her health quite soon began to show signs of strain due to the responsibilities of her position, so that all in all she was Headmistress for a very short period (September, 1919 to June, 1922) and most of the last year (School Session 1921 to 1922) she was absent from school due to illness and Miss Thwaites, the second mistress was responsible for running the school.

It was a short headship but during it Miss Baker carried on the good work on manners and conduct which Mrs. Holme had maintained over the years. Miss Baker had a striking personality—she was dramatic and when she pointed at one girl after another during a lesson in Scripture on the Kingdom of God saying, "The Kingdom of God is within you" with special emphasis on "you" the fear of God was also put into the person pointed at.

Besides being very keen on manners, she was a stickler for etiquette. Gloves had to be worn and woe betide any girl not wearing them as she approached the School from the gate in Halifax Road. Miss Baker would send her back to the gate with the order that she must put on the gloves and return. She personally watched that this was done.

With regard to etiquette, if she was asked why things had to be done she would reply, "Certain things have to be done because it is the thing to do them and one doesn't ask why and wherefore".[2]

Soon after Miss Baker became Headmistress, the ex-Army huts were

106

erected and this accommodation was shared between the two schools, an adequate brick barrier being erected between the two portions allocated to each school so that the two sexes were kept apart! The erection of these huts, the purchase of the Marlborough Estate by the Governors and the removal of the Kindergarten to Marlborough House eased the pressure on the accommodation in the main school. Part of Marlborough House (a sitting room and bedroom) was allocated for the use of Miss Baker.[3]

The House system had been introduced into the School by Mrs. Holme, the names of the Houses being Darling, Sommerville, Beale and Nightingale. For a time these houses were abolished and then the system was re-started under the names Angles, Saxons, Celts and Danes.[2]

Miss Baker was also responsible for introducing a system of school discipline which was at least fifty years ahead of its time. This was government by a School Council. Each Form had a representative or representatives on it along with representatives from the staff. Matters of School government were decided by this Council.[4] This idea has been the "pet" of modern educationists during the past few years, but it would appear that for good or ill, Wheelwright Grammar School for Girls under Miss Baker pioneered such a system of school government some fifty years earlier.

The financial embarrassment which was besetting the Governors began to be more apparent by July, 1920[5] which was the end of Miss Baker's first year as Headmistress. Being of a highly-strung nature, this worry in the background would certainly not help her at all.

Throughout 1921 and until the last meeting of the Dewsbury Endowed Schools Foundation in September, 1922, both schools were held to ransom whilst the decision was made to municipalise the schools and so make them a viable proposition again and remove the financial worry from the shoulders of the Governors. Like Mr. Sadler, Miss Baker had to face the increasing numbers of pupils in the school and with the financial collapse of the Governors it was obvious that unless something was done and the Local Education Authority took over the responsibility of the School there was no hope at all for a new girls' school and the cramped and over-crowded state of the school would have to be endured. This was not a good outlook for such a person as Miss Baker. Even though the Local Education Authority did take over the schools it was another twelve years before the girls were safely installed in their new school.

In June, 1921, Miss Baker applied for a French Assistant mistress to be attached to the school for one year under the Convention between the Board of Education and the French Ministry of Education.[6] This was a new departure from previous practice and illustrates Miss Baker's up-to-date methods.

All too soon after this Miss Baker's health deteriorated badly and she had long periods away from school. In January, 1922, she tendered her resignation due to the state of her health, to be effective from the end of July that year.[7]

It was hoped that Miss Baker would be able to be back at school for the summer term of 1922; but such was the state of her health that although Miss Thwaites had been appointed Headmistress as and from September, 1922, this was brought forward so that her appointment was dated from 1st June, 1922.[8]

Even though Miss Baker's tenure of office was so short, she left a mark on the school and laid the foundation on which Miss Thwaites built when she became Headmistress. The development of recreation groups was a special feature of Miss Baker's time.

It would seem that the post of Headmistress took too much energy from Miss Baker who was essentially a scholar and also a good teacher and so she found the strain of running the school too much her her. This is not surprising when she had an overcrowded school and no prospect of any change in these conditions and at the back of everything not knowing what the future held during this financial crisis of the Governors. It was only after her resignation that the school was taken over by the Dewsbury County Borough Education Committee and so the situation was saved. Major Walker's generosity regarding payment of salaries has already been mentioned in the section dealing with the Boys' School.

To some degree Miss Baker's reign at Wheelwright carried on the old traditions and introduced modern ideas far ahead of her time.

References

1. *The Dewsbury Reporter*	10th May	1919
2. Conversation with Mrs. A. Glover		1971
3. Dewsbury Endowed Schools Foundation (W.G.S. Committee)	8th Mar.	1920
4. Conversation with Miss M. Turner		1971
5. Dewsbury Endowed Schools Foundation (W.G.S. Committee)	12th July	1920
6. Dewsbury Endowed Schools Foundation (House Sub-Committee)	7th Jan.	1921
7. Dewsbury Endowed Schools Foundation (Special Meeting of Governors)	23rd Jan.	1922
8. Dewsbury Endowed Schools Foundation (W.G.S. Committee)	19th June	1922

CHAPTER IX

Miss I. Thwaites Headmistress (1922 to 1948)

Miss Isabella Thwaites was appointed Headmistress of the Wheelwright Grammar School for Girls in May, 1922, on the resignation of Miss Baker. She was originally appointed Mathematics Mistress in May, 1919, and she became second mistress in January, 1920, but little realised then how soon she would be called upon to carry the burden of a changing school in that capacity before being finally appointed Headmistress in 1922. Her promotion was certainly very rapid at this school.

Miss Isabella Thwaites, M.A. (Cantab.), was 32 years of age when she was appointed Headmistress. She was educated first at Halifax Secondary School for two years and then received private tuition under Dr. Clement Jones who was for many years the Senior Mathematics Master at Bradford Grammar School. She won an Open Scholarship at Girton College, Cambridge, awarded by the Goldsmith's Company, and entered the college in 1909, took a First in Mathematics in Part I of the Mathematics Tripos and a Second Class in Part II.

In 1912 she was appointed Mathematics Mistress at the Godolphin and Latymer School, Hammersmith, and she became Senior Mathematics Mistress in 1914 at Surbiton High School, Kingston-upon-Thames from which post she came to Wheelwright in May, 1919.[1]

During her period as assistant mistress, she helped greatly in organising the school on the modern lines adopted by Miss Baker and assisted in guiding the girls in adopting the principle of self-government already referred to, under Miss Baker. Miss Thwaites was very popular with both staff and girls in spite of her somewhat forbidding exterior.

She was a strict disciplinarian and due to her rather restricted education largely by private tuition, she did not always see a girl's point of view. She also had a sly sense of humour. She was known to the girls as "IT" (her initials). On one occasion some girls had been in trouble and she addressed the morning assembly on this point telling the girls, "Apparently some of girls think you are 'IT', but you are not".

By September, 1922, the Schools were taken over by the Dewsbury County Borough Education Authority and from that time onwards they have been run as a municipal grammar school, retaining as one member of the governing body a representative of the Wheelwright Trustees. Miss

Thwaites more or less started her headship simultaneously with this change in status of the school. Her big worry was the overcrowding which she had inherited from her predecessor and the set-back of the possibility of a new school as things would now have to begin again from the bottom. One thing which did help was that a few of the old governors were nominated on the new Board of Governors under the Local Education Authority, such as Major Walker, Miss H. B. Walker, Miss Kirk and Canon Wolde (Vicar of Dewsbury).

In 1923 Miss Thwaites applied again for a French Assistant mistress to be attached to the school for a period of one year,[2] the Governors being partly responsible for her maintenance allowance.

The "Top Field" was purchased by the L.E.A. in 1924[3]—it had been rented for some years previously, so that practice matches both by the boys and the girls (hockey) could be played and so ease the wear and tear on the "Front Field".

During 1924 the Harrison's Charity Trustees were finding themselves under some financial stress and it was finally decided that the Trustees would continue to pay the fees of the Harrison Scholars attending the School up to the age of sixteen, but would no longer pay for the books which were used.[4]

Miss Thwaites hit upon a novel idea with regard to the position of second mistress in the school. When Miss Head left in 1925, she decided to appoint both Miss Crankshaw and Miss McLeod to the post of second mistress, each to occupy the position for alternate years. The advantages of this system are not apparent, but it seems to have worked as it was maintained throughout Miss Thwaites' time.[5]

Miss Thwaites vacated her two rooms at Marlborough House in 1927 and this gave a little more room for the Kindergarten. One of the rooms was used as a staff room and the other as a classroom.[6]

Miss Thwaites carried on the Advanced Course in Modern Studies which had been initiated by Mrs. Holme and continued under Miss Baker. This Advanced Course consisted of English, History and French as principle subjects with Latin and Mathematics as subsidiaries. A rather odd arrangement was made by which girls wishing to do Mathematics and Science above Matriculation standard went down into the Boys' School and joined the Advanced Course in these subjects there. This appears rather strange as both Miss Thwaites and Mr. Sadler were Mathematicians. After 1928, she did take the Advanced Mathematics herself.

When the School was inspected by His Majesty's Inspectors in December, 1927, they at once stressed the need for a new school. At their previous inspection in 1920 they had made this point then and now the need was imperative. It would seem from the 1927 Inspection that they were somewhat annoyed that nothing had been done in the interim period.[7] There was also the problem facing all Local Education Authorities that by the 1930's the increased child population, a First World War "Bulge" would reach the secondary schools and this would put Dewsbury in a very bad position if nothing further were done.

The work of the Girls' School (always including the Kindergarten in this context) was carried on in four buildings, the main building, part of the ex-Army huts, Marlborough House and the Technical School and these separate divisions all added to the difficulties of organisation. It was obvious that the building was only capable of housing one school. There was no library, Art Room, Botany or Physics Laboratory, Rest Room, medical inspection room and no provision at all for the teaching of Domestic Science. The conditions in the huts have been fully described earlier under the Boys' School and the Assembly Hall at times had to accommodate two classes. This was also the only place where the Sixth Form private study could be done. All movement from one classroom to another took place through the Hall, which made it quite unsuitable for use as a classroom. To add to all these difficulties, music lessons took place here! These lessons naturally disturbed all work in the adjacent class-rooms.[7] Criticisms of the gymnasium and the basement by the H.M.I's were also adverse.

In spite of the lack of a Botanical laboratory, Miss Thwaites introduced Botany into the school in 1926. Her big worry was Housecraft and Domestic Science. Apart from Needlework, there was no Housecraft done in the school entirely due to lack of space. At one time the stables at Marlborough House were suggested as a possible site for conversion into rooms for Domestic Science. Due to lack of money (etc.) nothing was done and by 1927 the premises had deteriorated to such a degree that they were unsuitable for much use at all. Miss Thwaites was fully aware of these short-comings on the practical side of education as she realised that many, or most girls, are interested in the practical subjects rather than the pure academic ones.

All these aspects were criticised by the H.M.I's with one end in view, one suspects, that of jogging the L.E.A. into immediate action, namely the building of a new school for the girls. In spite of all the adverse criticism of the building, etc. the H.M.I's were satisfied with the standard of work being done at the school, the discipline, etc. and the manners and conduct of the pupils.[7]

It is significant that by October, 1928, the Borough Surveyor was instructed to prepare plans and lay-out for a new school for the girls. It would seem, therefore, that the H.M.I's report had stirred the authority into action.

During this period four girls out of eleven passed the Higher School Certificate Examination and 22 passed the School Certificate Examination (78%) with eight matriculating. This would indicate the amount of hard work which was done in spite of the cramped conditions.

By November, 1928, it was obvious that the Board of Education were on the tail of the L.E.A. subsequent to the Report by the H.M.I's in 1927. By this time the Board were enquiring as to what moves had been made towards the provision of a new girls' school.[8] From this date onwards, definite moves were made to erect the new Girls' School. A site was bought immediately north of Victoria Crescent, between it and Healds Road. This was only accessible by footpaths and so a new approach road had to be made from Halifax Road at the top of Hill Head and skirting the Boys' Playing Fields on the north side. Several sketch plans were drawn and various alterations made by all the parties concerned until in 1929 a final estimate was reached for a school to cost £48,900 which included £2,250 for the approach road and which was exclusive of the furnishings.[9]

In October, 1929, Major Walker and Ald. Shaw went to the Board of Education to discuss the plans for the new school. Naturally the Board made some alterations, which was not surprising.[10] The Board were finally satisfied with the plans as such but made a stipulation that the number of pupils under ten years of age should not be increased beyond the present figure. In other words, the new school was to be ultimately a secondary grammar school purely and simply. The Board of Education also requested that the present uniform fee for all pupils should be continued when the new school was completed.[11]

There were changes in the syllabus of the Northern Universities Joint Board in Domestic Science in 1930 and as there would be no provision for this subject until the new school was built, arrangements were made for this subject to be taken at the Victoria Central School for Girls.[12]

By September, 1930, the final plans for the new school were approved by the Board of Education with the proviso that the cost should not be more than £51,000.[12]

All then was set for the building of the new school. Progress with the foundations, etc. had proceeded sufficiently far so that by 11th July, 1931, it was possible for the Foundation Stone to be laid.

LAYING OF THE FOUNDATION STONE OF THE NEW WHEELWRIGHT GRAMMAR SCHOOL FOR GIRLS, 11th JULY, 1931

"This was a great day for the school. The proceedings commenced with a luncheon in the Town Hall to which distinguished men and women in the service of education were invited by the Mayor, Ald. P. B. Walker, V.D., J.P., and his sister Miss H. B. Walker, J.P. This was also an occasion to celebrate the long connection which Major Walker had had with the Wheelwright Schools.

"Major Walker presided over the function and was accompanied by both his sisters, Miss H. B. Walker and Dr. Jane Walker, C.H., M.B., LL.D., one of the first women in the country to qualify as a medical practitioner. Sir Percy Jackson, J.P., LL.D., representing the West Riding County Council Education Committee, local Members of Parliament, councillors from Batley as well as Dewsbury, the heads of the two Wheelwright Schools and the architect of the new school (Mr. T. Blakeley, A.R.I.B.A.), local clergy and the H.M.I. for the area (Mr. C. J. R. Whitmore, M.C., M.A.) were among the guests.

"Sir Percy Jackson made reference to the history of the school since 1888 and the deep debt of gratitude owed to the late Mr. S. J. Chadwick for his work in securing the Wheelwright money to build the school in Halifax Road.

"Miss Thwaites responded and referred to the congestion in the school. This was also aggravated to a considerable extent by the steady expansion of the Sixth Form and of more varied facilities for more advanced studies. 'It was not a case of where the shoe pinched—it pinched everywhere, in the classrooms, in the laboratory, in the gym. and in the playing fields'.[13] She went on to outline the history of higher education from the opening of Bedford College for Women in 1849 in Bedford Square, London, and of the general pioneering by London University for higher education for women. Others who spoke were Dr. Jane Walker, Mr. Whitmore, H.M.I. who paid the glowing tribute to the Boys' School, already referred to under that heading. He also suggested that a sum of £5,000 to £10,00 be spent on the Boys' School to make it adequate, once it was vacated by the girls.[13]

"After the luncheon was over, the entire company proceeded to the Wheelwright Schools in Birkdale Road by cars and a special bus. In the field in front of the School the girls and also the pupils of the Preparatory Department were assembled and they presented a very pleasing appearance, their school attire contrasting in a picturesque manner with the green of the playing field on such a bright sunny day. The mistresses and other members of staff and other graduate guests were robed in their academic gowns which gave a further touch of colour to the assembly. When all the guests had arrived, a procession was marshalled by the Chief Constable (Mr. F. E. Pritchard) and Chief Inspector Wilkinson, and this proceeded by way of Birkdale Road and over the top of the hill to the site of the new school, which was gaily decorated. Here a large crowd had assembled in specially reserved seats, while others crowded round the roped enclosure. Prior to the arrival of the procession, selections of music were provided by means of an amplifying apparatus operated by Messrs. Ward & Co. (Dewsbury) Ltd.

"The procession was headed by Thornhill Brass Band and was followed by the pupils of the Preparatory Department and those of the Girls' School, Major Walker and the Lord Bishop of Wakefield (Dr. J. B. Seaton who had taught at the Bond Street warehouse for a very short period during one Oxford Vacation), the Mayor and Mayoress of Dewsbury, Dr. Jane Walker and Sir Percy Jackson, guests and Governors of the School, Aldermen, Councillors and members of the Education Committee and officials of the Dewsbury Corporation followed.

"Ald. W. H. Shaw, J.P. presided over the proceedings which commenced with the singing of the hymn 'We build our School, on Thee, O Lord' by the pupils of the school, who were provided with special accommodation. The singing was conducted by Mr. Maurice E. Cooke (Music Master). An appropriate passage of Scripture was read by Rev. W. H. Pace, B.D. after which prayers were offered by the Bishop of Wakefield.

"Ald. Shaw then placed a number of documents containing information respecting the school in a special receptacle in the Foundation Stone prior to calling upon Major Walker to lay the Stone.

"The Borough Architect and Surveyor (Mr. T. Blakeley) then handed to Major Walker a silver trowel and the contractors presented a mallet, for the purpose of laying the Stone.

"After declaring the Stone 'well and truly laid' Major Walker then received at the hands of Miss Millie Turner (Head Girl of the School) a handsome silver rose bowl, the gift of Miss Thwaites, the staff and the pupils of the school, Miss Turner's voice, as she formally handed over the gift being reproduced by means of the microphone with considerable clearness.*

"Major Walker in his speech first of all outlined the events leading up to that day's ceremony from 1918 when under a scheme prepared by the L.E.A. the Wheelwright Governors proposed the erection of a new secondary school for girls to accommodate 500 girls but the proposal wasn't proceeded with. Then Major Walker outlined how the urgency of the position was realised after the report by the H.M.I's in 1927 and that the matter could no longer be delayed.[13] He then went on to give a brief statement about conditions in the school and the need for a good education.

"The Mayor of Dewsbury (Ald. Kitson Oldroyd) proposed the vote of thanks to Major Walker and paid tribute to the work for education which the Walker family had done. Major Walker had been chairman of the Governors for twenty three years and mentioned that besides that the whole family had been connected with most things in Dewsbury. Further speeches were made by Ald. Shaw and Rev. D. Tait Patterson and Mr. Ben Riley, the M.P. for Dewsbury.

"The hymn 'O, God our Help in Ages past' was then sung and this was followed by the Blessing by the Bishop of Wakefield and so the ceremony ended with the singing of the National Anthem.

"Afternoon tea was provided in the Girls' School and this concluded the proceedings."[13]

The architect (Mr. Blakeley) certainly used the site to the best of his ability. The concept was more or less based on a triangular plan. The style of architecture is a pseudo-Regency with Doric pillars flanking the main entrance. This was a style which was very much in vogue for schools at this time. It was the last word in design for the period. The main facade faces east, due to the slope of the land in that direction. This facade is the base of the triangle with the Assembly Hall bridging the centre gap between it and the apex of the triangle opposite. It is a two-storey building with space beneath the Assembly Hall for storage. On the ground floor flanking the entrance are the Headmistress's study and the Secretary's office. Corridors then go round the building on the inner side, the classrooms being on the outer sides of the building. The Staff Room is on the corridor immediately north of the Secretary's office and then the Domestic

*Amplification was in its infancy at this time, hence the interest.

Science room with the very well-equipped gymnasium on the north corner. To the South the medical and rest rooms, the cloak-rooms and changing rooms, showers, etc. are placed. On the first floor the library occupies the central position on the eastern face above the central entrance and the Headmistress's Study and the Secretary's office. Then on the north of this are the Chemistry and Physics laboratories, and the Art and Geography rooms, Biology laboratory along with the Needlework room. The dining hall is between the Assembly Hall and the classrooms. Besides being of a pleasing style with plenty of space, the building is enhanced by being freely ornamented with carved woodwork which is of very high quality particularly in the Assembly Hall and Library. This was the work of Mr. Kershaw and a local firm. The greatest draw-back to the whole scheme was, and is, the limited amount of playing field space. There is only one hockey pitch and until a lease was granted to use the sports field of Messrs. Joshua Ellis & Co. Ltd., the girls had to use part of one of the Boys' School pitches. As numbers increased there, this became no longer available for the use of the girls.[14] Some hard court tennis courts were laid; but they proved unplayable possibly due to the fact that the foundations had not had time to bed down.[14] Happily the late Mr. Henry Cullingworth gave some tennis courts and a Norwegian Pavilion to the school, in 1937, [14, 15, 21] and these provided a solution to the difficulty for the time being. These courts are known as "The Cullingworth Courts" and are situated some little distance from the school in Oxford Road. The site of the new Girls' School is atop one of the highest points in Dewsbury, being in a really bracing position.

In spite of the cramped conditions in the old school, the 1931,1932 and 1933 examination results showed an average of 82% passes at Higher School Certificate Examinations and an average of 68% passes at the School Certificate Examinations. Also there was a particularly high number of pupils obtaining places at the universities. In October, 1932, two girls went to Cambridge, one to Oxford, three to London and two to Manchester.[16]

About the same time there was a change in the School uniform, the actual choice being made by the girls themselves. Instead of the School colours of navy blue and red (with navy blue gym. slips), the colours were changed to maroon and white (with maroon gym. slips). In this the School colours now were nearer to those of the Wheelwright Family (old Claret and white). Instead of black woollen stockings, light coloured lisle ones were allowed, at first during the summer months, and then later during the whole year.[16]

On 28th May, 1933, the girls were transferred from the old building to the new school. In "The Dial" for 1933—(the School Magazine gets its title from the sun dial which stands in the cloister between one side of the school and the Assembly Hall) an eye-witness account of the move is given.

"For many weeks energetic work was done at the old school. Books were packed in parcels, pictures were taken down and packed, furniture was labelled. On the last day there, excited girls dashed about packing books and slamming desk lids, for at long last we were to occupy the wonderful new school that seemed mythical to us. On the morning 29th May, 1933, we collected our books, bade farewell (a fond one) to the school which had seemed so wonderful to the girls of forty years ago and set off on a pilgrimage to the new school. We managed to get there safely without dropping our books in Halifax Road and waited tense with excitement and expectation until the Kindergarten arrived. Then we went in, thrilled to know that at last we were crossing the threshold of our wonderful new school. Once inside, we eagerly took possession of the various form rooms with their different coloured walls and shining desks. It was hard to believe that we were really inside at last, really inside our new school in which it was possible to get lost! The space and light were exhilarating and the excitement grew and grew. We held our first Assembly in the hall 'built like a theatre' where we could sit on chairs, not crowded on the floor as in the old school.

"Although time has worn away the ecstacy of that first day, yet it has turned our excitement to sincere appreciation. Now, after being there a few months, we are beginning to understand more clearly how very lucky we are to have this wonderful school. Now, the oak-panelled hall and library, the Chemistry, Physics and Biology laboratories, the epidiascope in the Geography Room, the Needlework and Domestic Science Room, the new Gym., the shower baths, the net-ball court, the large, light Art Room and the form rooms are in full use. We thoroughly enjoy every minute of school life for this school makes work almost as attractive as play and we are really grateful for this second new school".

L. Addison[17]

"THE FIRST MORNING IN THE NEW SCHOOL

At the first morning Assembly in our new school, Miss Thwaites was accompanied by Major P. B. Walker, Chairman of the Governors, Miss Kirk, Vice-Chairman of the Governors, Miss H. B. Walker, Mr. L. Emmerson, Education Officer and Mr. T. Blakeley, the architect. The service began with the singing of the hymn, 'Fight the good fight' followed by a lesson and prayers. The choir sang the anthem, 'Except the Lord build the House' and the service closed with the singing of the hymn 'City of God'.

"In welcoming Major Walker, Miss Thwaites said the girls were delighted that Major Walker had come to join them in their first morning assembly in the new building. She gave a hearty welcome to Miss Kirk and Miss Walker who had taken such a lively interest in the work of the Girls' School and thanked the Governors for providing such a magnificent building to meet a need which had been felt for many years. She paid a warm tribute to the work of Mr. Blakeley and remarked that everywhere there was evidence of most careful attention to detail and the school was proud to enter such a nobly-planned building.

"Major Walker, who was received with great applause, said he felt overwhelmed by this occasion which was the realisation of an object for which he had striven for many years—adequate accommodation for the girls of Wheelwright Grammar School. This was a great day for the Governors, for Miss Thwaites and her staff and for the girls of the school. It was also a great day for the architect, Mr. Blakeley. At this point Major Walker whimsically contrasted the transience of his own labours as a blanket manufacturer with the permanency that crowned the thoughts and labours of the architect!

"Major Walker said he was sorry that the Governors had not been able to secure an outstanding person to open the School that day; but Lord Irwin, the President of the Board of Education and late Viceroy of India had promised to perform the official opening ceremony early the next year.*

On behalf of the Governors, Major Walker expressed the hope that the work of the School would progress in future as it had done in the past. He said that Miss Thwaites had reason to feel proud that she was the Headmistress of the School and on this special occasion he could not help thinking of Mrs. Holme, a former headmistress, who for a long time stressed the need for this new building.

In reply Miss Thwaites said that this day she felt very humble and yet very proud and she would endeavour to see that the School made a worthy response to its enlarged opportunity.

C. M. Ramsden"[17]

Parents were invited to view the new school and the Mayor and Corporation of Dewsbury visited the school on 18th July, 1933—this was the first time a Mayor of Dewsbury had visited the school since 1913. Head teachers of other Dewsbury schools were invited to view the school on Friday, 23rd July, 1933.[17]

With the advent of a new school Domestic Science was added to the curriculum and Miss M. Turner was appointed the first teacher of this subject in June of 1933.[18]

In December, 1933, a portrait in oils of Major Walker was presented to the Girls' School and now hangs in the Assembly Hall. This is in token of all the work which he did for the school.

When the girls moved to the new school they continued with the same working hours which had been the custom in the old school. Unlike the Boys' School the girls never attended on Saturday mornings; they worked a five-day week with no half-days. Any hockey matches with other schools were played on Saturday mornings.

The high standard of academic attainment was maintained in the new

*Lord Irwin was unable to perform this ceremony owing to illness on the day (17th July, 1934) and it fell to Major Walker to perform the ceremony.

school, in fact a very high percentage of passes at the Higher School Certificate Examinations were obtained in 1936 and 1938 when 90% passed, and 72% passed the School Certificate Examination in 1937.[21]

In 1937 also the "Holme Scholarships" mentioned earlier in this work were founded by two bequests of £1,000 each by Mrs. Holme for the foundation of two scholarhips of at least £30 per annum for three years at a university or other institute of higher education. The awards were to be open to boys and girls who have been for not less than two years scholars at Wheelwright Grammar Schools. The awards were to be made on the recommendation of the Headmaster and the Headmistress of the Wheelwright Schools.[19] The first one to be awarded was during this year to Joan R. Kemp.[20]

The new school was inspected for the first time by H.M.I.s in May, 1938. They were very pleased with the new buildings and congratulated the Governors on the school being "so excellently planned, well-fitted and carefully kept".[23] The library was praised by the H.M.I.s both for its size and equipment and mention is made that the senior English Mistress acts as librarian.[23] The good results of this English—library co-ordination is mentioned again later as Miss Truelove instilled a love of books in her pupils through this method. The H.M.I.s were worried about the shortage of out-door games facilities but otherwise only praise was given to the new school.[23]

In June, 1938, Miss Truelove was appointed Senior English Mistress. She was later destined to succeed Miss Thwaites as Headmistress.[22] November of that year saw the resignation of Major Walker from the Board of Governors. He had served twenty-five years as Chairman of the Governors of the School. It was a great loss to the two Wheelwright Schools.

This brings us up to the outbreak of the Second World War in September, 1939. When the school opened after the summer holidays there were more girls in it than ever before (499). This number included the evacuees from Isleworth Green, Nonsuch County School, Sutton High School, Richmond and East Cheam County Schools.[24] We get a good idea of what life was like at school from a contribution to the school Magazine, "The Dial" in 1943.

"The effects of the war upon Wheelwright Grammar School for Girls have not been so noticeable as upon schools in some other towns, since Dewsbury is a neutral area. The School opened within a week of the usual date in September, 1939, with about 100 pupils from the top forms, those forms taking external examinations in 1940.

"Work for these first hundred pupils went forward as usual except for air-raid practices. The School had then no built-in trenches, so that these hundred pupils took refuge in a deep ditch at the bottom of the hockey field, protected on one side by a wall and overhanging trees. By October the first trench unit to contain two hundred pupils was completed and the Middle School came back, but not in full session. Since the trench held two hundred pupils, there must be only 100 of the Middle School on the premises at any one time, so this part of the School attended only five days in a fortnight, 100 of them at a time. The majority of these girls were glad to end their prolonged summer holiday and settle down to work again. Attendance on alternate days did, however, have its disadvantages and the staff were a bit hard on delinquents (so the delinquents thought). By November, the second trench unit for 200 pupils was completed and the whole school was back in session again. Since then work has gone back to normal. Of course the syllabus cannot be completed, but the examining body of the Northern Universities will take that matter into consideration in assessing marks in the future.

"Apart from school work, the staff are taking an active interest in war work. Nearly all of them have full training in anti-gas and First-Aid work and are members of the Town's A.R.P.* units.

"It is regretted that the black-out has had such an adverse influence on our out-of-school activities. The Ambulance Corps ceased to meet, the Dramatic Society produced no plays, Language and Scientific Societies have held no meetings and school parties have been afternoon instead of evening functions.

"The societies have begun to meet again during the lighter weather and we try to go on as if the world were nearly normal."[25]

This passage has been quoted verbatim in order to give younger readers some small idea of the state of things in a school which, compared with many others, hardly suffered any disruption at all at the beginning of the War. Under modern conditions at school it is hardly possible to imagine now what things were like then. It is hard for people to realise that the girls went blackberrying in order that jam could be made from the berries for use at school dinners.

As the war proceeded the number of evacuees gradually dwindled as they returned home again. A shadow was cast over the school in the Autumn of 1940 when it was announced that along with the Templefield County Secondary School, the new school had been scheduled to be held as a possible military hospital should the need arise. However, this shadow was short-lived as by October of the same year, it was announced that some other place had been found for this purpose.[26]

In July and August, 1942, the first parties of girls to go fruit-picking accompanied by mistresses were arranged. They went to Wickhambrook, Suffolk on the estate owned by Mr. Justin Brooke (a well-known agriculturalist and writer). These parties were repeated there in 1943 and 1944.[27] During the Autumn term of 1943 and 1944 girls and staff camped in the Village Hall at Littlethorpe, near Ripon, for potato-picking. The living conditions here were very primitive and the work was really hard, but all added to the war effort.[27] These school camps for fruit-picking were

*A.R.P. – Air Raid Precautions. These were centres manned by civilians to deal with casualties from air raids.

continued under Miss Truelove when she became Headmistress (see later) at Broom near Stratford-upon-Avon from 1947 onwards.

The 1944 Education Act altered the school completely by abolishing fee-paying pupils. Those already in the school were allowed to remain and complete their courses. From now onwards admission to the school was dependent upon a pupil passing the Selection Examination at the age of eleven plus. The school was in the future to be solely a secondary grammar school. This Act was also responsible for the closing of the Preparatory Department. Miss Abbs had already retired several years before after some 45 years service. She was followed by Miss Lillie as Head until 1947 and Miss Evans 'till 1948. Miss Thwaites was very worried about all this and went to great lengths to see that neither staff nor children should suffer from the closure of this department. The children already in the department remained in the school until they were eleven years of age and then they had to take the Selection Examination along with all the other children of their age. By 1950 there were 12 pupils left in that department.[27]

It was arranged in the first instance as a result of the Selection Examination, that the first 55 girls and two over-age pupils would come to Wheelwright and that 10 places for girls living in the West Riding area could be reserved at the school.[28]

Miss Thwaites had some very difficult periods in the course of her headship. She took over when the school was bulging at the seams with overcrowding, then she had the worry of maintaining that school until the move to the new buildings. There she developed a new school altogether and finally, there were the war years and the staff shortages which followed it,[29] at a time when she could have been resting on her laurels to some extent.

Miss Thwaites for some time retained the system of self-government which she inherited from Miss Baker and which she had helped to make a success; but fairly quickly after she was appointed headmistress she dropped this system in favour of more conventional methods of maintaining control. She also experimented with the idea of having one afternoon per week to be spent in some activity of the pupils' own choice (already referred to) but this was also short-lived.

She was, however, the instigator of a Science side in the Sixth Form. Before her time any girls wishing to do Mathematics in the Sixth Form went down to the Boys' School but in 1928 she decided to do the Mathematics herself.[16] This late decision was somewhat strange, considering she was a mathematician. This did not mean that she made the school a specialist one in that subject as happened at the Boys' School, in fact she maintained a very wide and general all round education throughout her period of office.

Miss Thwaites had a long and momentous headship and she witnessed the fulfilment of the idea which had been in Mrs. Holme's mind when she first went into the Halifax Road Building from the Bond Street warehouse, namely a separate and fully-equipped girls' grammar school.

MISS I. THWAITES, HEADMISTRESS (1922 TO 1948)

References

1. *The Dewsbury Reporter* .. ..   13th May   1922
2. Dewsbury Education Committee Minutes (Governors W.G.S.)   14th May   1923
3. Dewsbury Education Committee Minutes
   (School Management and General Purposes Committee)   ..   14th Feb.   1924
4. Dewsbury Education Committee Minutes
   (School Management and General Purposes Committee)   ..   15th Dec.   1924
5. Dewsbury Education Committee Minutes (W.G.S. Governors)   12th Oct.   1925
6. Dewsbury Education Committee Minutes (House Sub-Committee) 3rd Feb.   1927
7. H.M.I's Report on Wheelwright Grammar School for Girls   December   1927
8. Dewsbury Education Committee (W.G.S. Governors)   ..   12th Nov.   1928
9. Dewsbury Education Committee (School Management Comm.)   21st June   1929
10. Dewsbury Education Committee (W.G.S. Governors)   ..   14th Oct.   1929
11. Dewsbury Education Committee (W.G.S. Governors)   ..   11th Nov.   1929
12. Dewsbury Education Committee (W.G.S. Governors)   ..   8th Sept.   1930
13. Brochure published to mark the Laying of the Foundation Stone Ceremony
    of the New Wheelwright Grammar School for Girls by Major and Alderman
    P. B. Walker, V.D., J.P., Chairman of the Governors, Saturday, July 11th,
    1931
14. Correspondence with Miss Truelove   1970
15. Dewsbury Education Committee (W.G.S. Governors)   ..   10th May   1937
16. Correspondence with Mrs. B. Nuttall   1971
17. *The Dial*   1933
18. Dewsbury Education Committee   ..   ..   ..   19th June   1933
19. Dewsbury Education Committee (W.G.S. Governors)   ..   14th June   1937
20. Dewsbury Education Committee (W.G.S. Governors)   ..   12th July   1937
21. Dewsbury Education Committee (W.G.S. Governors)   ..   11th Oct.   1937
22. Dewsbury Education Committee (W.G.S. Governors)   ..   30th June   1938
23. H.M.I's Report on Wheelwright Grammar Schools for Girls   1938
24. *The Dial* .. ..   July   1945
25. *The Dial* .. ..   May   1943
26. Dewsbury Education Committee (School Management and
    General Purposes Committee) ..   ..   11th Oct.   1940
27. Correspondence with Miss Truelove   1971
28. Dewsbury Education Committee (School Management and
    General Purposes Committee) ..   ..   13th July   1945
29. Dewsbury Education Committee (Secondary Education
    Committee) ..   ..   13th Jan.   1948

CHAPTER X

The School in Modern Times
Miss Truelove (1948 to 1963)

Miss Nancy Winifred Truelove, M.A. (Cantab.) first came to Wheelwright Grammar School for Girls as English Mistress in September, 1938. Like her immediate predecessor, she was promoted from the ranks to be Headmistress of the School in September, 1948.

Miss Truelove was educated at the King's High School for Girls at Warwick and she then went up to Newnham College, Cambridge, where she took a second class Honours degree in English. Her teacher-training was done at the Marie Grey Training College, London, where she took the Teacher's Diploma of the University of London. Before coming to Wheelwright she had held teaching posts in Queen's College, Barbados, W.1., Queen Anne's School, Caversham, Reading; and Greenhead High School, Huddersfield.

Miss Thwaites retired in July, 1948, as Headmistress of Wheelwright Girls' School and though she was a Mathematician, she did not let that subject dominate the School curriculum.[1] The appointment of Miss Truelove meant that for the first time Wheelwright Grammar School for Girls had an English Specialist for Headmistress.

Miss Truelove took over at a very difficult time, shortly after the Second World War had ended and there was a great shortage of teachers and in particular teachers of Science and Mathematics. So much was this so that in January, 1948, as there were no applicants for the post of Chemistry Mistress, an arrangement was made with the Principal of the Technical College at Dewsbury, Mr. H. Wright, to release Mr. M. Salont so as to undertake part-time Chemistry teaching at Wheelwright until a full-time teacher could be appointed. He was the first man to teach Chemistry in the School and there is still a man taking this subject at the present time (1970).[2]

Miss Truelove inherited this staffing problem from Miss Thwaites and as the "Post War Bulge" of pupils became more manifest as the years went by, her difficulties also increased. Luckily for a time classrooms which had been occupied by the Preparatory Department before its closure were able to contain the increased numbers.

Soon after Miss Truelove's appointment as Headmistress there was the changeover from the School Certificate Examination to the "O" Level General Certificate of Education (G.C.E.). As previously mentioned in the history of the Boys' School difficulties arose, especially under the original ruling that the candidates must be sixteen years of age. This meant that the four year "A" stream (a quick stream) which had been run in the School was no longer practical.[1]

All girls were given a reasonable foundation in Science in that all Forms studied three Science subjects to a certain level. One Science subject, Biology, was made compulsory up to "O" Level to provide a balanced curriculum, otherwise in the Fourth and Fifth Forms there were plenty of options. Art, Music, Needlework were all "O" Level subjects.[1]

Full use was made of School Radio programmes and later Television ones, Granada Television loaning the School its first set.[1]

The School joined in visits to Cliffe House from its opening. After trying different age groups, it was found that the fortnight's visit was of most benefit to the second year girls.[1]

There was no formal Parent-teacher Association in Miss Truelove's time but contact with the parents was made so that discussions on the progress of the girls could be held. The first year had a Parents' Afternoon with displays of work done, etc. At the Fourth year there were Parents' Evenings with talks on careers and discussions on the progress of the girls. In the Fifth year (the leaving girls) each one was interviewed at School by the Youth Employment Officer together with the parent, careers mistress and the Headmistress.[1] Also visits were arranged to local hospitals, etc. and talks were given by representatives of the various professions, and by Old Girls who worked in interesting occupations.

One of the first successes in Miss Truelove's time was the outstanding achievement by a Wheelwright Girl, Eileen Fenton, in winning the "Daily Mail" International Cross Channel Swimming Contest.[3] This was a feat of which the School was, is and always should be proud. Very few schools can claim a Cross-Channel Swimmer as one of its pupils. She brought credit both to the School and to the town of Dewsbury.

It would appear from the H.M.I's Report on the Girls' School in 1956 that Miss Truelove more or less carried on and expanded the School in the Thwaites' tradition. There were no momentous upheavals or the introduction of revolutionary ideas. Even if Miss Truelove had wished to develop one particular subject in the curriculum, that would have been impossible owing to the staffing problems in the late 1940's and early 1950's.[1] Repeated advertisements produced no response or at the most one applicant. Mention has already been made of the difficulty in Chemistry. Even essential subjects had to be dropped temporarily because of these difficulties. The time was filled in with extra lessons in other subjects, usually English, and it was hoped that later on the girls would be able to make up the time lost in this way.[1]

Like Miss Thwaites, Miss Truelove undertook considerable class teaching, up to 14 periods per week. As an English Specialist she developed the English but not at the expense of other subjects. It received careful attention all the way through the school. She was assisted by three mistresses in the teaching of English but her own contribution was best seen in the Sixth Form where she had a very deep influence.[4]

One thing Miss Truelove did was to inspire in her pupils a love of books and she showed them how to use them as well for the gleaning of knowledge as for pleasure. This was accomplished by the Third and Fourth Forms having specific library periods during which efficient guidance to make good use of books was encouraged.[4]

Miss Truelove inherited a very stable staff from Miss Thwaites. Once again we see the tradition amongst Wheelwright teachers of staying for long period of time and this is more remarkable in a Girls' School than in a Boys'. Miss Truelove's inheritance included six teachers who had been at the School for over twelve years and three who had been there over twenty-two years. These teachers gave the School great stability and they insisted on a high standard of work;[4] but this stability was not to last long. In common with schools throughout the country, this was soon to be shattered. Married teachers moved from place to place as their husbands moved jobs; then there was the national shortage of teachers already referred to.

The "Post War Bulge", as in the Boys' School, did not make itself felt until the late 1950's. When Miss Truelove took over there were about 340 girls in the School. This gradually increased until by 1956 it had risen to 360; but the real "crunch" came in 1959 with a peak of 432 in November of that year. However, this was still nearly 90 less than the Boys' School had to cope with, though it strained the School to capacity.

The high academic record which Miss Thwaites had achieved was carried on by Miss Truelove and during her tenure of office as Headmistress, which lasted fifteen years, 7 State Scholarships were obtained, 4 Dewsbury Major Scholarships, 2 County Major Scholarships, 1 Holme Scholarship and 25 other university exhibitions, bursaries, etc.[6]

As mentioned earlier in connection with the "Black-out" during the War, after-school activities had had to be curtailed and the times modified, so when Miss Truelove took over in 1948 things were not quite back to normal again. She set about expanding the School Societies. When War broke out there were Scientific, Geographical and Dramatic Societies and an Art Club as well as Dr. Barnado's Helpers' League.[5] In 1949 the Barnado's League was very flourishing and raised £122. The Scientific and Geographical Societies were also very flourishing.

In 1951 the Debating Society was formed, but this was not very well attended and the next year it had its foundations broadened to become a Literary and Debating Society in the hope that it would be better supported by the girls. In 1954 a Music Society was formed, but here again the support was not what was hoped for.

In 1950 the Council for Education in World Citizenship (a junior branch of the United Nations Organisation) was formed. This emphasised the importance of understanding current events and world affairs. Joint meetings with Leeds and Bradford Schools were held and an annual London Conference was usually attended by several senior girls.

The annual visit to Stratford and the Royal Shakespeare Theatre was first started by a few Sixth Form girls spending a week of the Summer Holidays with members of the staff at Stratford. This developed to become a coach-load going in term time for three crowded days of sight-seeing and plays. In 1959 The Student Christian Movement was formed as an extra society.

For several years previous to Miss Truelove becoming Headmistress, there had been fruit-picking camps at Stratford-upon-Avon and at Bidford-upon-Avon and in 1949 and 1950 these camps were at Broom in Warwick-shire.[6],[7]

The School had been divided into Houses for years and the House activities had been mainly concerned with competitive games, but Miss Truelove included handicrafts, hobbies, cookery and the organising of House concerts and plays to augment the sports competitions.[1]

It has been mentioned, much earlier in this history, how bazaars were held originally to re-pay the money loaned to help furnish and equip the Schools in Halifax Road. These bazaars became annual events under Mrs. Holme and they raised many hundreds of pounds for the Dewsbury and District General Infirmary. These Sales of Work, etc. were continued under Miss Thwaites and the amount raised was quite outstanding. From the time of entering the new School in 1934 to 1952 the sum of £1,526 had been raised for the Infirmary[4] as well as another £604 raised for other charities from 1953 to 1956.[4] Dr. Barnado's Helpers' League had its peak of contributions in 1961 and 1962 when £206 was raised.[8],[9] It had a membership of 206 girls out of an average of just over 400 girls. With the advent of the National Health Service, the voluntary donations that the School had given to the Dewsbury and District General Infirmary seemed less needed and it was decided to widen the scope of charitable efforts; part of the money raised went to "The School Fund" and part to good causes, e.g. in 1952 a fete raised £230 which was divided between the Infirmary and stage lighting for school, and in 1960 £325 was sent to World Refugee Year.[1]

In 1944 violin classes had been started by they faded out. Then in 1958 an opportunity presented itself whereby the school obtained a number of second-hand instruments. A Peripatetic music teacher was in charge and an orchestra was formed which was encouraged to play at the School Assembly, at concerts and at Speech Day.[1] This orchestra later became the core of the Dewsbury Schools' Orchestra.

In order to widen the outlook of the Sixth Form and to balance the academic side, "Talks for Sixth Forms", Radio broadcasts and Television Sixth Form subjects were included in the time-table. Another innovation was that one afternoon each week was set aside for voluntary Art and handicrafts. This proved very popular with the girls.[1]

The Joint Matriculation Board towards the end of Miss Truelove's time started an "A" Level course in General Studies. In 1962 ten girls were put in for the course and eight got through. The whole course was carried out without formal teaching, all the work being done with the aid of the library, book lists, etc., study themes only being given.[1]

Miss Truelove made a definite attempt to increase the number of girls seeking entrance to teacher training colleges. With the co-operation of local schools it was arranged that girls could spend a day observing teachers at work in different types of schools, Infant, Junior and Secondary. This was to help to give them an understanding of the work involved. The result of this was that eleven girls went to teacher training colleges in 1962 and the same number in 1963.[10]

In the year before Miss Truelove retired the Dramatic Society put on a very successful "St. Joan" by Bernard Shaw and by then all the various School societies were in a flourishing state. The "Bulge" had just passed its peak so that there were actually more pupils in the school to be attracted to the societies.

The last year of Miss Truelove's reign as Headmistress saw a real breakthrough in relations with the Boys' School. During that year a combined Revue was put on with the help of the Boys' School. This was indeed a great step forward in the right direction. Up to now only small numbers of pupils had gone to the Boys' School for Mathematics and a few boys had come to the Girls' School to do Biology; but there had not been a free movement of the sexes between the two schools. One is bound to wonder why the two schools were kept so separate all these years, when in the original Foundation one boy and one girl were to benefit by the bequest, no segregation was hinted at, yet it was only towards the end of Miss Truelove's time that more co-operation was indulged in. This co-operation between the two schools became more and more operative when Miss Levitt and Mr. Lancaster became the heads of the respective schools shortly afterwards.

In the year that Miss Truelove retired yet one more girl swimmer made a name for herself and the school. She was Jennifer Thompson, who represented Great Britain at the European Games at Leipzig in 1963.

During Miss Truelove's time some 50 girls went to the various universities, a marked preference being for the provincial ones, only one to each of the older universities. There has been a steady stream of girls to the teacher training colleges (some 89), and so it would seem that Miss Truelove's aim to increase the flow to these colleges has succeeded. An increasing number of girls have joined the ranks of the nursing profession, Radiographers and Pathological technicians, etc., there being twenty-two from 1957 onwards.

Both Mrs. Holme and Miss Thwaites had the task of opening a new school at some time in their respective careers. This sort of upheaval did not present itself during Miss Truelove's time as the school had been in the new buildings for fourteen years and was settling down after the Second World War when she took over the reins. Though she had no such upheaval she had her share of difficulties in the shape of getting the "Post War Bulge" through the school and at the same time coping with the gross shortage in teaching staff. The two circumstances occurring simultaneously certainly called for effective and efficient administration from the top.

The scope of education was as broad as possible under the circumstances and at the same time great emphasis was placed on the training for good citizenship and duty to others over and above the excellent academic successes.

When Miss Truelove retired, she handed over a good school which was running very smoothly, one of which the Founder would have been proud.

References

1. Correspondence with Miss N. W. Truelove 1970
2. Minutes of the Governors of Secondary Education Sub-Committee 13th Jan. 1948
3. *The Dial* 1950
4. Report of H.M. Inspectors of Schools Wheelwright
   Grammar School for Girls .. .. Jan. and Feb. 1956
5. *The Dial* 1939
6. *The Dial* 1949
7. *The Dial* 1950
8. *The Dial* 1961
9. *The Dial* 1962
10. *The Dial* 1963

CHAPTER XI

Miss D. M. Levitt (Headmistress 1963 to ——)

Miss Truelove retired from the Headmistress-ship of the School in July, 1963, after being at the School for 25 years, ten of them as Headmistress. We have seen that she aimed at giving her pupils a sound secondary education, with high academic standards, and also aimed to give them the realisation that they had duties and responsibilities with regard to the community in which they lived.

She was followed as Headmistress by Miss Dorothy May Levitt, B.A. (Leeds). Miss Levitt received her education at the Greenhead High School for Girls, Huddersfield, and then proceeded to the University of Leeds where she took a second class honours degree in Classics and also the Diploma in Education. Miss Levitt's first post was at the County School for Girls at Chatham. It is quite coincidental that she should occupy this post, which was held by Miss Baker forty-four years ealier and from which school she came to Wheelwright in 1919. Little did Miss Levitt think that she would step into Miss Baker's place as the Headmistress of Wheelwright so many years later. She came to Wheelwright from Hulme Grammar School for Girls at Oldham where she had held the post of Senior Classics Mistress.

Miss Levitt is the second head of the School to be a graduate of one of the so-called "Red-Brick" Universities as opposed to Oxford and Cambridge. Miss Baker was the other one.

When Miss Levitt became Headmistress of the School the "Post War Bulge" had arrived at the Lower Sixth Form and there were still three Fifth Forms and three Fourth Forms lower down the School. Below these the School was becoming completely two-stream.[1] The total numbers on the roll dropped from 390 to 350 in 1965; the passing of the "Bulge" and the opening of the Technical Secondary School both helped to create this drop.

One of the first things to happen after Miss Levitt came was the effort made to get more playing fields for the School.[2] An agreement was drawn up with Messrs. Joshua Ellis & Co. Ltd. for the School to be allowed the use of their playing field in Healds Road for £25 for the Christmas and Easter terms.[3] This was so that the heavy wear and tear on the hockey pitch in front of the School could be eased considerably. The site on which

128

St. Joseph's R.C. School stands was also used for many years prior to 1963.

During practically the whole of Miss Levitt's time to date, there has been repeated staff movement. The most settled period was 1969-70.[1] The factor which has saved the School many a time is the substantial core of long serving members who certainly give real stability to the School.[1] The years 1965-6 and above all 1968-9 were times of rapid changes of staff; this is not to be wondered at when the number of married teachers there at the time is considered. There have been men on the staff, particularly for the science subjects, all Miss Levitt's time, the number varying between four and six; two of these were already there when she came. Fortunately there have always been quite a few former members of staff living in the district who were able to help in times of crisis.

Miss Levitt introduced several changes. From 1964 the children in the first two years have been unstreamed, i.e. not all the best in one form and the others in a parallel form beneath it. It is the intention to gradually extend the unstreaming throughout the School. Since 1968 all the girls staying on after taking their G.C.E. examinations have gone into the Sixth Form whatever their number of passes, even if they mainly do "O" level work there.[1]

The Upper Sixth Form itself has now a proper Sixth Form Common Room where the girls have facilities for making hot drinks. There is quite a collection of arm-chairs which have either been bought for the room or are throw-outs from elsewhere.[1] The Lower Sixth Form Room has tables and curtains but at the time of writing there is no means of producing hot drinks.

With the idea of giving the girls much more freedom and with it more responsibility, since 1968 the Sixth Form has been able to wear any combination of maroon or grey uniform and during the dinner time they can go out of the School precincts.

Since 1969 there has been in existence a Sixth Form Committee. This is still in its infancy and mainly concerned with co-ordinating and organising extra-curricular activities. It is already making suggestions and taking on quite a lot of responsibilities.[1] It is interesting to find such a development again in the history of the School as one remembers that Miss Baker introduced a similar system (the School Council) in 1920 which applied to the whole School. It is rather ironic that some outstanding educationists should think that this idea is progressive, or is it that they are some fifty years behind Wheelwright School in their outlook?

The main change in the curriculum has been the addition of "A" Level Housecraft which has been made possible by the sharing of lessons with the Dewsbury Technical Secondary School.[1] In 1967 groups of pupils were entered for the C.S.E. Examination (Certificate of Secondary Education) in Mathematics and French and since 1968 a few girls have taken Chemistry and Physics in that examination. This has coped with girls who might have dropped these subjects feeling they were not of G.C.E. standard.[1]

One big change has been that all Second Form girls now begin Latin.

This is one result of running an unstreamed school.[1] This would seem to be the only place where Miss Levitt's Classical speciality has asserted itself. Otherwise the curriculum is much as it was under Miss Truelove.

Almost all the time since Miss Levitt's appointment, and definitely since 1966 there has been the shadow of reorganisation hovering over the School.[4]

Holiday parties have been a feature of Miss Levitt's regime. In 1965 a party went to Germany, in 1966 one to Lugano, Switzerland, in 1968 another to Italy and in 1969 one to Tarragona, Spain.[1] In 1969 and 1970 there were walking parties at Easter to the Lake District with Mr. Butts.[1] The girls have continued to go on the Yorkshire-Lille Exchange Scheme and each year a party has gone to Stratford-upon-Avon.[1]

When Miss Levitt took over in 1963, Miss Harrison was the Deputy Headmistress and she had held the post since 1957 and continued in it until she retired in 1965 when Mrs. Tuxford was appointed Deputy Head. One of the very few teachers to die whilst connected with the School was Miss A. M. Shaw in August, 1965. She joined the staff in 1939, and was one of the solid core of teachers in the School. In the same year Miss M. Turner retired after teaching at the School for 32 years to which number she could add her years as a pupil there. She belongs to a family which has had more and longer connections with the two departments of the School than any other.

In 1964 the Dewsbury Schools' Orchestra was formed. The core of this orchestra has always been formed by the Wheelwright Girls. The music department under Mrs. Waller had had its scope greatly extended and there is now tuition in woodwind as well as in stringed instruments.[1]

Miss Levitt has further fostered the work begun by Mrs. Holme and Miss Thwaites and carried on by Miss Truelove in helping charities by efforts at School. From 1967 onwards an annual Charity Week has been organised in which each Form by some effort has raised money to be distributed to charities chosen by the Sixth Form. This was extended to actual practical help in 1968 when arrangements were made for Fifth Formers to spend a week helping in schools, hospitals and Old People's Homes.[1]

A feature of Miss Levitt's time has been the greater interest in the careers of the girls. In 1966 a careers meeting was held in the School attended by both parents and senior girls at which people representing various professions spoke.[1] This was repeated in 1967; but in the Autumn of 1969 a Careers Convention was held at which different professions had stalls and displays to which parents and girls went to discuss the merits, etc. of each. There have been many talks and visits connected with careers throughout the years.[1]

No Parent-teacher Association as such exists but regular parents' meetings are held so that they have a chance to discuss with teachers matters concerning the girls. Each School year has one such meeting from the Third Form upwards.[1] The First Form has an Open Afternoon during the summer term instead of the parents' meetings.[1]

No new School Societies have been formed but all those in existence in 1963 have flourished.

By 1964 Eileen Fenton and Jennifer Thompson had represented Great Britain in swimming contests four times and June Hanby swam Morecambe Bay, Tor Bay, Whitby Bay and Lake Bala.[5]

At least fifty girls have proceeded to universities, seventy-four to teacher training colleges as well as to the School of Librarianship, nursing, etc.[6] So the School is a sound all-round training ground both academically and for citizenship as well.

Since 1965 there has been more and more co-operation with the Boys' School, chiefly at Sixth Form level. In November of that year the First Sixth Form Conference (jointly with the Boys' School) was held at Cliffe House and this has been repeated each year.[1]

More co-operation in dramatic productions and also some interchange of Sixth Formers in music lessons has been carried out and a joint Boys' and Girls' committee arranges dances, folk evenings, hockey matches, etc., and the Student Christian Movement and the Archaeological Society are both joint activities. This greater co-operation between the two schools is one of the chief facets of the development of the schools under Miss Levitt's and Mr. Lancaster's guidance.

References
1. Correspondence with Miss Levitt 1971
2. Minutes of the Education (Governors of Secondary Schools)
   Sub-Committee .. .. 17th Sept. 1963
3. Minutes of the Education (Governors of Secondary Schools)
   Sub-Committee .. .. 15th Oct. 1963
4. Report by the Working Party established by Dewsbury
   Education Committee .. .. October 1966
5. *The Dial* .. .. July 1964
6. *The Dial* .. .. issues from 1964 to 1970

CHAPTER XII

The Preparatory Department or Kindergarten

The year following the opening of the Wheelwright Grammar Schools in the Bond Street premises saw the establishment of the Kindergarten. This department of the school was always under the control of the Headmistress of the Girls' School.

The first Kindergarten mistress was Miss P. Snowdon. To this preparatory department came Miss Louisa Abbs as a pupil in 1891. Before proceeding further it might be as well to mention here that there are some discrepancies with dates at this period. Miss Snowdon was appointed mistress in charge of the Kindergarten in 1890 and Miss Abbs appears to have attended as a scholar from 1891 to 1895.[1] In her speech when she was presented with her retirement present she says that the Governors opened a preparatory department in 1894-5[2] but Miss Huckwell's Annual Report for 1893 states that the Kindergarten was started in that year.

According to Miss Abbs, besides the girls present on the first morning there were three fair-haired little boys, all very smart in their "sailorsuits", and it would seem that they received a good deal more attention that week than was good for them.[2]

Miss Abbs was far and away the most popular and certainly the longest serving member of staff in the department, in fact she was the longest serving member of the whole of the Wheelwright school staffs with 45 years service to her credit. The next best record was set up by Mr. Perkins in the Boys' School with 42 years. When Miss Abbs was about to leave school as a pupil, Miss Huckwell asked her to stay on and help in the Preparatory Department, as she definitely had a gift for dealing with and teaching young children.[2] Miss Abbs agreed and started work under Miss Snowdon. Some time later when Miss Huckwell realised that just to be able to do the job without any recognised qualification would be a disadvantage, she suggested to her that she should take some academic qualification and assisted her in every way possible to gain her L.L.A. of the University of St. Andrews.

The Preparatory Department in its early years was somewhat peripatetic, travelling round the school to occupy any classroom which was vacant. Miss Abbs said that she had had a class of babies (first year prep. children) in the old gym. the old library (which was a small room in the Boys' School), and in the basement.[2]

Under Miss Abbs and two assistants, after Miss Snowdon left, the Preparatory Department grew and flourished, so much so that she became almost a legendary figure and instead of parents saying they were sending their children to the Wheelwright Grammar School Preparatory Department, they simply said they were sending them to Miss Abbs,[2] who was regarded as being as firm as a rock or the Bank of England.[2]

Under Mrs. Holme there were several highlights in the Preparatory School year, one of which was the invitation to the Boys' School Sports Day, during which they ran an eighty yards race. This race was called "The Veterans' Race" and it really proved to be the great event of the afternoon. Every child ran and Mr. Holme was adamant that everybody got a prize.[2]

The other great event was the Christmas Party and the visit of the ventriloquist who, strangely enough, knew all the daily happenings in the school.[2]

After the first World War space was at a premium in the Main School and something had to be done about accommodating the Preparatory Department, and luckily for the Governors the Marlborough Estate on the opposite side of Halifax Road to the School came on the Market in January, 1920.[3] At a special meeting of the Governors in the following month, the Estate was purchased from Miss Hunter for £8,625.[4] The detached double-fronted house which faced south over the grounds was used to accommodate the Preparatory Department. Four rooms were used as classrooms and one as an Assembly Hall. By 1927 there were 82 children of both sexes and a teaching staff of four in the building.[5]

The move to Marlborough House gave the Preparatory Department a settled home for some years and it also gave it room to expand, the grounds being used to the full advantage.[2] The Preparatory Department also helped in providing a stall at the annual bazaar which was held by the Main Girls' School to raise funds for the Dewsbury and District General Infirmary. Later it had its own bazaar and sold handwork made by the children themselves and had hoopla stalls, cake stalls, etc.

When the new Wheelwright Girls' School was opened in 1934, the Preparatory Department had one more and final move, back to the Main School where it was accommodated in one of the wings of the Main School building. It used three classrooms which were both well-planned and airy and had excellent furniture and equipment. Here Miss Abbs was assisted by two well qualified Froebel trained mistresses. In 1938 there were 24 boys and 33 girls in the department.[6]

Soon afterwards the Second World War broke out and though there were no after-school activities to be curtailed, there was the general disorganisation of air precaution practices, etc.

In 1941 Miss Abbs retired from the post of Head of the Preparatory Department. Actually it had not many more years to run as by the Education Act of 1944 the Wheelwright Girls' School became the grammar school for the Dewsbury County Borough and so only secondary education was carried on there. This meant the closure of the Preparatory Department. After Miss Abbs retired Miss Alice Lillie became the Head until 1947 and Miss Evans left in 1948. Miss Thwaites was very worried about the closure of the department and went to great lengths to see that neither the staff nor the children would suffer by this event. The children stayed on until they were eleven years of age; but no new entrants were admitted, so the numbers gradually decreased, there being 12 there in 1950. These were under the control of the new Headmistress of the Girls' School (Miss N. W. Truelove). This small number of children in the department created considerable staffing difficulties.[7]

In effect, then, the Preparatory Department and Miss Abbs were practically synonymous and co-existent as it had been in existence only a few years before she came to it as a pupil and lasted only a few years after her retirement.

References

1. The Staff Register of the Wheelwright Grammar School for Girls
2. *The Dewsbury Reporter* .. .. 18th Jan. 1941
3. The Minutes of the Dewsbury Endowed Schools Foundation 26th Jan. 1920
4. The Minutes of the Dewsbury Endowed Schools Foundation 2nd Feb. 1920
5. Board of Education H.M.I's Report on the Wheelwright Grammar School for Girls 1927
6. Board of Education H.M.I's Report on the Wheelwright Grammar School for Girls 1938
7. Correspondence with Miss N. W. Truelove 1970

CHAPTER XIII

Conclusion

In the main body of the book almost 250 years' history of the Wheelwright Schools in Dewsbury, both as elementary and grammar, has been covered. This has followed the growth of a school founded by John Wheelwright for one boy and one girl (poor children of tenants of his estate) before he died in 1724, to the two schools which are the successors of that school in which there are about now 350 boys and the same number of girls (1971).

Through all the vicissitudes of the schools both as elementary and grammar, the name of the founder has been held in great esteem, so much so that the grammar schools have always been known simply as "The Wheelwright".

The school founded by John Wheelwright on the site of the present Central Library remained as an elementary one until 1888 when the new Scheme to establish the school as a grammar school with separate boys' and girls' departments received the Royal Assent. From 1889 until 1922 the schools were administered under a board of Governors on which the Dewsbury Town Council had a majority of members. In 1922 the schools were fully municipalised.

We know very little indeed about the scholars who attended the original charity school in Wellington Road and in order to find out what life was like liberty was taken to quote fully from the minutes of the Daw Green Charity School which was contemporary with the Wheelwright School. Not until the grammar schools were founded in 1889 does the success story of the schools begin and this has gained momentum from that time to the present day.

The first success was in 1892 (three years after the school opened) when Margaret Auty and Ella Walker gained a County Scholarship Class B and a County Free Studentship respectively. The next year Ellen (Nellie) Bishop gained a County Scholarship Class B and went on to gain a B.A. (Victoria) in 1896. The first boy to start the long list of successes was the late Prof. W. G. Fearnsides, F.R.S. Other boys quickly followed with names like F. A. Hepworth and later Dr. D. A. Wray leading the way to the "Red-Brick" universities. Wray was appointed to the Geological Survey, T. Lister became Private Secretary to the Lt. General of Tangoon and W.

135

Secker became Senior Chemical Assistant to the Government Laboratories along with J. E. Scatcherd, who became the General Manager of the Foreign Auxiliary of Lloyds and the National Provincial Banks; these are but a few of the early Wheelwright boys to make names for themselves and the School.

After the first World War the number of Wheelwright successes mounted steeply. Names like P. B. Walker who gained the first Ph.D. awarded by the University of Cambridge for research into aeronautics and G. E. Walker who became the Secretary of the Thames Conservancy Board, W. G. Senior who held the post of Chief Dental Officer to the Ministry of Health, C. R. Addinall, one of the first boys from Wheelwright to obtain research degrees at Havard, come to mind.

Then the Sadler Mathematicians won fame for the school both at home and abroad. D. H. Sadler (no relation to the Headmaster of that name) became Superintendent of the Nautical Almanac Office and produced the first edition of the Air Almanac, R. Frith at the National Physics Laboratories and many others till we come to the two giants of computer science, Leslie Fox and Tom Kilburn, holding professorships at Oxford and Manchester respectively (the last named becoming our second F.R.S.). They have blazed the Wheelwright name through modern scientific spheres.

Even though mathematicians were specially treated, other branches of knowledge claimed successes. M. H. Scargill took the Wheelwright banner to Canada, where he holds the chair of Linguistics at the University of Victoria, British Columbia. Turning to journalism, two names take Wheelwright to the top ranks, H. Keeble who became Editor of the "Sunday Times" and E. L. Iddon ("Don Iddon") whose famous column in the "Daily Mail" was syndicated to 117 newspapers in seventeen countries.

Others took Wheelwright into the Church, many to the established Church. One, the late B. A. Smith, became Canon Treasurer of York Minister, others like G. V. Jones and M. Furness favoured the Congregational and Methodist sects respectively. Two boys took Wheelwright to Westminster and became M.P's (the late Col. E. W. Pickering, D.S.O, and Marcus Fox). Another (John Stansfield) almost did in the 1970 Election.

Not all the fame was in the Boys' school though it must be realised that up to the last World War, although girls had an equal opportunity with them to enter the universities, etc., once there, most of the professions were dominated by men, except that of teaching and to a less extent Medicine.

One has to allow for this outlook towards girls when one finds that the success lists are not so long in the Girls' School as in the Boys', although as we have seen, Margaret Auty and Nellie Bishop were among the first successes the School ever had. In 1899 Louisa Abbs took her L.L.A. at St. Andrews. She was also the first old pupil of the school to become a permanent member of the teaching staff of the school. This precedent was followed almost immediately by Edith Annie Pickersgill, who gained a B.A. at Oxford and then returned to teach at the school, and this has been followed by many other Old Girls and Old Boys. Present day teachers who are in this tradition are Miss E. Secker, Mrs. G. Waller, Miss Dawson, Mrs. Killey, Messrs. R. B. Crowther, G. Robinson, D. Butterfield and D. B. Crawshaw.

An authoress who was a one-time scholar in the Girls School was the late Miss Ella Pontefract who joined forces with Miss Marie Hartley to give us their famous books on Life in the Yorkshire Dales.

Naturally with the growth of the two schools, the success lists have grown even longer and longer. A notable feature of the lists of the Girls' School is the increase in the number of girls going to Teacher Training Colleges, evident success of Miss Truelove's policy.

Turning to the Boys' School names of sportsmen which come to mind equal in honour to those of the girls mentioned earlier are Victor Metcalf, who became outside-left with Huddersfield Town and who gained International Caps for England against Argentina and Portugal in 1951, Ian Anderson, the English Schools Long Jump Champion and also Scottish International, and Tony Nicholson who plays with the Yorkshire County Cricket Team.

Besides all these there is a multitude of old pupils from both schools who have been and are indebted to Wheelwright for having given them their start on the road to becoming doctors, dentists, lawyers, solicitors, engineers, chemists, pharmacists, scientists and teachers of all types. The great names have been picked at random and no slight or insult is intended to any one whose name has not been mentioned as all of us, great and small have need to thank John Wheelwright in the first place for having founded his school by 1724 in Dewsbury, S. J. Chadwick for having the foresight to fight for and gain money from the Wheelwright Trustees in order to build the school in Birkdale Road, Dr. Matthew Hinchliffe for his munificence in 1897 and Major P. B. Walker as Chairman of the Governors for twenty-five years for guiding Wheelwright through many difficult times.

Lastly we all owe a great debt of gratitude to all the teachers who have been at Wheelwright be their stay long or short, some great teachers and some not so great, but each adding his or her bit to help make the Schools the successful educational institutions they have been for so many decades and still are. We have all gained something at one time or another which we should have missed had we not been pupils at Wheelwright.

APPENDIX 1. ASSISTANT MASTERS AND MISTRESSES IN THE BOYS'
SCHOOL

*Details from Dewsbury Endowed Schools Foundation Minutes 1900–1922.
†Temporary teachers.
‡Dewsbury Endowed Schools' Foundation Year Book, 1902–1903.
§Second Master or Deputy Headmaster.
‖Headmaster's Report to Governors, 1895.

Name	Dates	Degree and University
*Hayden, Stafford R.	1889–1905	M.A. Cambridge
*Owen, C. H.	1889–1891	M.A. Edinburgh
Schoenemann, Hugo (Herr)	1889–1891	University of Prague
*Reynolds, P.	1889–1902	B.A. London
Batley, Walton	1889–1919	A.R.C.O. London
Knowles, T.	1891–1900	Inter B.Sc. London
‖Loffler (Herr)	1891–1895	
*Gledhill, James	1893–1919	B. of E. Art Masters' Certificate
Leumann, J., Dr.	1895– ?	Strasbourg
‖Long, Mr.	? –1897	
*Leng, Mr.	1898–1902	
‖Gamble, H.	1897– ?	
Tolson, T.	1897– ?	Swimming Instructor
‡Heath, Mr.	1900–1902	
‡Shorter, H. V. S.	1901–1902	B.A. Oxford
Walker, (Capt.)	1901– ?	Drill Sgt.
‡Burnett, T. R.	1902–1902	B.Sc. (Victoria) Ph.D. Basle
*Cowburn, A. B.	1902–1903	
*Harrison, J. W.	1902– ?	Drill Sgt.
*Harrison, F. C.	1902–1905	A.R.C.S., F.G.S.
*Dunstan, A. C.	1902–1904	A.K.C. London
*Thomas, W. J.	1903–1905	
*Thorpe, J.	1903–1906	
Birkhead, Mabel (Miss)	1903–1911	Art Masters' Certificate
*Taylor, Herbert John	1903–1909	F.C.S.
*Fraser, J. C.	1904–1905	
*Buckley, Joshua	1905–1911	Art Teachers' Certificate
*Bunnett, W. E.	1905–1905	B.Sc.
§Hawkes, Geoffrey	1905–1916	B.A. Cambridge
§Evans, John Hugh	1905–1920	B.Sc. Wales, Inter B.Sc. London
Thompson, George Henry Main	1905–1910	B.A. Wales
Williams, A. P.	1906– ?	
*Upton, W. E.	1906–1907	
Peel, Albert Edward	1906–1914	Teachers' Certificate
*McPhie, Mr.	1906–1907	
Graham, Herbert	1907–1919	D.S.M.
Pickersgill, Edith Annie (Miss)	1907–1919	B.A. Oxford
Griffin, John	1908–1911	B.A. Cambridge
Hibbert, Thomas	1908–1910	Inter B.Sc. London
Morgan, Walter	1910–1921	M.A. Wales

Name	Dates	Degree and University
Frost, Dalma Maud (Miss)	1910–1914	B.A. Cambridge
Harrison, Muriel Kathleen (Miss)	1910–1914	B.Sc. London
Nicholas, Sidney Diggery	1911–1917	B.A. Oxford
Lorryman, Percy Wilfrid	1911–1919	B. of E. Certicate in handwork
Hirst, Alice	1911–1912	
Magan, Emily Arthington (Miss)	1911–1912	Art Teachers' Certificate
Moore, Katherine K.	1913–1918	Art Teachers' Certificate
Hemstead, Mark Ignatius	1914–1920	B.A. London, A.C.P.
Connold, Mildred (Miss)	1914–1915	B.A. London
French, Dora Elizabeth (Miss)	1914–1917	B.A. London
Patterson, Dorothy Christine (Miss)	1914–1916	B.Sc. Glasgow
Blackburn, Harold	1915– ?	City and Guilds Certificate
Cooper, Constance May Farquharson (Miss)	1915–1917	B.A. London
Currie, John Brown	1916–1917	Dip. Chemistry
Birtwell, Elizabeth Winifred (Miss)	1916–1917	M.A. Manchester
Thornton, Christopher	1916–1919	Teachers' Certificate
Hebson, Mary Elizabeth (Miss)	1916–1917	B.A. Leeds
Orgill, Handell	1917–1922	B.A. London
Jennings, Charles	1917–1919	Teachers' Certificate
Beck, Beatrice (Miss)	1917–1918	B.A. Birmingham
Brechin, Ivy (Miss)	1917–1919	M.A. Leeds
Brookes, Selina (Miss)	1918–1918	B.A. Manchester
Parnell, Kathleen (Miss)	1918–1919	Teachers' Certificate
Crankshaw, Elizabeth	1918–1919	B.A. Cambridge
White, W. H.	1918–1919	
Sorrell, Henry Thomas	1919–1931	B.Sc. London
Budd, Phyllis Marjorie (Miss)	1919–1928	Inter B.Sc. London
Clark, Mabel Laidlow (Miss	1919–1919	L.L.A. St. Andrews†
Gilbert, Evelyn Mary (Miss)	1920–1943	Teachers' Certificate
Lewis, Peter Albert	1919–1922	M.A. Wales
Maudsley, Henry	1919–1920	A.R.C.A.†
Cooke, Maurice Edward	1919–1938	F.R.C.O.
Pickles, John Arthur	1919–1940	P.T. Certificate
James, William Thomas	1919–1943	Teachers' Certificate
§North, Alfred Edgar	1920–1923	M.A. Oxford
§Browne, Barrington	1920–1955	M.A. Cambridge
Bradshaw, Frank	1920–1948	A.R.C.A. London
§Williams, Caradoc	1920–1959	B.Sc. Wales
Alexander, John Dow	1920–1921	Inter B.L.
Kirwan, Joseph	1921–1922	Dip. R.C.S. Dublin
Bodenham, Robert John William	1921–1928	B.A. Birmingham
Robinson, Harold S.	1921–1944	Inter B.A. Liverpool
Byrne, Richard Hugh Garrett	1922–1926	M.A. Leeds
Clark, Geoffrey	1922–1925	M.A. Cambridge
Hamilton, Horace Charles	1922–1928	M.A. Birmingham
Perkins, Harold	1922–1964	B.Sc. London
Franklin, John Dingley	1923–1960	B.A. London
Mewse, Ewart	1925–1926	B.Sc. Durham

Name	Dates	Degree and University
Oldroyd, James Henry	1925–1948	City and Guilds Certificate
§Chester, Charles Vincent	1926–1967	M.A. Oxford
Seed, Walter	1926–1957	B.A. London, B.A. Reading
Boyer, Thomas	1926–1940	M.Sc. Manchester
Down, Wilfrid Charles	1928–1941	B.A. London, Ph.D. Cambridge
Newton, Ethel (Miss)	1929–1941	L.R.A.M.
Docton, Horace Martin	1929–1945	M.A. Cambridge
	1949–1963	
Jones, Clifford Merton	1932–1948	M.A., M.Sc. Leeds
Barlow, Nellie (Miss)	1938–1939	L.R.A.M.
Spencer, John Marshall Cecil	1938–1939	B.A. Leeds
	1939–	
Rhodes, Florence (Miss)	1940–1940	B.A. Leeds
Crosland, George Lindley	1940–1940	B.A. Leeds
Dixon, Helen (Miss)	1940–1942	B.A. Leeds
Thompson, James Anderson	1940–1946	B.A. Leeds
Stansfield, Clifford Maxwell	1941–1967	M.Sc. Leeds
Garthwaite, Elizabeth Anne (Mrs.)	1942–1947	Teachers' Certificate
Richards, Henry	1942–1968	Teachers' Certificate
Kaye, Harold	1943–1967	Teachers' Certificate
Williamson, Reginald	1944–1957	Handwork Teachers' Certificate
Wall, Kenneth Lester	1944–1945	M.A. Sheffield
Roberts, Walter John	1945–1946	M.A. Cambridge
Challiner, William Herbert	1945–1945	B.A. Birmingham, Inter B.Sc.†
Jones, Lynn Daniel	1946–1949	1st M.B. Certificate P.T. College, Fredenbourg
Berkoff, Nelson Abraham	1947–1948	M.A. Cambridge
Brooke, Gwenneth (Miss) (Mrs. Waller)	1947–1948	L.R.A.M.
Hamilton, Samuel Greenlees	1948–1971	B.Sc. Liverpool
Berry, Clement	1948–1965	City and Guilds Certificate
Bushell, P.	1949– ?	Art Master's Certificate
Dickens, Eric	1949–1964	B.A. Reading
Avison, Marion (Miss)	1949–1953	Teachers' Certificate
Evans, Denis	1950–1965	Teachers' Certificate and P.E.Dip.
Crowther, Ronald Butler	1952–	M.A. Cambridge
Benton, Herbert	1953–	B.A. Leeds
Dutton, David Wynne	? –1953	Teaching Diploma (Art)
Harrap, George Maurice	1954–	B.A. Manchester
Thornton, Percy	1954–1954	Nat. Dip. (Design)†
Saxton, Colin	1954–1954	Dip. in Fine Art
Malpas, John Anthony	1955–1961	B.A. Belfast
Wilcock, George	1955–1956	Teachers' Certificate
Staynes, Thomas	1955–	M.A. Oxford
Hemer, Colin John	1955–1955	B.A. Oxford†
Regan, John Charles	1956–1961	B.Sc. London
Tattersall, Peter	1957–1961	B.Sc. London
	1962–1963	
Bamford, Keith	1957–1968	B.Sc. Durham

APPENDIX

Name	Dates	Degree and University
§Crompton, John Stuart	1957–	M.A. Manchester
Farrar, Peter Thornton	1957–1958	B.A. Durham
Swain, James David	1957–1961	B.A., A.K.C. London
Doyle, Brian	1958–1961	B.A. Liverpool
Smith, Eric David	1958–1964	B.A. Hull
Smith, Norman Geoffrey	1958–1961	Teachers' Certificate
Lyne, Julian Roger Maxwell	1959–	B.A. London
Parker, Percy Philip	1959–1961	B.Sc. Manchester
Wilcock, Clive	Temporary†	
Fletcher, Malcolm Frank	1961–1963	B.A. Manchester
Ingram, William Anthony	1961–1965	B.A. Liverpool
Moss, Peter	1961–1967	B.A. London
Daniel, Ruth (Miss)	Sept. to Dec. 1961	B.Sc.†
Stansfield, John M.	1961–	B.Sc. Birmingham
Harrison, John Raymond	1961–1963	B.A. Nottingham
Newberry, John Kelvin	1962–1969	B.A. Leeds
Wilby, Edmund David	1962–1963	Inter. Dip. Arts and Crafts
Ellis, John David	1963–1967	
Cass, T. A.	1963– ?	
Buckley, Colin	1963–1964	B.A. Leeds
Carruthers, John Allistair	1963–1963	Teacher's Certificate†
Hainsworth, Gordon	1964–1965	M.A. Cambridge
Kharhar, Dalputram Chotalal	1964–1967	B.A. Bombay
Chadwick, Antony Ronald	1964–1965	B.A. Manchester
Coast, Colin Reginald	1964–1967	B.Sc. Hull
Ramsden, John Theodore	1964–1967	B.A. Durham
Mawhinney, Samuel Frederick	1965–1966	B.A. Dublin
Biggin, Peter	1965–	B.Sc. Manchester
Brook, Richard Laird	1965–1969	B.A. Leeds
Craven, Daniel Stephen	1965–1970	Dip. in Education
Woodrow, Kenneth Jack	1966–	M.A. Cambridge
Womack, Robert	1966–	Dip. in P.E. Carnegie College
Appleby, Keith	1967–1967	B.Sc. Leeds†
Butterfield, David	1967–	B.Sc. Durham
Donald, Robert William	1967–	Teacher's Certificate
Heard, Michael Edmund	1967–	B.A. Manchester
Hubbard, Brian Trevor	1967–	Teachers' Certificate
Throp, James Michael	1968–	B.A. Birmingham
Dunning, Geoffrey Arthur Ormiston	1968–	B.Sc. Manchester
Wood, Raymond Hugh	1968–	M.A. Cambridge
Lynnes, Michael Willis	1968–1969	Certificate of Education
Morris, Geoffrey	1969–1970	B.A. Leeds
Stephenson, D. M. (Mrs.)	1969–1970	Certificate of Education†
Widdows, Peter Andrew	1970–	B.A. Leeds
Crawshaw, David Barrie	1970–	B.Sc. Durham

APPENDIX 2. THE ASSISTANT TEACHERS IN THE GIRLS' SCHOOL

*From Dewsbury Endowed Schools' Ledger
†Temporary Teachers
‡Dewsbury Endowed Schools' Foundation Year Book.
§Second Mistress or Deputy Headmistress.

Name	Dates	Degree and University
*Hovey, Rosa (Miss)	1889–1893	B.A.
*Oakshott, Florence (Miss)	1889–1892	
*Mitchell, L. (Miss	1889–1892	
*Bever, J. (Fraulein)	1889–1891	
Batley, Walton (Mr.)	1889–1919	A.R.C.O.
*Snowdon, F. (Miss)	1890– ?	
*Wohlmann, M.	1891– ?	†
*Athya, F. (Miss)	1891–1895	
*MacDonald, (Miss)	1892–1894	
*Harden, A. M. (Miss)	1893–1898	B.A. London
Gledhill, James (Mr.)	1893–1919	Board of Education Art Masters' Certificate
*Agar, W. (Miss)	1894–1895	
Wormald, (Miss)		
Sgt. Barry (Drill)		
Harrison, J. W. (Mr.) (Drill)		All teaching in the School before 1895,
Miss and Mrs. Ash (Dancing)		dates uncertain.
Miss H. Beaumont		
Miss Ellis (Swimming)		
Miss S. Wommersley		
*Tennett, (Miss)	1895– ?	Newnham College, Cambridge
*Abbs, Louisa	1895–1940	L.L.A. St. Andrews
*Rowland, (Miss)	1896–1899	
*Parlby, P. (Miss)	1897–1898	
*Lisben, (Miss)	1898–1899	
*Barnard, (Miss)	1898–1899	
*Ellison, (Miss)	1899– ?	
*Parr, (Miss)	1899– ?	
Fordham, Helen (Miss)	1901–1919	National Froebel Union
‡Wales, E. (Miss)	1901–1907	B.A. Cambridge
Birkhead, Mabel (Miss)	1901–1911	Art Teachers' Certificate
‡Cook, E. M. (Miss)	1902–1907	B.A. London
‡Eldred, E. (Miss)	1902–1907	B.A. London
Watts, M. (Miss)	1902– ?	
Law, Ruth Mayson (Miss)	1903–1915	B.A. London
Aimers, M (Miss)	1903–1907	B.A. Royal University of Ireland
Newberry, E. (Miss)	1903–1907	B.A. Cambridge
Weaver, E. (Miss)	1903–1907	Inter. B.A. London
Smith, Bertha (Miss)	1905–1918	B.A. Oxford
Hawkes, Geoffrey (Mr.)	1905–1916	B.A. Cambridge
Crowther, Eveline (Miss)	1906–1908	
Mackay, Sarah Ann (Miss)	1906–1910	
Houghey, Margaret Angela (Miss)	1907–1910	

Name	Dates	Degree and University
Pickersgill, Edith Annie (Miss)	1907–1919	B.A. Oxford
Roberts, Rose Ethel Turton	1907–1908	B.Litt. Durham
Marsh, Mildred (Miss)	1908–1918	P.T.Dip. Liverpool
Frost, Dalma Maud (Miss)	1910–1914	B.A. Dublin
Harrison, Muriel Kate (Miss)	1910–1914	B.Sc. London
Hirst, Anita (Miss)	1911–1913	Board of Education Certificate
Magaro, Emily Arthington (Miss)	1912–1913	Art Class Teachers' Certificate
Moore, Katharine Kenyon (Miss)	1913–1918	Art Teachers' Certificate
Connold, Mildred (Miss)	1914–1915	B.A. London
Patterson, Dorothy Christina (Miss)	1914–1915	Inter. B.Sc. London, B.Sc. Glasgow
French, Dora Elizabeth (Miss)	1914–1917	B.A. London
Howard, Nora Adeline Mary (Miss)	1915–1918	B.A. London
Blamires, Florence Mary (Miss)	1916–1919	B.Sc. London
Coults, Marion Charlotte (Miss)	1916– ?	M.A. Aberdeen
Hobson, Mary Elizabeth (Miss)	1916– ?	
Evans, John Hugh (Mr.)	1916–1919	B.Sc. Wales
Birdwell, Elizabeth Winifred (Miss)	1916–1917	M.A. Manchester
Bruce, Sybil (Miss)	1916– ?	B.A. London†
Bick, Beatrice (Miss)	1917–1918	B.A. Birmingham
Brady, Catherine Elizabeth (Miss)	1918–1920	B.A. London
Quarmby, Ethelyn (Miss)	1918–1918	B.A. London†
Cooke, Gertrude Elizabeth (Miss)	1918–1918	Inter. B.A. London†
§Head, June (Miss)	1918–1925	M.A. Leeds
Parnell, Kathleen (Miss)	1918–1920	Teachers' Certificate
Oates, Dorothy Richardson (Miss)	1918–1932	Dip. of Physical Training
Turner, Ethel (Miss)	1918–1919	M.Sc. Sheffield, B.Sc. London
§Crankshaw, Elizabeth May (Miss)	1918–1957	M.A. Cambridge
Giles, Doris E. (Miss)	1918–1919	Inter. B.A. London
Jenkins, Isabel Maud (Miss)	1918–1920	Teachers' Certificate
Blakey, Louisa (Miss)	1918–1919	
Pownall, Phyllis (Miss)	1919–1920	Inter. B.Sc. Manchester
Audsley, Edith (Miss)	1919–1919	Teachers' Certificate†
§Thwaites, Isabella (Miss)	1919–1948	M.A. Cambridge
Lightowler, Hilda (Miss)	1919–1920	B.A. Birmingham
Maudesley, Henry (Mr.)	1919–1920	A.R.C.A. London†
Trevorrow, Polly (Miss)	1919–1921	(Help in Kindergarten)
Cooke, Maurice Edward (Mr.)	1919–1938	F.R.C.O.
Fortune, Mabel (Miss)	1919–1921	B.A. Manchester
§Noble, Elizabeth (Miss)	1920–1945	Ph.D. Dublin
Wood, Amy Louisa (Miss)	1920–1926	M.A. Manchester
Scott, Blanche Ethel (Miss)	1920–1920	Teachers' Certificate
Evans, Dorothy Wheatcroft (Miss)	1920–1947	N.F.U.
Ingle, Slea May (Miss)	1920–1920	†
Moore, Hilda Mary (Miss)	1920–1922	B.A. Oxford†
Moore, Hilda Mary (Miss)	1920–1922	B.A. Oxford
Morahan, Dorothy (Miss)	1920–1922	B.A. Manchester
Foster, Edna (Miss)	1920–1957	B.A. London
Moore, Dorothy Winifred (Miss)	1920– ?	Dip. Edinburgh College of Art

Name	Dates	Degree and University
Gentry, Kathleen Ida (Miss)	1920–1948	
Armstrong, Jessie (Miss)	1921–1922	N.F.U.
Lillie, Alice (Miss)	1921–1947	N.F.U.
Exley, Elsie (Miss)	1922–1922	B.Sc. London†
Tollit, Beatrice Eveline (Miss)	1922–1926	N.F.U.
Senior, Lucy (Miss)	1922–1928	
§MacLeod, Muriel Clare Wroughton (Miss)	1922–1928	
Hill, Kathleen (Miss)	1922–1928	B.A. London
Collins, Eva Muriel (Miss)	1923–1957	B.A. London
Hirst, Miriam (Miss)	1923–1923	M.A. London†
Ballaster, Renee May (Miss)	1925–1926	B.A. London
Davis, Freda Bessie (Miss)	1926–1927	B.A. London
Whittaker, Helen (Miss)	1926– ?	B.A. Cambridge
Brierley, Muriel (Miss)	1926–1958	N.F.U.
Birch, Elsie (Miss)	1927–1927	B.A. Manchester†
Lewis, Phyllis Mary (Miss)	1927–1927	B.A. Bristol†
§Harrison, Ethel Hulme (Miss)	1928–1965	B.A. Birmingham
Grylls, Rosemary Florence (Miss)	1928–1929	B.A. Cambridge
Waugh, Marjorie Walthall (Miss)	1928–1930	B.Sc. Liverpool
May, Elma Lillian Annie (Miss)	1929–1929	B.Sc. London†
Crout, Marian (Miss)	1929–1932	B.A. London
Kayley, Constance Ruth (Miss)	1930–1933	B.Sc. Liverpool
Peters, Kathleen Mary (Miss)	1930–1930	M.A. Manchester†
Clarkson, Elsie Mary (Miss)	1930–1947	B.Sc. Liverpool
Withers, Grace (Miss)	1932–1932	Dip. P.T. Liverpool P.T. College†
Law, Elizabeth (Miss)	1932–1938	B.A. Manchester
Hobson, Dorothy Florence (Miss)	1932–1938	Dip. in P.T.
Turner, Martha (Miss)	1933–1965	Dip. Dom. Sci.
Cooke, Edna Clare (Miss)	1934–1939	B.Sc. Birmingham
Hart, Kathleen (Miss)	1937–1939	B.Sc. London
Barlow, Nellie (Miss)	1938–1939	L.R.A.M.
Oxley, Doreen Evelyn (Miss)	1938–1940	Dip. P. College, Liverpool
Hadfield, Jessie Margaret (Miss)	1938– ?	B.A. Cambridge
§Truelove, Nancy Winifred (Miss)	1938–1963	M.A. Cambridge
Clapham, Ethel Mary Pickering (Miss)	1938–1940	Dip. R.C.A.
Cooper, Marjorie (Miss)	1939–1939	B.Sc. London†
Rhodes, Florence Margaret (Miss)	1939–1947	L.R.A.M.
Doran, Margaret Mary (Miss)	1939–1944	Dip. Fine Art, London
Secker, Ethel (Miss)	1939–	B.A. Cambridge
Shaw, Alice Mary (Miss)	1939–1965	B.A. London
Smith, Doris (Miss)	1940–1943	B.Sc. Manchester
Cooper, Elizabeth M. (Miss)	1942–1945	B.A. London
Auty, Agnes Elaine (Miss)	1943–1961	B.Sc. Leeds
Briggs, Winifred Mary (Miss)	1943–1952	B.Sc. Liverpool
Walford, Kathleen (Miss)	1943– ?	
Critchley, Mabel Mary (Miss)	1943–1946	N.F.U.
Coulson, Clarice Mary (Miss)	1944–1961	B.Sc. Leeds
Estevez (Mrs.)	? –1944	

Name	Dates	Degree and University
Galloway, Kathleen (Miss)	1944–1970	Board of Education Art Teachers' Diploma
Wordsworth, M. (Miss)	1946– ?	
Wilson, Monica Ruth (Miss)	1946–1947	B.A. Manchester
Smith, Betty Haiste (Miss)	1946–	B.Sc. Leeds
Gillander, Margaret (Mrs.) (née Wordsworth)	1946–1950	
Waller, Gwenneth (Mrs.) (née Brooke)	1947–	L.R.A.M.
Forster, A. M. (Miss)	1947–1952	B.A.
Cowling, Dorothy Brenda (Miss)	1947–1952	Dip. P.T. Liverpool College
Salont, Mark (Mr.)	1948–1951	Inter. B.Sc. London
Nuttall, Barbara (Mrs.)	1948–1954	B.Sc. Leeds
Yates, Betty (Miss)	1949–1965	M.A. Durham
Adshead, Betty (Miss)	1949–1952	B.Sc. Inter. Leeds
§Tuxford, Rita (Mrs.) (née Needham)	1950–	Teachers' Certificate
Dawson, Marjorie (Miss)	1951–	Dip. P.T. London
Taylor, Joan (Mrs.) (née Nelson)	1951–1954	B.Sc. Nottingham
Benfell, Jean (Miss)	1952–	B.A. Bristol
Lawson, Freda (Miss	1952–1955	B.A. Durham
Palmer, M. M. (Mrs.)	1952– ?	
Hay, Pauline (Mrs.) (née Oates)	1953–	B.Sc. Leeds†
Dransfield, Dorothy (Mrs.) (née Hardcastle)	1953–1954	B.Sc. Leeds
Doherty, Robert (Mr.)	1954–1956	B.Sc. Dublin
Thornton Christine Mary (Miss)	1955– ?	Dip. Dom. Sci.
Broadhead, Mary (Miss)	1956–1957	B.D. London†
Fletcher, Bernard (Mr.)	1957–1959	B.Sc., M.Ed. Leeds
Tweed, Brenda Mary (Miss)	1957–1959	B.A. Nottingham
Hampshire, Betty Monica (Miss)	1957–1962	B.A. Belfast
Ramsden, Lucy Ann (Mrs.) (née Ede)	1957–1959	B.A. London
Sykes, Barbara Joyce (Mrs.) (née Stones)	1958–1965	Teachers' Certificate
Ashworth, Margaret (Mrs.)	1958–1964 1968–1969	B.A. Liverpool†
Willshaw, Margaret (Mrs.) (née Holroyd)	1958–1961	Ministry of Education Tech. Dip.
Patterson, Hetty Ebba (Mrs.) (née Strachen)	1959– ?	B.A. London†
Reed, Sybil Edna (Miss)	1959–1960	B.A. Durham
Jackson, Molly (Mrs.)	1960–1960	M.A. Cambridge†
Stansfield, Stella Catherine (Mrs.) (née Dawson)	1960–1966	B.A. Durham
Healey, Maureen (Mrs.)	1960–1962	B.A. Durham
Robinson, Geoffrey (Mr.)	1960–	B.Sc. Manchester
Bamford, Marion (Mrs.) (née Williams)	1960–1964	B.A., A.K.C. London
Marshall, Ann Patricia (Mrs.) (née Archer)	1961–1962	B.A. Leeds
Lister, John (Mr.)	1961–	B.Sc. Nottingham
Lister, Marjorie (Miss)	1961–1963	Dip. P.E.

145

L

Name	Dates	Degree and University
Andrassey, Lillian Margaret Ethel (Mrs.) (née Asquith)	1961–	Dip. Dom. Sci.
Lupton, Thomas Anthony (Mr.)	1962–1968	Inter. B.Sc. Manchester
Le Sage, Marie (Miss)	1962–1965	B.A. Leeds
Jenkinson, Patricia (Mrs.) (née Yelland)	1962–1968	B.A. Bristol
Martin, Frederick Ronald (Mr.)	1963–1968	B.A. London
Bowker, Christine (Miss)	1963–1967	Dip. Ed. Cambridge
Powell, Eric (Mr.)	1964–1966	M.A., B.D. Leeds
Hay, Beryl Enid (Mrs.) (née Chard)	1965–	B.Sc. London†
Harrison, Kathleen Joyce (Mrs.)	1965–	B.A. Oxford†
Greenald, Patricia Lesley (Miss)	1965–1966	Certificate of Education Liverpool
Hodgson, Margaret Elizabeth (Miss)	1965–	B.A. Hull
Crabbe, Eileen Muriel (Mrs.)	1965–1967	Technical Teachers' Certificate
Corby, Mary Rosalyn (Mrs.)	1965–1966	B.A. London†
Neville, Edith Chloe (Miss)	1965–1968	B.A. Sheffield
Kirklaw, Tessa (Mrs.)	1965–1965	B.A. Durham†
Stirk, Anthea Hilda (Miss)	1965–1965	B.A. London†
Ibson, Roger (Mr.)	1966–1967	B.A. Leeds
Carmichael, Jean Helen	1966–1966	B.A. Leeds†
Greensmith, J. B. (Mrs.)	1966–1968	
Whitley, Shirley (Mrs.)	1966–1966	B.A. London†
Taylor, Geoffrey Herbert (Rev.)	1966–1966	M.A. Oxford†
Grainger, Mollie (Miss)	1966	B.Sc. London†
Foster, Mary Beardsworth (Miss)	1966–1967	M.A. Cambridge
Ashton, Carol (Mrs.)	1966–	B.A. Hull
Senior, Marjorie (Mrs.)	1966	Teachers' Certificate
Beckwith, Hilary Anne (Mrs.)	1967–1967	B.A. Leeds†
Banks, Barbara Bronwyn (Mrs.)	1967–1968	Teachers' Certificate
Heard, Elaine (Mrs.) (née Taberner)	1967–1968	B.A. Manchester
Copperthwaite, Nigel Hardy (Mr.)	1967–1967	B.Sc. Bradford†
Richards, Nancie (Mrs.)	1967–1968	B.A. Cambridge†
Butts, David (Mr.)	1968–	B.A. Nottingham
Armstead, Elsie (Mrs.)	1968–	B.A. London†
Robinson, Susan Margaret (Mrs.) (née Bailey)	1968–1970	Teachers' Certificate
Preston, Anthony Waring (Mr.)	1968–	M.A. Cambridge
Johnson, Joyce (Mrs.)	1969–	B.Sc. Hull†
McFadyean, Joan Margaret (Mrs.)	1969–	B.A. Manchester
Robinson, Muriel (Miss)	1969–	B.A. London
Cunliffe, Judith Anne (Mrs.)	1969–	B.Sc. Leeds
Loughran, Vera Patricia (Miss)	1969–	B.A. Leeds
Benfield, Margaret (Miss)	1969–	Teachers' Certificate Durham
Wenham, Angela (Mrs.)	1970–	B.A. London
Siggs, Heather Elizabeth (Miss)	1970–	B.A. Leeds
Fairweather, Daphne Hazel (Mrs.)	1970–	B.Sc.(Eng.) London

APPENDIX 3. SUMMARY OF HONOURS GAINED BY THE SCHOOLS 1889 to 1910

Name of Examination	*No of passes*
University Local Examinations	772 Certificates
London and Northern Universities Matriculation, Victoria Preliminary	97
Open Entrance Scholarships and Studentships to the universities and other places of higher education	71 (Total value upwards of £9,000)
Degrees at Oxford, Cambridge, London and Northern Universities	46
Honours in the Cambridge Triposes	13
University Graduate Scholarships	16
University Lectureships	2
Examinership for the Science Tripos	1
Indian Civil Service	1
Gold Medal of the Gas Institute	1
College Fellowships	1
Fellowship of the Royal College of Surgeons	1

In addition to the above a large number of passes have been obtained in different Professional Examinations (Institute of Bankers, Civil Engineers, Incorporated Law Society, Institute of Chartered Accountants, The Royal College of Surgeons and Physicians, Teachers' Certificates, etc., but exact statistics are not available.

APPENDIX 4.

Besides the wonderful academic record this school holds there is another record which must not be forgotten. In the two World Wars, Old Boys took their places in the Armed Forces, many to give their lives for their country; some of these and others more fortunate gained military honours because of bravery and devotion to duty. Old Girls took their share in the Second World War along with Old Boys. The School can claim some credit for this as the basic disciplines taught there laid the foundation for the type of life lived and devotion given by pupils of both schools.

Below a list of the names of the Fallen on the War Memorial in the porch of the Boys' School is given and also the names on the brass plaque fixed to the Island book case which was given to the school in memory of those Old Boys who gave their lives in World War II. Following this is a list of Old Boys who gained military honours. If any names are inadvertently omitted the Author apologises as every effort was made for this to be as accurate as possible.

TO THE MEMORY OF THE WHEELWRIGHT GRAMMAR SCHOOL BOYS WHO LAID DOWN THEIR LIVES IN THE GREAT WAR (1914-1918)

P. Archer
H. Armstrong
B. W. Batley
L. E. Brook
A. C. Chadwick
N. Cleveland
H. Cooke
H. Dawson
A. Day
L. M. Evers
H. Fell
J. C. Fitton
S. P. Fletcher
H. Fothergill
R. E. Gate
L. Giggal
A. E. Gott
G. G. M. Green
F. B. Hinchcliffe
H. Hirst
F. Holmes
T. A. B. Kitson
D. Lawson
A. Liversedge
J. W. Marsden

R. L. Mayman
J. A. Moorhouse
R. F. Morton
C. Oxley
G. R. Peace
G. G. Phillips
S. Pollitt
R. H. Pope
D. Pritchard
W. Risdon
J. E. Rowley
R. H. Simpson
G. Spedding
A. Tattersfield
F. Taylor
F. Tomlinson
G. Townend
C. Walker
D. W. S. Watts
W. Whitehead
E. A. Whittles
N. Wilkinson
A. Williams
G. Wilson
H. Woods

BOOKCASE PRESENTED BY THE OLD BOYS OF THE SCHOOL IN MEMORY OF THOSE WHO FELL IN THE WORLD WAR 1939-1945

S. Adams
D. B. Asquith
K. Beevers
W. Boot
J. Booth
R. Brown
R. Campbell
C. C. Child
J. R. M. Critchley
E. Diss
G. G. Etchells
A. Handley
H. Hooper

M. Howley
W. Lockwood
H. Lupton
R. S. Manson
A. Palmer
J. Quinn
C. V. Ramshaw
R. J. Sampson
R. B. Shires
C. Summerscales
D. Sykes
A. Turner
G. C. Wilby

OLD BOYS WHO HAVE WON MILITARY HONOURS

Captain H. J. Adshead,	M.C.
Lieut. R. D. Ambrose,	M.C.
Gnr. P. Barraclough,	M.M.
Cpl. J. Campbell,	M.M.
Capt. T. Chadwick	M.C.
Capt. A. M. Deane,	Mentioned in Dispatches
2nd Lieut. E. Field,	D.S.O.
Cpl. F. W. Flatow,	M.M.
Gnr. J. B. Gledhill,	D.S.C.
Gnr. E. Hemingway	D.C.M.
Lieut. C. Hirst,	M.C.
L/Cpl. G. W. Kaye	M.M.
Capt. N. Lee,	M.C.
Capt. H. E. Pickersgill,	M.C.
Col. E. W. Pickering,	D.S.O.
Capt. H. E. Pickering,	Belgian Croix de Guerre
Major B. I. Rolling,	D.S.O.
Sgt. H. T. Saville,	M.M.
Sgt. J. A. Sconce,	M.M.
A. Shaw (L.T.M.B.),	M.C.
Capt. L. Shaw,	M.C.
Gnr. H. Shirreff,	M.M.
L/Cpl. M. Wood,	M.M.
Sgt. T. Woodcock,	M.M.

LIST OF SUBSCRIBERS

Armitage, J. A. (Mrs.), 9, Staincliffe Close, Dewsbury.
Atack, V., 3, Eskdale Close, Windermere Road, Dewsbury.
Aveyard, T., 18, Lamplands Grange, Batley (Yorks.).

Baker, J. F. Havard, "Mayfield", 16, Birkdale Road, Dewsbury, WF13 4HH.
Batley Public Libraries, Market Place, Batley, WF17 5DE.
Beckwith, W. F., 248, Headfield Road, Dewsbury.
Benn, H. M. (Mrs.), 114, Old Bank Road, Dewsbury.
Bentley, F., Long Range, Albert Promenade, Halifax.
Benton, H., 1, Northfield Street, Dewsbury.
Biddle, B., 21, Woodburn Avenue, Earlsheaton, Dewsbury.
Bingley College of Education, Bingley (Yorks.).
Blackburn, E. H., "Gwylfa", 99, Oxford Road, Dewsbury.
Blackburn, A. N., "Brymer", 21, Pinfold Lane, Mirfield (Yorks.).
Bolton, W., 58, Alexandra Crescent, Dewsbury.
Bowers, M. (Mrs.), "Housesteads", 52, Brunswick Street, Dewsbury.
Bradford Grammar School, Bradford, 1BD 4JP.
Bradford Central Library, Prince's Way, Bradford, BD1 1NN.
Bretton Hall College of Education, Bretton, Wakefield.
Broadbent, P. G., 363, Bradford Road, Chain Bar, Cleckheaton.
Broadhead, C. A., "Cleveleys", Healds Road, Dewsbury.
Brook, L. A., M.B.E., Wharfedale, St. Mary's Avenue, Carlton Grange, Batley.
Brook, N., 3, Bell Hill, Petersfield, Hants.
Brown, M. R., 25, Caulms Wood Road, Dewsbury.
Brown, Raymond Lamont, 25, Ladywell Road, Tweedmouth, Berwick-upon-Tweed (Northumberland).
Brown, T. R., 46, Willow Green, Ingatestone, Essex.
Butterfield, D., 3, Fox Royd Avenue, Mirfield, WF14 9SW.
Binns, A., The Hall, High Hoyland, Barnsley (Yorks.).

Carden, S. G., 21, Hobart Road, Dewsbury.
Chapman, W., 25, Ashworth Green, Moorlands Road, Dewsbury.
Cleveland, A., 334, Upper Elmers End Road, Beckenham, Kent.
Clitheroe, J. Marlborough House, Dewsbury, WF13 4HD.
Collins, E. M. (Miss), "Gaytons", Sewards End, Saffron Walden, Essex.
Cooper, R., 15, Marlborough Road, Parkstone, Dorset.
Cowell, J., 76, Park Lane, Allerton Bywater, Nr. Leeds.
Croft, J., 3, Wakefield Crescent, Dewsbury.
Crompton, J. S., 5, Judy Haigh Lane, Thornhill, Dewsbury.
Crowther, R. B., "The Hollies", Scopsley Lane, Whitley Lower, Dewsbury.
Cullingwoth, J. (Miss), Skell Cottage, Borrage Green Lane, Ripon, HG4 2JH.

Day, D. (Miss), 4, Ash Grove, Earlsheaton, Dewsbury, WF12 8HA.
Day, G. (Mrs.), Thornhill Lees C.E. Junior School, Thornhill Lees, Dewsbury.
Dennison, F. (Mrs.), Barn Cottage, Hunsingore, Wetherby (Yorks.).
Dewsbury Education Authority, c/o Chief Education Officer, Municipal Buildings, Dewsbury.
Dewsbury Public Library (4 copies), Central Library, Wellington Road, Dewsbury.

Dixon, E. (Mrs.), "Rowans" 49, Heaton Avenue, Dewsbury
Docton, H. M., 44, Church Hill Avenue, Warton, Carnforth, Lancs.
Dunford, E., 2, Edge View, Thornhill, Dewsbury, WF12 0ES.
Dunning, J. E. P., Church Farm House, Westcott, Aylesbury, Bucks.

Elliott, H., 14, Upleatham Street, Saltburn-by-Sea, N. Yorks.
Ellis, D. R., Pollard Old Hall, Gomersal (Yorks.).
Evans, D. 78, Headfield Road, Savile Town, Dewsbury.
Evans, D. W. (Miss), Cefn-Glanlwrch Cottage, Wanrhaeadr-ym-Mochnant, Oswestry, SY10 0DS.
Exley, F., (3 copies), "Portelet", Church Lane, Thornhill, Dewsbury.
Exley, G. F., 34, Albion Road, Thornhill Edge, Dewsbury.

Foggo, R., "Crown Cliff", 318, Leeds Road, Dewsbury.
Foster, P. (Mrs.), 42, Huddersfield Road, Barnsley, S75 1DW.
Fox., L. Prof., 24, Sandfield Road, Headington, Oxford, OX3 7RQ.
Fox, Marcus, M.P., House of Commons, London, SW1A 0AA.
France, M. R. (Miss), 2, South View Terrace, Hill Head, Halifax Road, Dewsbury, WF13 4JE.
Furness, G., 29A, West Hill, Epsom, Surrey
Furness, J. M. (Rev.), The Manse, West Avenue, Gosforth, Newcastle-on-Tyne.
Furness, W. (Dr.), 32, Edinburgh Gardens, King's Road, Windsor, SLA 2AW.

Garforth, M. (Mrs.), 40, Westacres Crescent, Newcastle-upon-Tyne, NE15 7PB.
Garrett, P. A., "Helston", Main Street, Askham Bryan, York, YQ2 3QS.
Garthwaite, E. A. (Mrs.), 125, Oxford Road, Dewsbury.
Gee, P. M. (Mrs.), Boston View, 40, Northgate, Hunstanton, Norfolk.
Gibson, A. K., "Gwent", 24, Oak Tree Road, Kendal, Westmoreland.
Gill, C. H., 94, Heaton Road, Paddock, Huddersfield, HD1 4JJ.
Gill, M. J. (Mrs.), 54, Bradley Road, Bradley, Huddersfield (Yorks.).
Gill, W. S., 204, Soothill Lane, Batley (Yorks.).
Glover, A. D. (Mrs.), 190, Kingsway, Ossett (Yorks.).
Grason, W., 12A, Ashburnham Road, Tonbridge, Kent.
Greaves, A., 427, Lees Hall Road, Thornhill Lees, Dewsbury, WF12 9EX.
Green, R., 5, Salisbury Avenue, Baildon, Shipley (Yorks.).
Greenwood, J. (Mrs.), Thornhill Lees C.E. Junior School, Thornhill Lees, Dewsbury.

Halliwell, A. B., Flat 3, Holmdene, Springfield Terrace, Halifax Road, Dewsbury, WF13 2JW.
Hamilton, S. G., 5, Rock Terrace, Hipperholme, Halifax, HX38 P13.
Hanson, N. (Mrs.), 624, Leeds Road, Dewsbury, WF12 7QH.
Heard, M. E., 9, Nixon Close, Thornhill, Dewsbury.
Heylings, M. R., 371, Lees Hall Road, Thornhill Lees, Dewsbury.
Hirst, W., 19, Jackson Avenue, Roundhay, Leeds 8.
Hodgson, E. (Miss), 6, Carr Manor Parade Leeds, LS17 5AA.
Hodgson, M. F. (Mrs.), 53, Selbourne Road, Savile Town, Dewsbury.
Hodgson, N. L., 13, Carlton Avenue, Carlton Grange, Batley.
Howarth, D., 102, Savile Road, Savile Town, Dewsbury.
Howgate, V. E., 41, Birkdale Road, Dewsbury.
Huddersfield Central Library, Princess Alexandra Walk, Huddersfield, HD1 2SU.

Huddersfield Polytechnic, Queensgate, Huddersfield, HD1 3DH.

I. M. Marsh College of Physical Education, Barkhill Road, Liverpool, L17 6BD.
Ingram, J. D., 3, Northfield Street, Dewsbury.
Isles, G. L. (Dr.), 100, Bywell Road, Dewsbury.

Jones, C. M., 35, West Park Street, Dewsbury (Yorks.).
Jury, S., Oak Cottage, Briestfield Lane, Dewsbury.

Keeble, H., I. M. Portman Mansion, Baker Street, London, W.1.
Kershaw, D. (Dr.), Department of Mathematics, Cartmell College, University of Lancaster, Lancaster.
Kerrod, N., 16, Woodlands Drive, Lepton, Huddersfield, HD8 0JB.
Ketton, J., 2A, Marsden Terrace, Crackenedge, Dewsbury.
Kilburn, T. (Prof.), F.R.S., Department of Computer Science, The University, Manchester, M13 9PL.
Knott, M. A. (Miss), Wakefield Girls' High School, Wentworth Street, Wakefield (Yorks.).
Knowles, N. (Mrs.), "Storolea", 4, Valley Road, Thornhill, Dewsbury.
Koteen, H. T. (Mrs.), 46, Grace Leather Lane, Soothill, Batley (Yorks.).

Lancaster, W. B. (2 copies), Wheelwright Grammar School for Boys.
Lansdale, B., 54, Scotchman Lane, Morley, Nr. Leeds.
Lawton, J. Harrap, 15, Chevet Lane, Sandal, Wakefield.
Leeds University Institute of Education Library.
Leeds City Libraries, Central Library, Municipal Buildings, Leeds, LS1 3AB.
City of Leeds and Carnegie College, Leeds.
Levitt, D. M. (Miss) (2 copies), Wheelwright Grammar School for Girls, Dewsbury.
Lock, K. R., 46, Smithy Brook Lane, Thornhill, Dewsbury.
Lonsdale, N., "Prestwood", Butts Road, Ashover, Chesterfield, Derbyshire.
Ludlam, H., 11, Fountain Street, Halifax, HX1 1LU.
Lyles, S., "Fieldhurst", Liversedge Hall Lane, Heckmondwike (Yorks.).

Macorison, M., 19, Brunswick Drive, Westborough, Dewsbury.
Martin, L. (Mrs.), 7, Hazel Drive, Chickenley, Dewsbury.
Manley, M. (Mrs.), 6, Lowdale, Bennett Lane, Dewsbury.
Merson, M. (Miss), Newfield Lodge, Halifax Road, Dewsbury.
Mitchell, A. L. (Dr.), "Nyanja", Bark Lane, Addingham, Nr. Ilkley.
Moore, E. (Miss), c/o Messrs. Finn, Gledhill & Co., 1 & 2, Harrison Road, Halifax, HX1 2AG.
Morley Public Library, Commercial Street, Morley, LS27 8HZ.
Morrell, P. K., 14, Rich Close, Emscote Gardens, Warwick (Warwicks).
Morris, C., 12, Brecks Lane, Kippax, Nr. Leeds.

Newbould, H. C., 124, Soothill Lane, Batley (Yorks.).
Newsome, J., 4, The Oaks, West Byfleet, Surrey.
Newton, G., 26, Edge Top Road, Thornhill, Dewsbury.
Noble, E. (Dr.), 46, York Road, Dunlaoghaire, Ireland.
Nowell, J., Seacroft Cottage, Hillcrest Road, Hythe, Kent.
Nuttall, B. (Mrs.), 14, Red Hall Avenue, Leeds, LS17 8NQ.

LIST OF SUBSCRIBERS

Oldroyd, B. S., 13, Fir Avenue, Ravensthorpe, Dewsbury.
Ossett, Borough Library, Ossett (Yorks.).

Parkinson, M. G., 38, Grasmere Road, Dewsbury, WF12 7PG.
Patchett, P. M. (Miss), 16, Heaton Avenue, Wakefield Road, Dewsbury (Yorks.).
Pearson, J. A. (Mrs.), The Elms, Wakefield Road, Heckmondwike (Yorks.).
Peel, H., 1, Stonefield Street, Halifax Road, Dewsbury (Yorks.).
Popplewell, D. E. (Miss), 54, Stockhill Street, Dewsbury, WF13 2JD.

Ramsden, A. (Mrs.), 19, The Town, Thornhill, Dewsbury, WF12 0RB.
Ramsden, G., "Greenlands", 127, Oxford Road, Dewsbury.
Raynor, M. W., 18, Higher Drive, Purley, Surrey, CR2 2NE.
Ripon: The College, Ripon, Yorks. (The Librarian).

Sadler, C. A. N., 21, Fordwich Hill, Hertford (Herts.).
Sampson, F. V. E., "Wayside", 527, Halifax Road, Hightown, Liversedge (Yorks.).
Sanderson, R. C., 101, Dark Lane, Batley (Yorks.).
Saynor, E. (Miss), 8, Stonefield Street, Dewsbury.
Scatcherd, J. E. (2 copies), 3, Pump Court, Temple, London, E.C.4.
Secker, B., 217, Uxbridge Road, Harrow Weald, Harrow, HA3 6TW.
Secker, E. J. (Miss), Yew Tree House, Mollyhurst Lane, Woolley, Nr. Wakefield.
Senior, N. (Mrs.), 36, High Street, Carrville, Durham, DH1 1AS.
Sheard, J. L. (Mrs.), 6, Kingston Drive, West Park, Lytham-St. Annes, Lancs.
Smith, D. M. (Cr.), Hill Head House, Dewsbury, WF13 HJA.
Smith, F. M. (Miss), 11, Brunswick Drive, Dewsbury, WF13 4NG.
Smith, H., "Fir-don", 15, Uplands Drive, Mirfield (Yorks.).
Smith, J., "Linksway", 13, Ennerdale Road, Dewsbury (Yorks.).
Smith, M. (Ald. Mrs.), 516, Leeds Road, Dewsbury (Yorks.).
Spencer, J. M. C., Briestfield, Dewsbury.
Spenborough Public Library, Cleckheaton, BD19 3DX.
Spurr, C. L., 20, Penn Drive, Hightown Road, Liversedge (Yorks.).
Squires, V. (Mrs.), 38, North Park Street, Dewsbury (Yorks.).
Stansfield, C. M., "Higburg", 28B, Hopton Hall Lane, Mirfield (Yorks.).
Stapleton, A. E., 9, Slaithwaite Road, Thornhill Lees, Dewsbury (Yorks.).
St. John's College, York, YO3 7EX.
Swift, J. H. (Mrs.), 7, Mansion Court Gardens, Thorne, Doncaster, DN8 5BN.
Sykes, A., 7, Robin Royd Croft, Mirfield (Yorks.).
Sykes, C., Manea County Primary School, Manea (Cambs.).
Sykes, O. (Miss), Wheelwright Grammar School for Girls, Dewsbury (Yorks.).
Swithenbank, N., "Fieldhead", Hillcrest Road, Savile Town, Dewsbury (Yorks.).

Tattersfield, D., 10, Beverley Gardens, Woodmancote, Cheltenham, Glos., GL52 4QD.
Tattersfield, K., 69A, Knowle Road, Mirfield (Yorks.).
Taylor, H., King James's Grammar School, Almondbury, Huddersfield (Yorks.).
Temlett, L., 13, Bar Lane, Garforth, Leeds.
Thomas, E., "Kirklands", 65, Towngate, Clifton, Brighouse (Yorks.).
Thompson, S. P., "Sunnyacre", Horton Road, Ringwood, Hants, BH24 2EB.
Thornes, J. (Mrs.), Ash Tree Close, Baghill, West Ardsley, Wakefield.
Thornhill Secondary School (c/o A. S. McAllister), Valley Drive, Thornhill, Dewsbury.
Thornton, G. B., 15, Northfield Road, Dewsbury.

Tillotson, M., Lantern Cottage, 16, Middle Street, Nafferton, Nr. Driffield, E. Yorks.
Tolson, A. M., 14, Headland Lane, Earlsheaton, Dewsbury.
Townend, R., 17, Fortescue Chase, Thorpe Bay, Southend-on-Sea, Essex.
Truelove, N. W. (Miss), 55, Avon Crescent, Stratford-upon-Avon (Warwicks.).
Turner, T. C., 125, Sunnybank Road, Mirfield (Yorks.).

Underwood, H., 13, Ventnor Close, Ossett (Yorks.).

Vollans, R., 22, Windermere Road, Dewsbury.

Wakefield (The Lord Bishop of), Rt. Rev. E. Treacy, Bishop's Lodge, Woodthorpe
  Lane, Wakefield.
Wakefield Historical Society, 11, College Grove Road, Wakefield.
Walker, G. (Dr.), 37, Water Royd Avenue, Mirfield, WF14 9LT.
Walker, G. E., O.B.E., 4, St. Andrew's Walk, Cobham, Surrey.
Walker, P. B. (Dr.), White Walls, 58, Park Road, Camberley, Surrey.
Walker, P. M. (Mrs.), 54, Speeton Avenue, Horton Bank Top, Bradford, BD7 4NQ.
Waller, G. (Mrs.), 14, Park Road, Birkdale Road, Dewsbury.
West Riding County Library (2 copies), Balne Lane, Wakefield, WF2 0DQ.
Wheelwright, J. M. H., Sigsworth Lodge, Wath, Pateley Bridge, Harrogate.
Whitaker, J. G. D., "Woodcroft", The Promendade, Arnside, via Carnforth (Lancs.).
Wigglesworth, G., 11, North Park Street, Dewsbury.
Widdowson, H., 51, Ullswater Avenue, Dewsbury.
Williams, J. (Rev.), Headmaster, Rishworth School, Ripponden, HX6 4PZ.
Willoughby, B. G. (Dr.), 100, Town Street, Earlsheaton, Dewsbury.
Wilkinson, R. (Miss), 44, St. Catherine's Road, Harrogate, HG2 8LA.
Winterbottom, L., 38, Heaton Avenue, Wakefield Road, Dewsbury.
Withers, M. (Mrs.), 12, Grasmere Road, Dewsbury (Yorks.).
Wright, R. K., 159, West Town Lane, Bristol, BS14 GEA.
Wilde, K. (2 copies), 26, Highfield Crescent, Overton, Wakefield, WF4 4RA.
Waterhouse, R. & J., 34, Moorcroft, Staincliffe Road, Dewsbury.

INDEX
PROPER NAMES

(G) after a number indicates a Girls' School society